focus ON SCIENCE

LIFE & LIVING

JAN

For my family, who are always supportive.

Acknowledgements

The author would like to thank Edie Threadgold and her son, David for information on haemophilia, and Dr Edmund Flach and Dr Margaret Williams of Whipsnade Wild Animal Park for their assistance in writing this book. The publishers would like to thank Lynda King and Chris Halls for design work, and Tom Cross and Jeff Edwards for the illustrations.

The publishers would like to thank the following individuals, institutions and companies for permission to reproduce photographs in this book. Every effort has been made to trace ownership of copyright. The publishers would be happy to make arrangements with any copyright holder whom it has not been possible to contact:
Cover, main photo: false-colour transmission electron micrograph of a mitochondrion in a cell, courtesy Science Photo Library/Bill Longcore. Cover, small photo: courtesy Planet Earth/Peter Scoones/Telegraph Colour Library.
Focus openers: pages 4-5 frog spawn, courtesy J Allen Cash Ltd; pages 22-23 fruit and vegetable market in Arusha, Tanzania, courtesy J Allen Cash Ltd; multiple image of gymnast performing a beam exercise, courtesy Science Photo Library/Jerry Wachter; pages 76-77 light micrograph of xylem vessels in a palm, courtesy Science Photo Library/J C Revy; pages 92-93 sow and piglets, courtesy J Allen Cash Ltd; pages 116-117 wildebeest and flamingoes in the Ngorongoro Crater, Tanzania, courtesy Tanya Piejus.
Heather Angel (2 bottom left and right, 68 bottom right, 99 top right, 106 both, 133 right); Ardea (128 top right), /John Beames (83), /R J C Blewitt (136 top left), /John Daniels (3 top right), /Eric Dragesco (72), /Francois Gohier (7, 80 bottom, 131 bottom), /Edwin Mickleburgh (118), /Stefan Meyers (125 centre right); BBC Natural History Unit/Neil Nightingale (113 bottom); Biofotos/Andrew Henley (124 top left), /Geoffrey Kinns (133 left); Biophoto Associates (10 both, 53, 99 bottom right, 120 top); John Birdsall (94); Debra Bourne/Whipsnade Wild Animal Park (45); Bruce Coleman/Trevor Barrett (73 top), /Jane Burton (80 top, 99 top middle, 136 bottom), /John Burton (109), /R I M Campbell (3 bottom left), /John Cancalosi (108 middle, 112 bottom left), /Nicholas De Vore (44 bottom), /Stephen J Doyle (82), /Frank Greenaway (124 top right), /Harald Lange (6 top), /Luiz Claudio Marigo (129), /Dr Eckart Pott (56), /Hans Reinhard (51, 73 bottom, 125 left, 125 centre left), /Frieder Sauer (68 right middle bottom), /D & R Sullivan (108 middle), /Kim Taylor (26), /Rod Williams (101 left), /Gunter Ziesler (124 bottom right); Collections/Anthea Sieveking (44 top left); Jenny Eggleton (19 top right); Dr Edmund Flach, Whipsnade Wild Animal Park (45); FLPA (6 bottom) /David T Grewcock (78 left), /Life Science Images (29), /M B Withers (122), /J Zimmerman (78 bottom right); Frank Spooner Pictures/Olivier Blaise/Gamma (19 bottom); Hulton Deutsch (44 top right); Images of India/Roderick Johnson (130 bottom); B & G Ingram-Monk (95); John Ledger (62); Dr Graham Lenton (128 bottom right); Dr Harry Moore, University of Sheffield (101 middle); Moviestore Collection (112 top); Nature Photographers Ltd/Peter Craig-Cooper (121 top), /Paul Sterry (101 right); NHPA/Anthony Bannister (121 bottom), /Stephen Dalton (18 top, 50), /Nigel J Dennis (120 bottom), /Rich Kirchner (123 bottom), /Steve Robinson (131 top), /SCRI (137 top), /Morten Strange (132), /M I Walker (98), /David Woodfall (128 left); Oxford Scientific Films/Kathie Atkinson (68 right middle bottom), /G I Bernard (124 bottom right), /Scott Camazine (107 right), /Gene Cox (36 bottom right), /C G Gardener (32), /R L Manuel (30), /Hans Reinhard/Okapia (14 bottom), /George Reszeter (136 top right), /Survival (18 middle), /Harry Taylor (99 top left), /Harry Taylor/British Museum (Natural History) (108 top), /Steve Turner (125 right); Roddy Paine (14 top, 19 top left, 36 both left, 39, 41 left, 58, 68 top right, 78 top right, 79, 85, 104); Tanya Piejus (17, 102); Press Association Ltd/Agence France Presse (112 bottom right); Rex Features Ltd (130 top); Belinda Richardson (66); Royal Brompton Hospital, London (113 top); Science Photo Library/Dr Jeremy Burgess (2 top right, 100 bottom), /J Croyle/custom medical stock photo (64 left), /Dr Don Fawcett (96 bottom right), /Simon Fraser/Royal Victoria Infirmary, Newcastle (41 right), /John Greim (86 top), /Adam Hart-Davis (15 left, 60, 100 top), /Bruce Iverson (86 top right), /Mehau Kulyk (64 right), /Hank Morgan (18 bottom), /Dr P Marazzi (31), /Profs P M Motta and S Correr (38), Prof P Motta/Dept of Anatomy/University 'La Spaienza', Rome (63 bottom), /NIBSC (40 top), /Novosti (87 middle), /Gary Parker (107 left), /Chris Priest (86 middle), /Dr H C Robinson (37), /Secchi, Lecaque, Roussel, UCLAF, CNRI (63 top), /Jim Selby (61), /St Bartholemew's Hospital, London (86 bottom), /David Vaughan (87 top); Still Pictures/Mark Edwards (137 bottom); Trip/H Rogers (126); John Urling Clark (15 right, 40 bottom) with thanks to Centeon Ltd; Prof Larry Venable (123 top).

We would also like to thank the following for permission to reproduce copyright material: ABPI (from *Medicines and Drugs - The Facts*), the Midlands Examining Group, the University of London Examinations and Assessment Council, and the Welsh Joint Education Committee.

British Library Cataloguing in Publication Data

Vellacott, Jane
Life and living – (Focus on science)
1. Life sciences
I. Title
570

ISBN 0 340 655062

First published 1996
Impression number 10 9 8 7 6 5 4 3 2 1
Year   2000 1999 1998 1997 1996

Copyright © 1996 Jane Vellacott

All rights reserved. No part of this publication may be reproduced or transmitted in any form or by any means, electronic or mechanical, including photocopy, recording, or any information storage and retrieval system, without permission in writing from the publisher or under licence from the Copyright Licensing Agency Limited. Further details of such licences (for reprographic reproduction) may be obtained from the Copyright Licensing Agency Limited, of 90 Tottenham Court Road, London W1P 9HE.

Typeset by Wearset, Boldon, Tyne and Wear.
Printed in Great Britain for Hodder & Stoughton Educational, a division of Hodder Headline Plc, 338 Euston Road, London NW1 3BH by Cambridge University Press, Cambridge.

Contents

Acknowledgements	ii
Biology – the study of living things	2

Focus 1 Introducing living systems — 4

Being alive	6
Body systems	8
The human plan	10
Skin deep	14
The plant body	16
About living things	18
Summary	20
Questions	20

Focus 2 Blood and guts — 22

Food for life	24
Eat yourself healthy	26
Dealing with food	28
Cutters, choppers and grinders	30
More about the small intestine	32
Gut reactions	34
Blood structure and function	36
Life blood	38
Blood disorders	40
Activities	42
Blood and guts explored	44
Summary	46
Questions	46

Focus 3 Coordinating life processes — 48

Sensitivity	50
A closer look at nerve cells	52
Reacting and learning	54
A sensitive eye	56
Drugs and sensitivity	58
Chemical coordinators in animals	60
Becoming an adult	62
Human reproduction	64
Hormones and fertility	66
Chemical coordinators in plants	68
Activities	70
A coordinated approach to life	72
Summary	74
Questions	74

Focus 4 The body in balance — 76

Controlling change	78
Regulating water	80
About body temperature	82
Controlling body temperature	84
Activities	86
The body in control	88
Summary	90
Questions	90

Focus 5 Past and future — 92

Variety of life	94
Coding for life	96
Making more cells	98
Making sex cells	100
Inheritance	102
Inherited diseases	104
A change of code	106
Past and future	108
Activities	110
The genetic link	112
Summary	114
Questions	114

Focus 6 Ecosystem Earth — 116

Spread around the world	118
Ecology	120
Adapting, competing and surviving	122
Predator and prey	124
Human impact on the Earth	
1 Pollution	126
2 Using the land	128
Protecting the planet	130
Activities	133
Interacting, competing and adapting	136
Summary	138
Questions	138

Glossary	140
Index	142

Biology – the study of living things

The pictures on the front cover of this book give you an idea of what biology is about – living things. The smaller picture shows a shoal of fish swimming around a coral reef. The coral itself is alive. In the larger picture you can see part of a cell through a microscope.

A large part of biology is concerned with what living things are like. Biologists find out how living things are made up and how their bodies work. This often means using microscopes or other methods to see parts which are too tiny to see otherwise. You will probably be reading some biological terms (shown in **bold** print) for the first time. If you need to check their meanings, use the glossary on page 140.

An exciting discovery in biology was finding out the structure and nature of DNA. DNA (deoxyribonucleic acid) is sometimes called the *molecule of life*. It contains the genetic code, which acts as a set of operating instructions for a cell. This discovery was a landmark because it has helped scientists to understand how cells work, and has opened the door to many other discoveries.

The genetic code controls how a living thing grows and develops. DNA is inherited from one generation to the next, and so shapes what a new individual is like. It is now possible to take part of the genetic code from one living thing and give it to another. This is called genetic engineering. It means that scientists can transfer useful characteristics from one living thing to another – 'designing' in new features.

Picture 1 This is a false colour photograph taken through an electron microscope. The tentacles on this leaf have sticky glands that trap the fly. Enzymes ooze from the glands. The enzymes are chemicals which digest the fly, providing food for the plant.

Knowing about living things is useful, because we can use biological knowledge to find solutions. If something goes wrong, e.g. a crop does not grow, someone becomes ill or a batch of cheese 'goes bad' during production, biological scientists can help.

Discovering how living things have changed over the millions of years that Earth has existed, also involves biology. It is detective work which uses clues from the past, such as fossils of all types. The features of fossils can be compared to living things that exist today.

Just as important is knowing how living things behave and how they interact within their environment. All parts of Earth

Picture 2 A giant in the plant world. The redwood tree lives for up to 2000 years or more, and grows to a mighty 80 metres in height. Many of the world's forests are being attacked by the chainsaw – just one impact of human activity on the natural environment.

Picture 3 These apple trees were grown from seeds that have been given some useful extra genes. The genes mean the trees grow close to the ground, making it easier to pick the apples.

Introduction

are linked together, and what happens in one part affects what happens elsewhere. Looking to the future, we need to know how to protect our planet from the impact of human activities.

Why is biology important?

Here are some examples of a wide range of jobs that biologists do:
- finding out how diseases spread
- helping to develop new medicines
- protecting species from becoming extinct
- monitoring the environment, e.g. checking water quality in rivers
- breeding new and more successful species of plants and animals
- helping to feed the world's hungry people
- producing useful materials from living things.

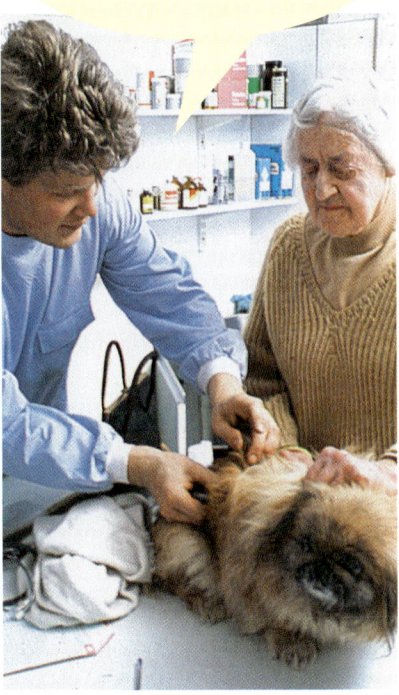

I love working with animals. Pets are great friends to people, and they're good workers too. We need to look after them.

Picture 4

Picture 5 Dian Fossey spent many years studying a group of gorillas. Their behaviour and society mimics humans in many ways.

To think about

Each of the following jobs requires some knowledge of biology. Suggest reasons why this is so.
- **a)** doctor
- **b)** farmer
- **c)** dietician (an expert on diet)
- **d)** safari park manager
- **e)** fishery manager
- **f)** veterinary surgeon
- **h)** Greenpeace investigator
- **i)** dairy manager

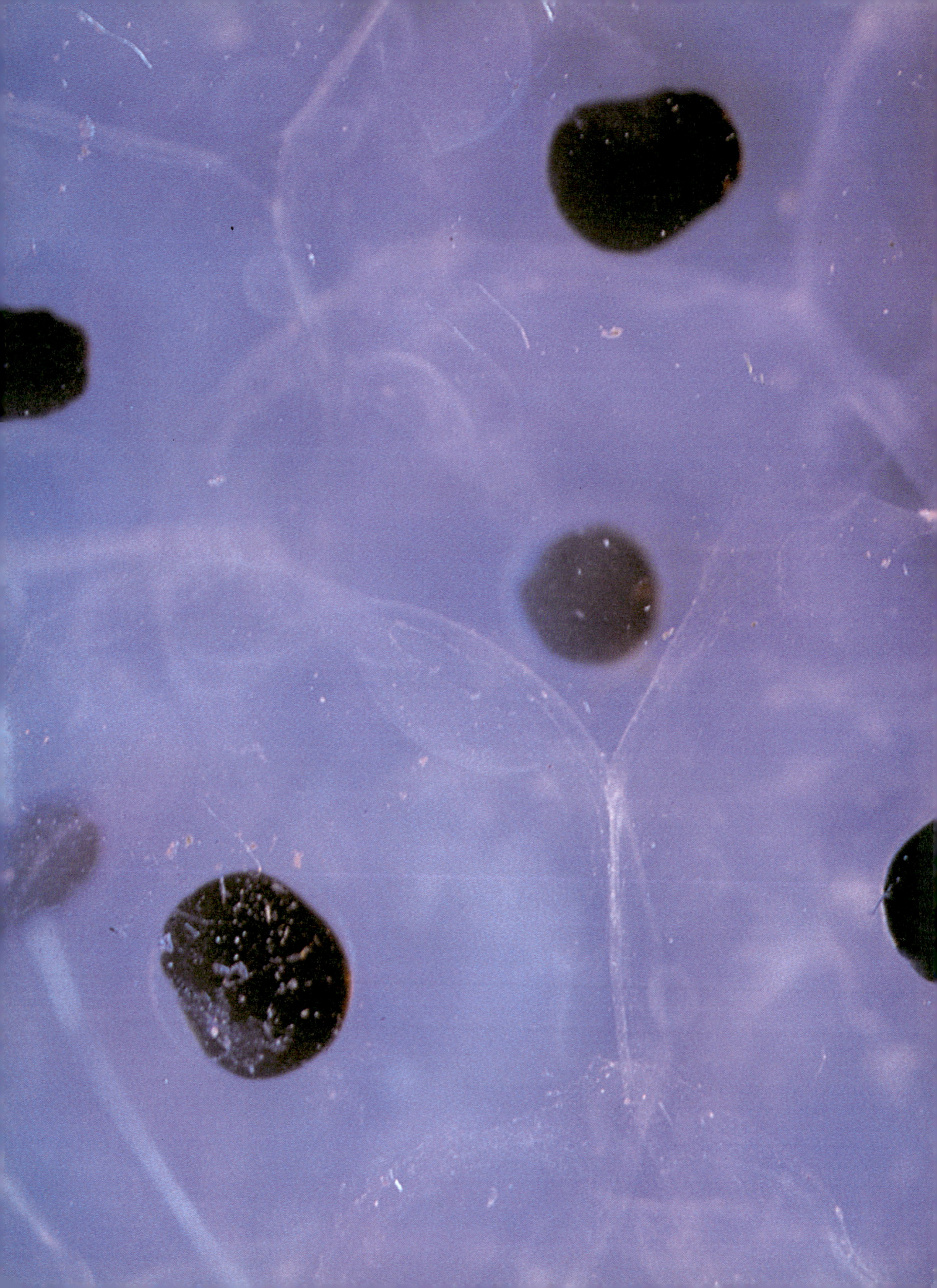

focus 1

Introducing living systems

Being alive — 6
Life is about the processes that living things can *do* which non-living things can't.

Body systems — 8
Body systems are the parts of the body that carry out the life processes.

The human plan — 10
Describing how human body systems are organised.

Skin deep — 14
A closer look at one human body system.

The plant body — 16
Describing how plant body systems are organised.

Being alive

Life processes

Living things are very active. It may not look as though the limpets in Picture 1 are doing much, but beneath their shells the cells are full of life. **Life processes** are the activities which living things do, for example, feeding. The life processes work together and you can read more about this in *Body systems*, pages 8–9.

Picture 1 Limpets fix themselves to rock surfaces where they stay for the whole of their lives.

Food is something that no living thing can do without – they all need **nutrition**. Food is an energy source. It is used by the human body to keep warm and to move.

Animals feed on foods which are mostly made of large and complex particles. Foods must be broken down into smaller particles before we can use them. This is called **digestion**. The digested food provides both the energy and the raw materials essential for life processes.

Even the plants in Picture 2 are having a picnic! As long as they are in the light, plants can feed themselves. During **photosynthesis** they make food from a gas in the air and water. Any food that isn't used up straightaway is stored, either in the leaves or other parts of the plant such as the root.

Respiration transfers the energy in food to the body. All living things carry out respiration and most living things need oxygen for this process (see page 38 and *Materials*, Focus 4).

Picture 2 Students need a good rest and a good feed after the morning's climb.

Growth is an increase in size which happens to young living things as they get older. Not all living things grow in the same way. They may grow different amounts at different times. For example, some plants such as daffodils grow only in the early spring and summer. The leafy part of a plant may die at the end of the summer.

Activity	Energy needed to carry out activity kJ/min
sleeping	4.5
running	42.0
playing football	36.5
standing	7.1
walking slowly	12.6
sitting	5.9

Table 1 How much energy is needed?
Source: The Living World, Michael Roberts.

Introducing living systems

Humans only grow for about the first twenty years of life, as Picture 3 shows.

The chemical reactions that happen in cells make **products**. Some products are wastes, and we need to get rid of them. Getting rid of waste is called **excretion**. **Urea** is a waste product from proteins which the body doesn't use. We excrete urea in urine. A waste that's not so obvious is the carbon dioxide gas we breathe out. Yet an adult human breathes out about one hundred thousand litres of carbon dioxide a year. There are other wastes too, and you can read more about them in *Controlling change*, pages 78–79.

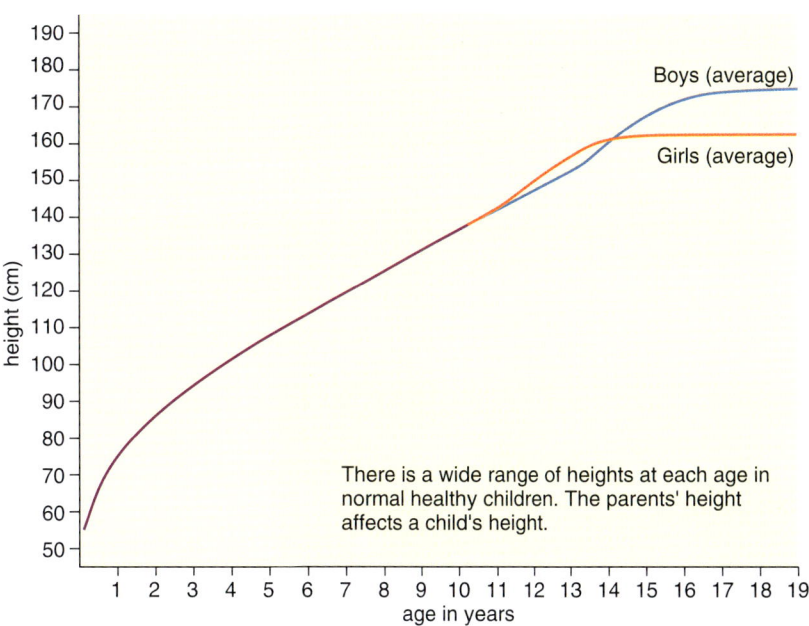

Picture 3 Patterns of growth for boys and girls. Nuffield–Chelsea Curriculum Trust, 1990.

Living things are sensitive, which means they can detect what's happening around them. The insides of bodies are sensitive to changes too. As a result, living things can respond to changes inside and outside their bodies. In fact survival depends on **sensitivity**.

Animals look lively when they are moving. Plants also make movements by growing in a certain direction. **Movement** is a life process.

When living things are mature they reproduce. **Reproduction** is the process of making new lives. The newborn replace those that have died. A population decreases if there are more deaths than births. Earth's human population is increasing greatly. Between 1980 and 2060 the population is expected to double to 10 billion people. Yet the population of many plants and other animals is decreasing rapidly. Pages 118–119, *Ecosystem Earth*, look at why the balance of living things on Earth is changing.

Picture 4 This anteater wouldn't last long if it wasn't sensitive to its food source – ants.

Questions

1. Make a list of all the important life processes mentioned above, and write a sentence to explain what each life process is.
2. What differences are there between how plants and animals get food?
3. How is food used in the human body?
4. Suggest some different ways of measuring growth in **a)** plants and **b)** animals. What are the advantages and disadvantages of each method?
5. What effects do you think an increase in the human population might have on the world?
6. What information did your sensitivity allow you to detect today, between getting up and arriving at school?

Body systems

Building blocks of life

Cells are very tiny units of life. Some living things are made of only one cell. Many cells together can build up a bigger living thing. Most cells are so small that you need a microscope to see them. Even then it takes experience to see the features shown in Picture 1.

The structure of cells varies. This is because they are designed to carry out different jobs. Although there are many different types of cell, they all have some features in common.

Picture 1 What are cells like? Both the cells shown here are types of surface cells. a) is a cell from inside the human cheek, b) is a cell from a leaf.

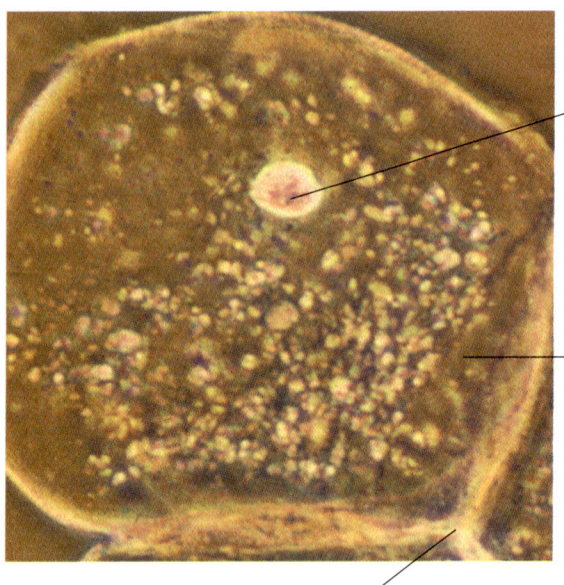

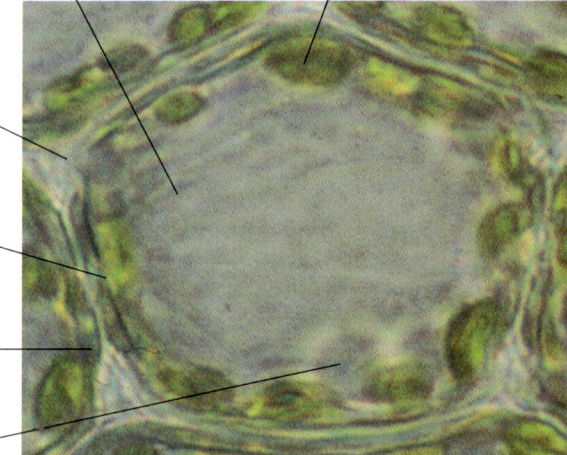

the **nucleus** contains a set of instructions for the chemical processes that happen in cells; these instructions are **inherited** and decide what a living thing is like

cytoplasm is the living contents of a cell where all the chemical processes happen

cell membranes control the movement of substances in and out of cells

chloroplasts are where the plant's food supply is made

the **cell wall** gives support

the **vacuole** contains a watery solution

Introducing living systems

How is a body system built up?

A **body system** carries out major jobs in the body. Picture 2 is an example of a human body system, showing how it is built up from cells, tissues and organs. There are many body systems and the main ones are described in *The human plan*, pages 10–13 and *The plant body*, pages 16–17.

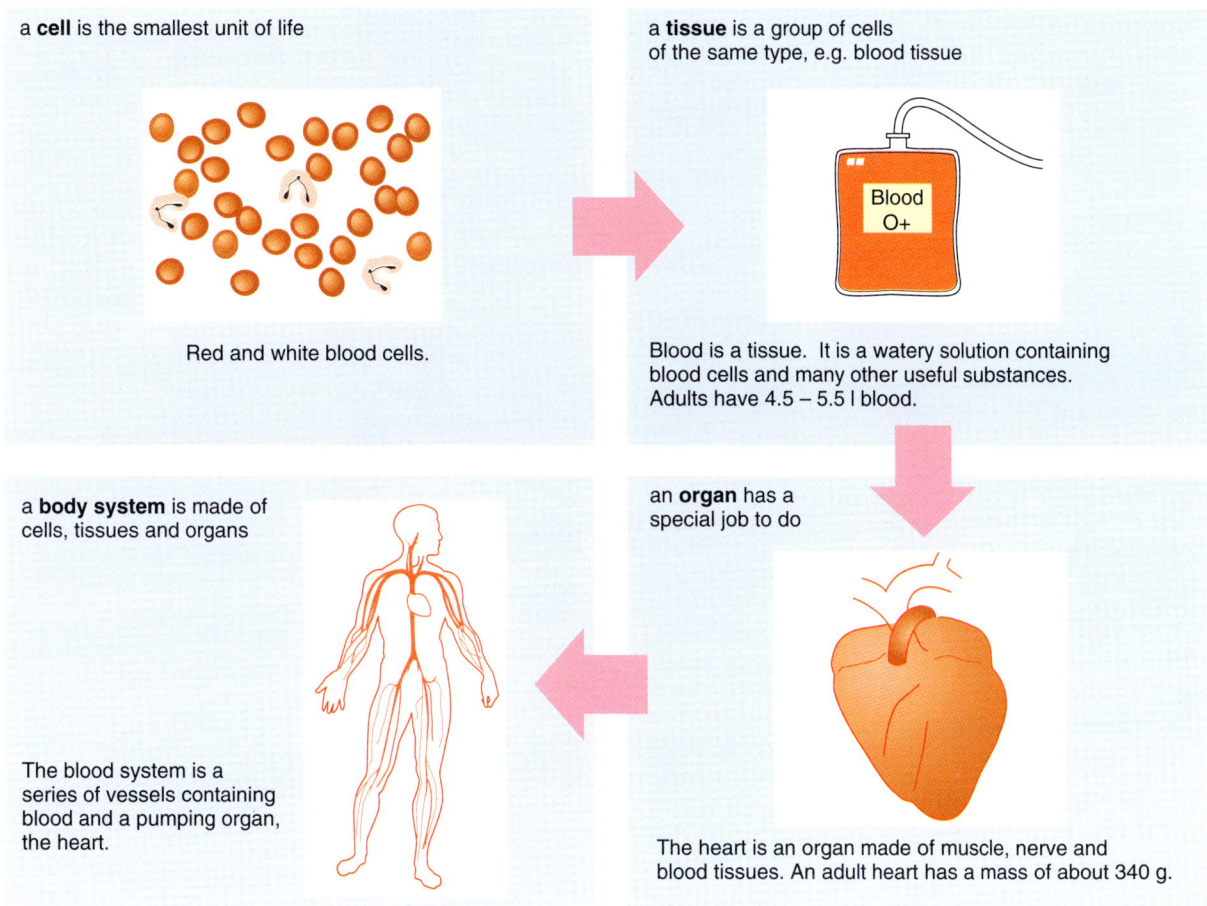

Picture 2   The **circulatory system** is built of cells, tissues and organs.

a **cell** is the smallest unit of life

Red and white blood cells.

a **tissue** is a group of cells of the same type, e.g. blood tissue

Blood is a tissue. It is a watery solution containing blood cells and many other useful substances. Adults have 4.5 – 5.5 l blood.

an **organ** has a special job to do

The heart is an organ made of muscle, nerve and blood tissues. An adult heart has a mass of about 340 g.

a **body system** is made of cells, tissues and organs

The blood system is a series of vessels containing blood and a pumping organ, the heart.

Transport in water

Water is the liquid in all body fluids such as tears, saliva and the tissue fluid that is found between cells. Blood carries dissolved oxygen and carbon dioxide, sugar and salts and many other substances such as hormones, as well as blood cells. Transport systems in plants rely on water too.

Questions

1. Which parts of a cell are common to both plant and animal cells? Which features are only found in plant cells?
2. Which tissues make up the circulatory system?
3. What is an organ? Name five human organs.
4. The main job of the circulatory system is to transport substances around the body. What features make the circulatory system good at transporting?

The human plan

Focus 1

Outlining the human body

The human body is a very complex machine. There are many body systems which work together, performing the processes of life. Picture 1 on this page and continuing overleaf shows the main body systems. Not all the details can be shown in the available space.

The **skeletal system**: Most tissues in the body are soft and they need strong bones to give them support. The skull, ribcage and hip girdle are places where bone surrounds and protects organs. The arms and legs have long bones running down the centre. Muscles are attached to bones and can pull them, causing movement.

The **nervous system**: Seeing and hearing are just two ways we can sense what's going on around us. The nervous system links different parts of the body and helps us to
- detect changes
- decide how to react
- cause a reaction to happen.

Sense organs such as the eye, nerves and the brain make up the nervous system.

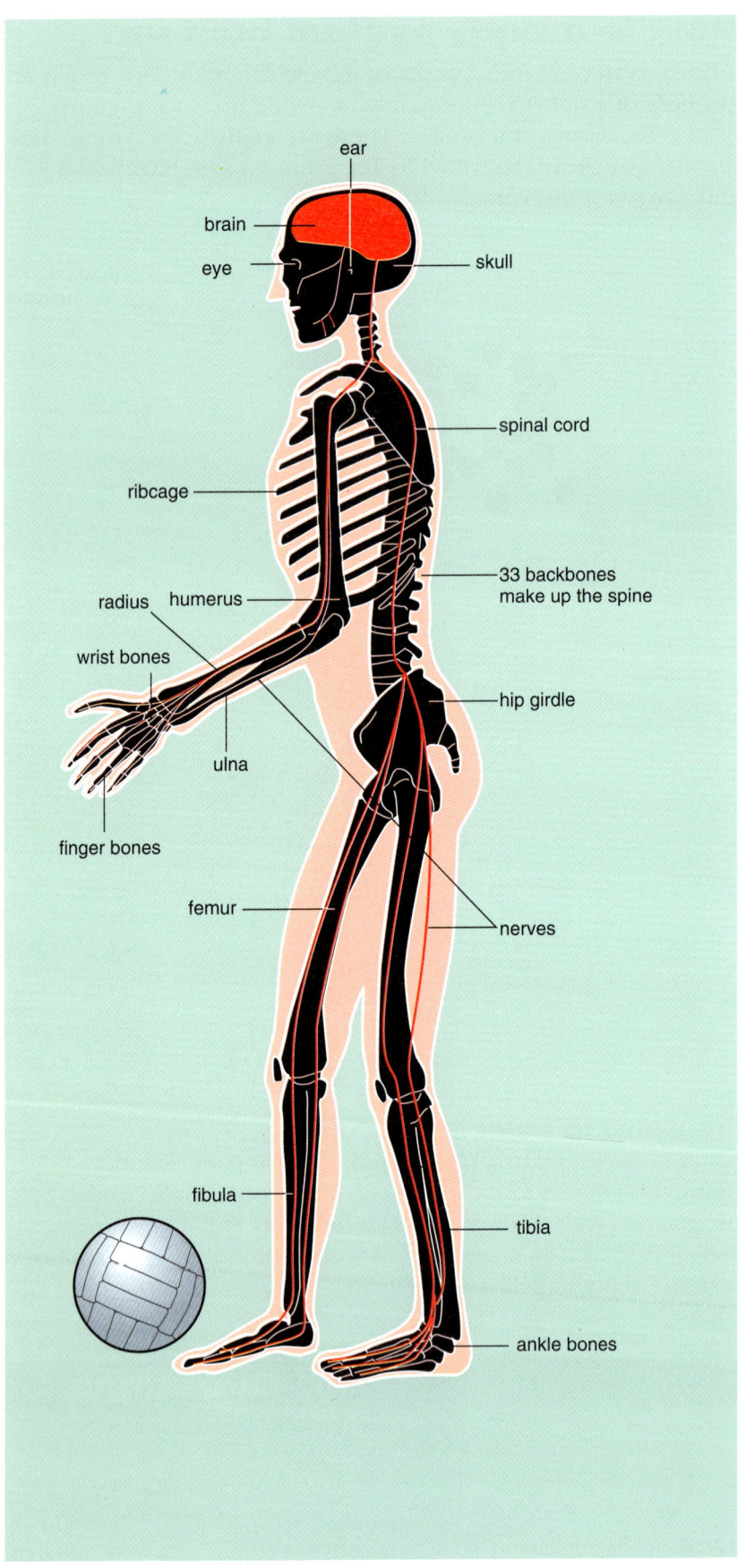

Picture 1   Skeletal and nervous systems.

Introducing living systems

The **breathing system**: Air moves in and out of the chest cavity when we breathe. To make this happen, we change the size of the chest cavity and the pressure inside it. Breathing movements involve the ribs and diaphragm. Air moves in and out of the lungs through tubes. The tubes branch many times, and then end in tiny air sacs. In the air sacs, gases pass into and out of the bloodstream.

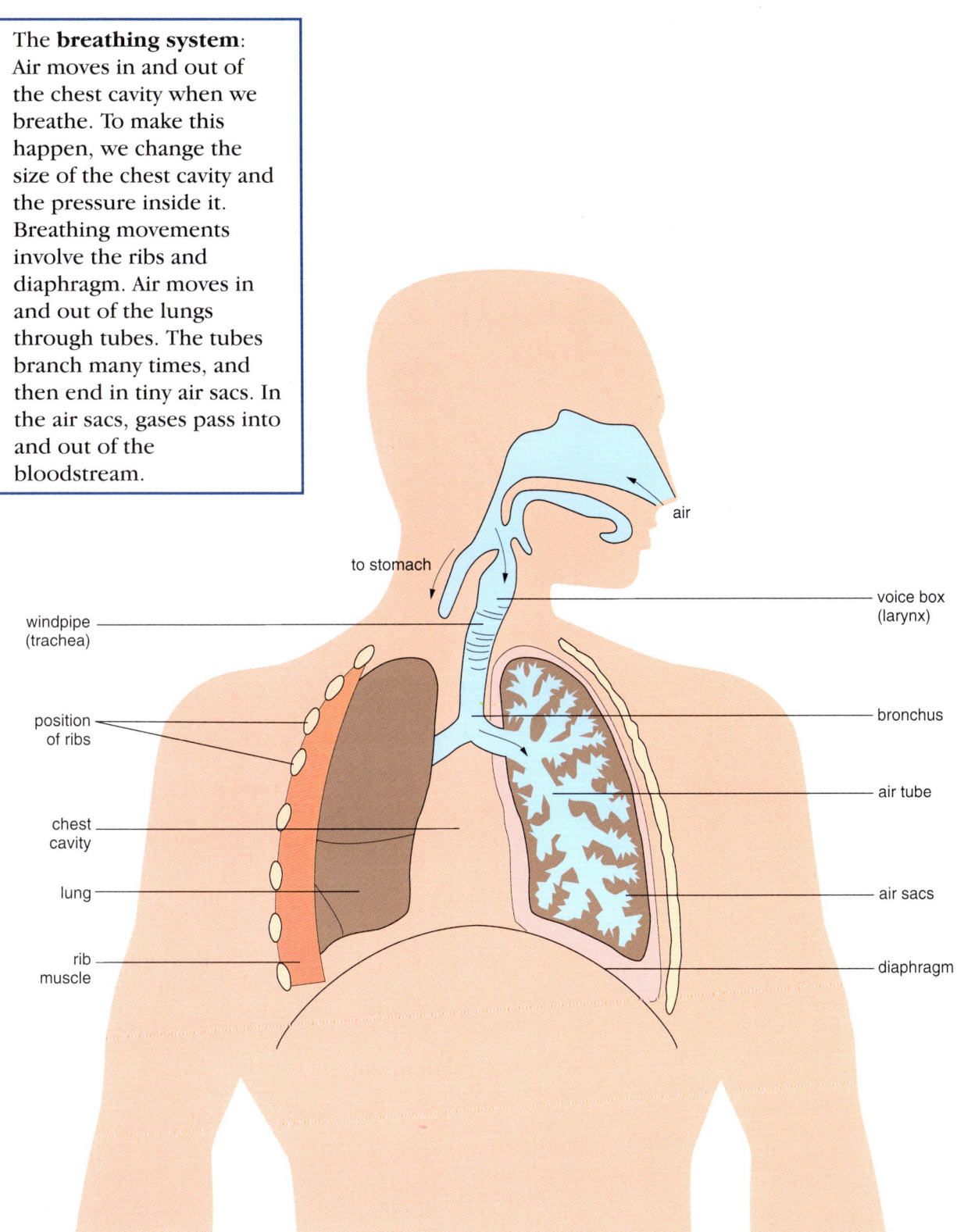

Picture 2   Breathing system.

The human plan

The **digestive system**: Packed up inside the abdomen are the organs that deal with the food we eat. Food is broken down into smaller and smaller particles until it can pass through into the bloodstream. Any food that is not digested passes out of the body through the anus. The liver works alongside the digestive system, controlling the level of food in the blood and removing toxic substances.

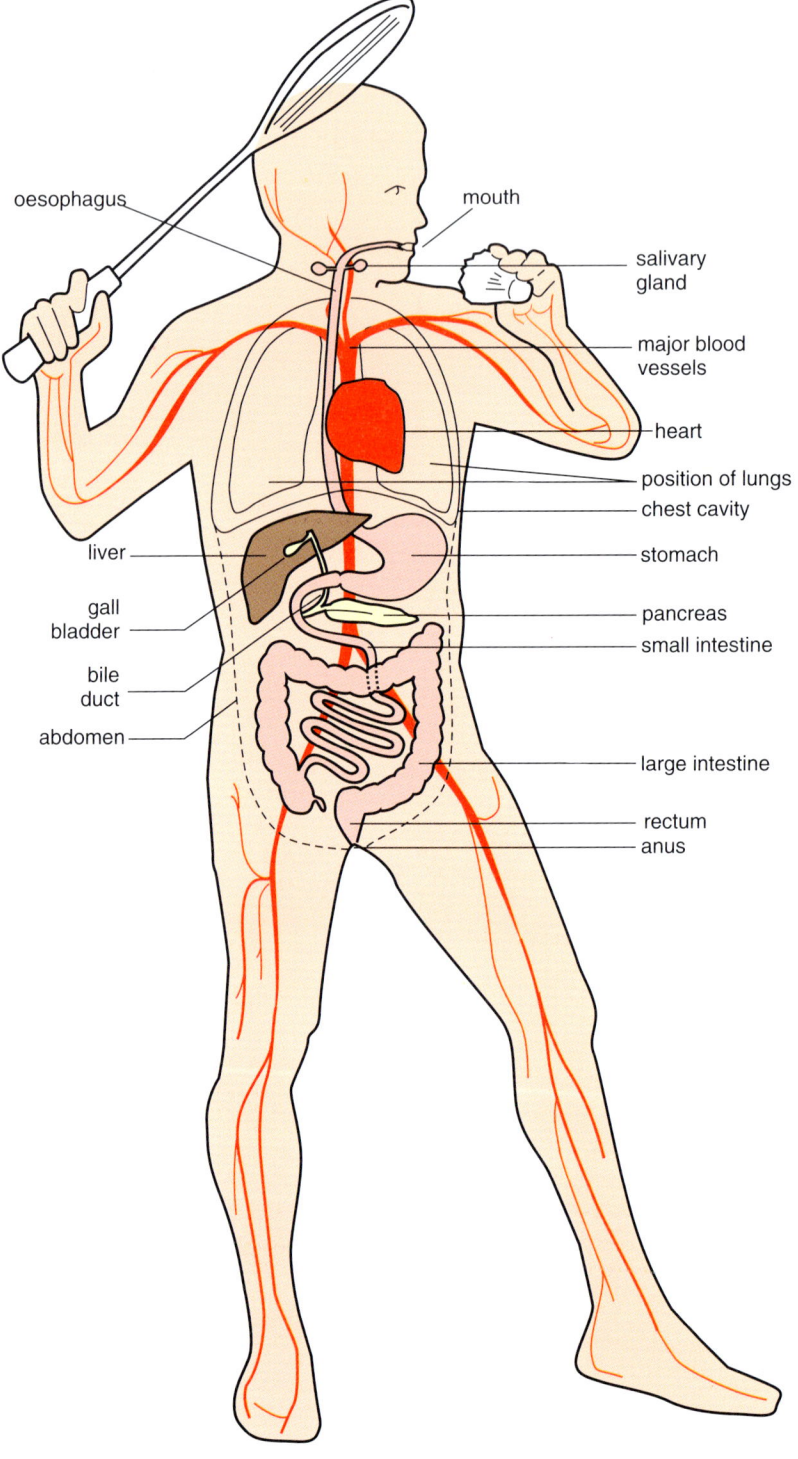

The **blood system**: The blood carries useful substances to cells as it flows through all parts of the body. At the same time blood collects waste products that need to be got rid of. The blood system keeps the blood flowing and its major job is transport. Fighting bacteria which cause infection is another important job of the blood.

Picture 3 Digestive and blood systems.

Introducing living systems

The urine system: The kidneys have the job of keeping the right balance of water and salts in our bodies. As the blood moves through the kidneys, any unwanted water and salts, and waste products such as urea, pass into urine. Urine collects in the bladder. Every now and then urine passes out of the body through the urethra.

The reproductive system: Sex cells are made in the sex organs. In males, sperm cells are made in the testes. They move out of the body along the sperm tube and urethra. In females, egg cells (or ova) are made in the ovaries. They move along the oviducts to the uterus. Fertilisation happens when sex cells fuse. A fertilised egg develops into a baby in the uterus and at birth it leaves the body through the vagina.

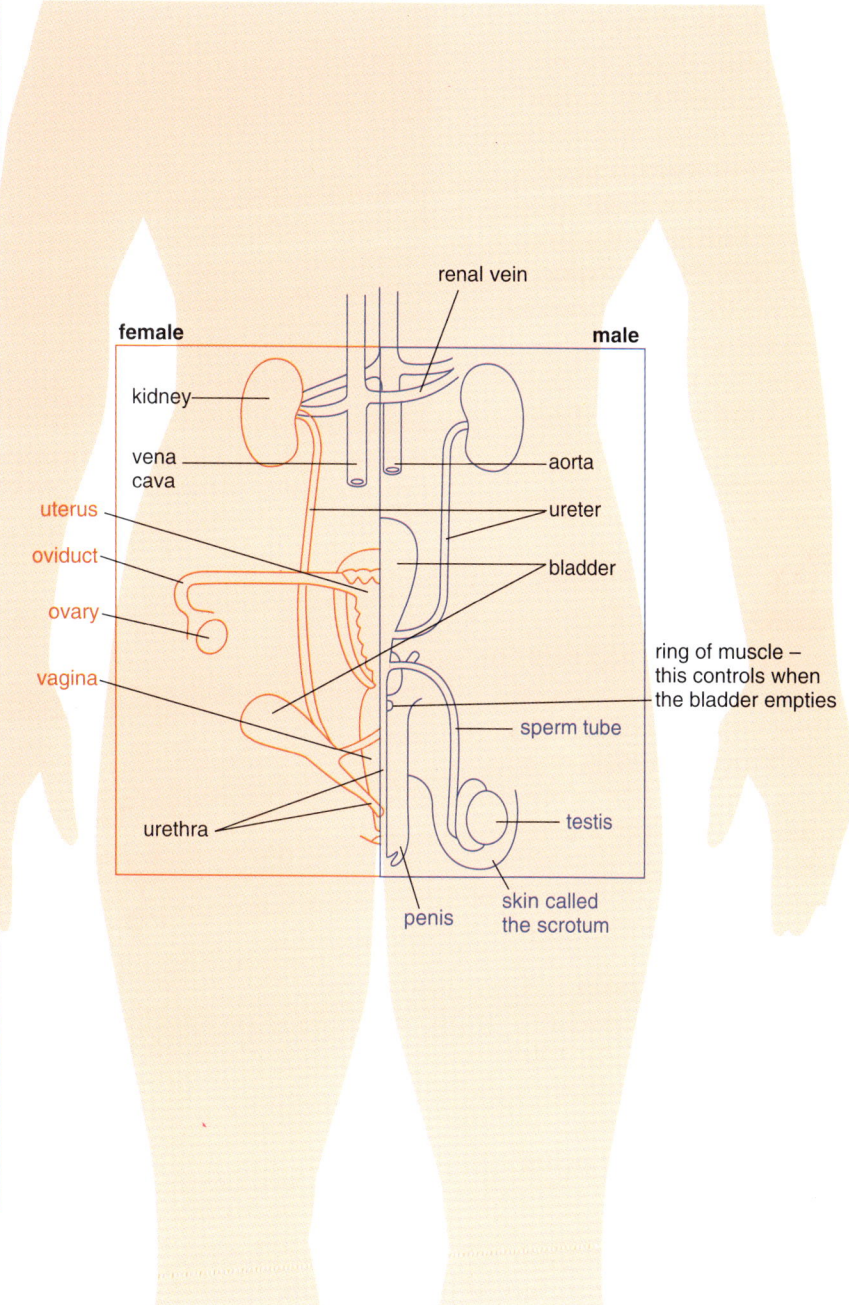

Picture 4 Urine and reproductive systems.

Questions

1. Which body system helps to get oxygen into the body?

2. The circulatory system transports substances around the body. Name two body systems which are closely linked to the circulatory system.

3. a) What are the functions of the skeletal system?

   b) Name two tissues which help to form the skeletal system.

4. a) Which body system is concerned with reproduction?

   b) Which organs produce sex cells? In which organ does the baby develop?

5. Which part of the nervous system deals with information collected by the sense organs?

Skin deep

What is skin?

Skin is more than a pretty covering. Skin is an 'organ' because it is specially designed to carry out many vital jobs. Although skin is quite tough it may get damaged. If a large area is injured, the major danger is that fluid leaks out, which can cause death. Bacteria can get in through a wound and cause infection.

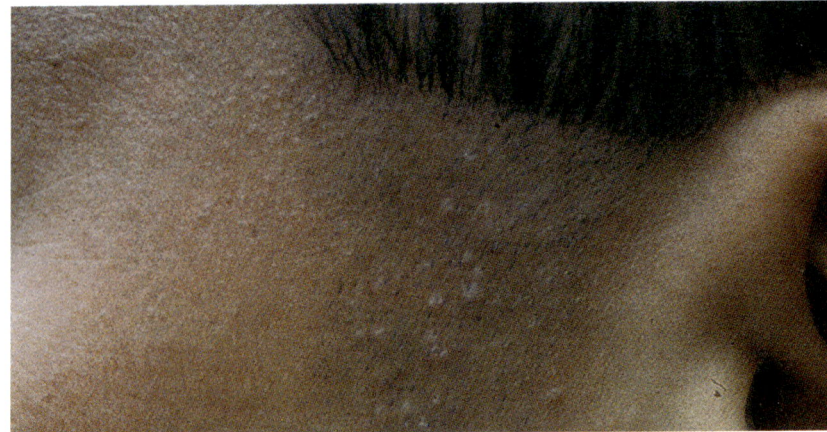

Picture 1 Skin is about 0.5–4.0 mm deep and consists of many layers of cells along with other tissues such as blood, nerves and fat.

Why is skin so important?

Skin is protective and helps to prevent injury. It is made of several layers of cells closely packed together. Bacteria can't get through the skin easily. If the skin is cut it can mend itself, because new cells keep growing from the lower part of the epidermis.

A 2.5 cm³ block of skin contains about 650 sweat glands, 100 oil glands, 1500 sensory receptors and 3 million cells which are constantly dying and being replaced.

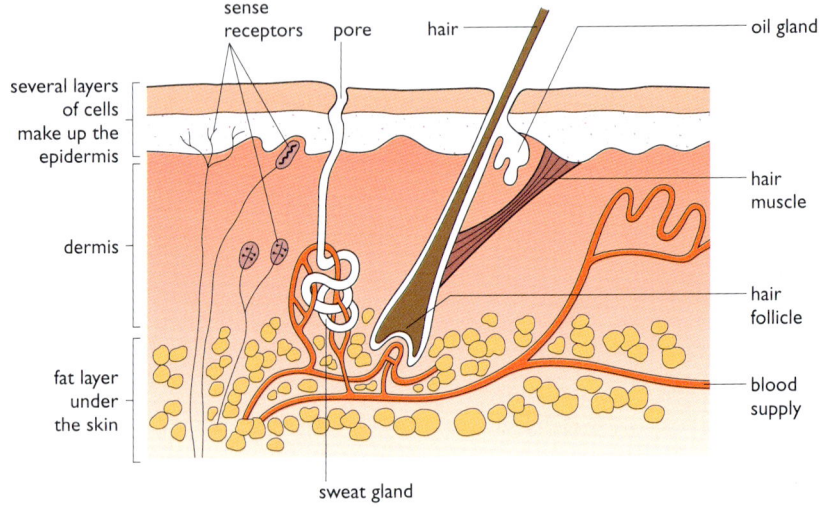

Picture 2 An illustration of the skin.

New cells are made in the lower part of the epidermis. They move up towards the surface of the skin as they get older. The older cells become waterproof and stop the underlying tissues drying out. The oldest layers of cells die and later flake off. Oils from the oil gland keep the skin in good condition.

Heating is needed to make water evaporate, so evaporation at the body surface has a cooling effect. Picture 3 shows how a dog can cool itself by lolling out its tongue and panting. Sweating has the same cooling effect when the water in sweat evaporates.

One major job of the skin is to help regulate our body temperature. This is partly due to sweating. The amount of blood passing near the skin surface can be increased or decreased, causing more or less cooling. Although we are not very hairy in comparison to some other animals, the hairs can stand up and

Picture 3 Panting may look like hot work but it actually cools the dog.

Introducing living systems

trap air. This helps to insulate the body and keep us warmer (see pages 84-85 and *Physical Processes*, Focus 6).

Because our skins are sensitive we can perform delicate tasks. The fingertips have many sense **receptors** so we can feel what we're doing. Pain is an early warning system that may stop skin being damaged.

Picture 4 The Braille system can be used by people with blindness. It involves a pattern of raised dots. Sense receptors in Lara's fingertips can detect the pattern of dots.

Picture 5 Sunbathing is not good for pale skin. It may cause sunburn, and ages the skin. Exposing pale skin to the sun, especially in childhood, increases the risk of skin cancer. It is 200 times more frequent in parts of Australia than in India for this reason.

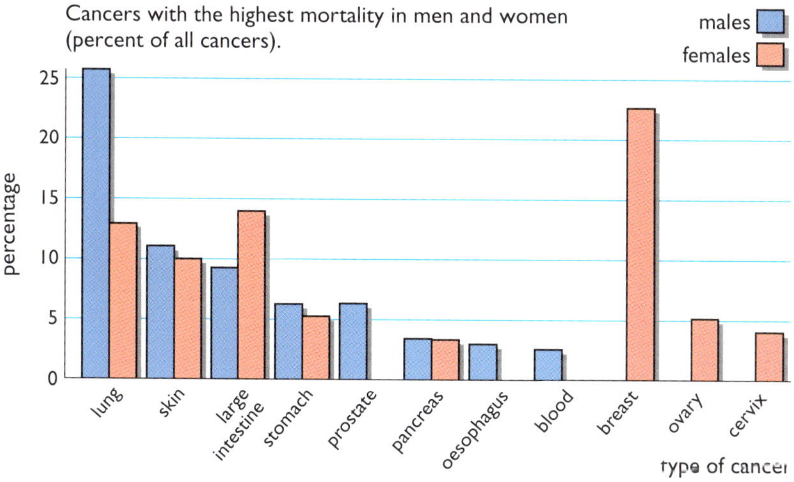

Human skin usually contains a brown colour. Some people have much browner skin than others, especially if they come from a hot country. Skin is sensitive to sunlight. It makes more brown colour (gets more tanned) in the sun. The brown colour helps to stop the sun damaging the skin. Sunscreen lotion filters out or blocks some sunlight, and can stop sunburn altogether.

Picture 6 Skin cancer is the second most common type of fatal cancer. There are many different types of skin cancer.
From *Target Cancer*, ABPI.

Questions

1. What are the main layers in the skin? In which layer do cells divide, replacing dead ones that flake off at the surface?
2. How does skin help to protect us against disease?
3. Why is nerve tissue an important part of skin?
4. Describe three ways in which skin is involved in controlling body temperature.
5. Which features help to keep skin waterproof?
6. a) Why can sunbathing be dangerous to the skin?
   b) Suggest why the number of cases of skin cancer is increasing now that air travel is cheaper.

The plant body

The parts of a plant

The main parts of the plant body are leaves, stems and roots, and the reproductive structures (flowers or cones). Different tissues make up the whole plant. For example, a transport tissue links all the regions of the plant's body. Picture 1 shows the main parts of a plant.

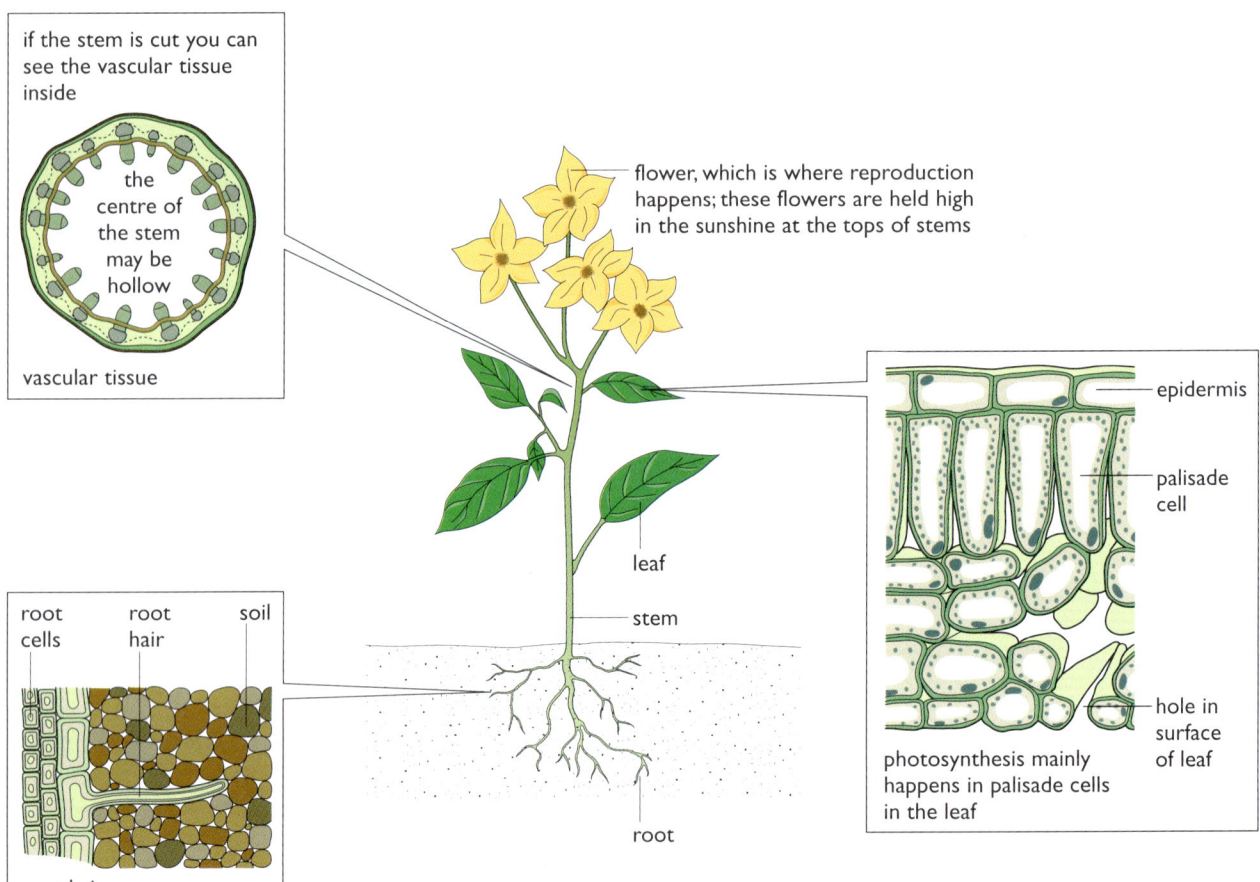

Picture 1   Plan of a plant.

Leaves are like food 'factories'. They produce a simple carbohydrate food (sugar) from carbon dioxide and water. This process is called **photosynthesis**. Plants convert around 3.5×10^6 kg of carbon dioxide into sugars each year.

Leaves vary in shape and size, but whatever their design, they need the sun as an energy source. Each leaf is like a thin sheet, so all the cells are near to either the upper or the lower surface. Light can shine through to the cells. Some leaf surfaces have tiny holes, where gases can move in and out. Plants are cooled when water evaporates through pores in the leaf surfaces.

Stems are a link between the roots and all other parts of the shoot. Water and food supplies move through stems. Stems usually hold the leaves and flowers above ground level. Some stems trail, and others creep along the ground surface, sometimes rooting at intervals.

Introducing living systems

Vascular tissue carries water and dissolved food around the plant. It is made of different types of cells including some which are like tubes.

Roots spread away from the base of the main stem, growing between stones and soil particles. They act like an anchor, holding the plant in place. Picture 1 shows a root hair which forms near the tips of roots. The **root hairs** are cells which are shaped like a finger on the outer surface. There are many root hairs, and they give roots a big surface area for absorbing water and minerals from the soil.

Seed-producing plants have **flowers** or **cones** for reproduction. The male parts make **pollen** and the female parts contain egg cells called **ovules**. **Fertilisation** involves a pollen grain and an ovule. A seed develops when the nuclei of these cells join.

Sometimes plants die during the winter. Seeds make sure that when spring comes, new plants will grow. Seeds also spread away from the parent plants to new places.

Picture 2 These yellow iris flowers are brightly coloured to attract insects, which will carry pollen from them to fertilise other flowers.

Growing points

The **buds** at the tips of stems are places where growth happens. The buds may give rise to leaves and more stem, or to flowers. Growth is rapid at the tips of young roots too, causing an increase in length. Increase in girth is due to cells dividing in a layer called the **cambium**. Bark forms from several layers of cells at the surface of tree stems.

Water supports

Aquatic plants and animals live in water. Water is denser than air and gives support to things that live in it. Aquatic animals don't have such a large bony skeleton as land animals for this reason. Aquatic plants often have very long, thin stems that trail in the water which supports them.

Water can support bodies from the inside too. Imagine a plant in dry soil. If the plant loses more water than it takes in, it starts to wilt.

Questions

1. a) Which part of the plant carries out photosynthesis?

   b) Why does a plant carry out photosynthesis?

2. a) Name some substances that move into and out of a leaf.

   b) Why do leaves have a thin shape?

3. a) Insects visit plants to get pollen. They carry pollen from flower to flower which helps seeds form. How do tall stems help in this process?

   b) A student grew some bean seeds. He noticed that the roots got longer very rapidly. Suggest how he might show that a root grows at its tip.

4. Suggest reasons why water is important in living things.

About LIVING THINGS

'There is a wealth of life in the world. To begin to understand this life is to begin to wonder at its beauty and complexity.'

Margaret Williams, Biologist

A quick squirt brings food into reach for this archer fish

The woodpecker finch is using a twig to extend its beak

The fight for food

For many people, getting food is simply a matter of going to the supermarket. Other people hunt or farm. In some cases, animals have developed very clever ways of collecting food. An archer fish can direct a squirt of water to take its prey by surprise. The water jet knocks the insect into the water, and the fish eats it.

Notice the skill of the woodpecker finch. It's using a twig as a tool to dig insects out from tiny cracks in the bark.

Life support

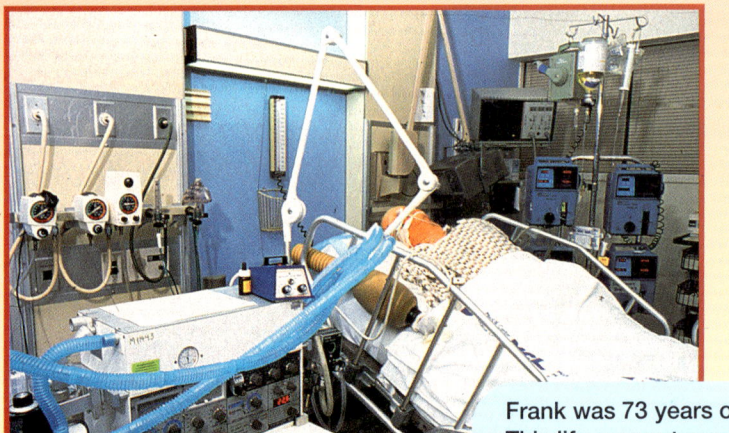

The body may stop working if an important organ is damaged. A life support machine takes over the job of the damaged organ. Sometimes a machine like this is used during an operation. For example, the heart must stay still while a surgeon works on it. A life support machine is used to pump the blood round the body while the heart is not beating.

Frank was 73 years old when his heart failed. This life support machine kept him alive for the first few critical hours, while a medical team worked to save his life.

DEAD or ALIVE?

Sometimes the life processes slow down so much it's difficult to tell if something really is alive. Many small animals, such as dormice, hibernate in winter (see pages 82–83). They go into a deep sleep called hibernation, so their bodies are transferring less energy.

Dormant seeds

Plants may survive difficult times by producing seeds, which can stay dormant. This means they are not actively growing. The peanuts are still alive and might grow into new peanut plants. The dry roasted peanuts are dead. Why?

Dry roasted peanuts

Peanuts fresh from the plant

Growing

Did you grow out of your clothes very fast at certain times in your life? A spider can do better than that – it outgrows its own skin. This is an old skin left behind by a tarantula. After pushing its way out of the skin, a spider expands in size before the new skin hardens.

Cast off – the old skin shed by a tarantula

On the *move*

Aquafit for elephants? Exercising in water is good for the body because there is less impact on the joints

An adult male elephant can weigh a hefty 6 tonnes, and is not really a fast mover on land. But perhaps it's not surprising that they can be good swimmers. The water gives support to their massive bulk. What's more, an elephant has a ready-made snorkel (its trunk) if it needs to breathe underwater.

Introducing living systems

Summary

► A life process is an activity of living things. The main life processes are:

- *Nutrition:* food is a source of raw materials and energy. Animals feed on ready-made food. Plants make their own food during photosynthesis.
- *Respiration:* transfers energy from food to the body.
- *Growth:* an increase in size such as mass or length, but not just an increase in water content.
- *Reproduction:* making new individuals.
- *Excretion:* getting rid of waste materials such as urine, faeces, and carbon dioxide.
- *Sensitivity:* being able to detect changes inside and outside the body.
- *Movement:* most animals can move from place to place by themselves.

► A cell is the smallest unit of life. Cells have a surface membrane, and cytoplasm with a nucleus. Plant cells also have a cell wall, a vacuole and chloroplasts.

► Tissues are made of many cells of the same type, e.g. muscle tissue is made of muscle cells.

► An organ such as the heart is made of several tissues. It has special jobs to do. Skin is an example of an organ.

► Body systems such as the digestive system are made up of organs and tissues. The body systems work together.

► The main parts of a plant are the stem, bud, leaf, root and flower or cone.

Questions

1. There are seven life processes common to living organisms. These are:

   **excretion   feeding   growth   movement
   reproduction   respiration   sensitivity**

   The table describes some of these processes in humans.
   Finish the table by writing in the correct process for each description.
   The first one has been done for you.

2. The diagram shows a section through Alan's skin.
   a) Add labels to the diagram to show which is
      i) the fatty layer
      ii) the epidermis.
   b) Alan feels cold. Suggest **two** things which happen in Alan's skin when he feels cold.
   c) Describe how messages travel from the skin to the brain.

   MEG

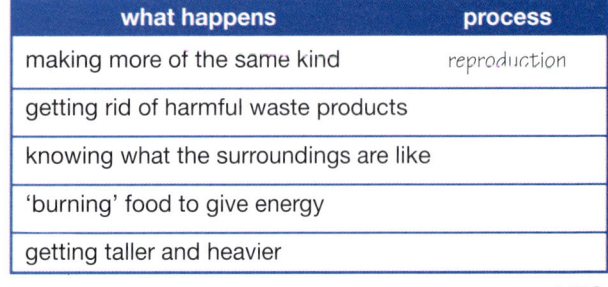

what happens	process
making more of the same kind	reproduction
getting rid of harmful waste products	
knowing what the surroundings are like	
'burning' food to give energy	
getting taller and heavier	

MEG

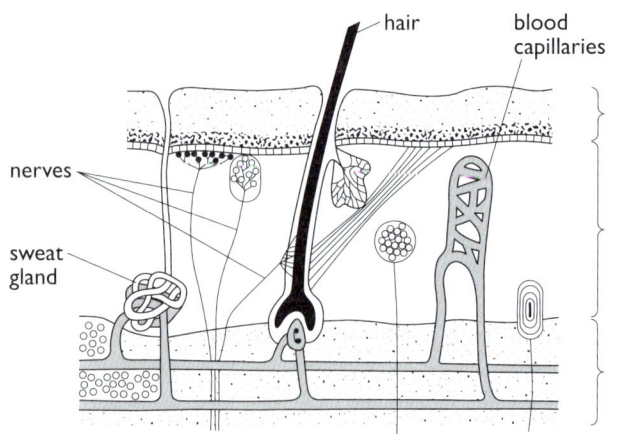

Questions continued

3 The diagram shows a plant.
  a) Which part of the plant labelled in the diagram
   i) contains reproductive organs?
   ii) takes in minerals?
  b) The leaves contain green chloroplasts.
  Why are most of these chloroplasts found in the palisade layer of the leaf?
  c) i) Which labelled part of the plant loses most water?
   ii) What would happen to the leaves if the roots stopped taking in water?
  d) Explain why plants grown from seeds are similar to the plants the seeds came from.
  e) A farmer collected some seeds from one plant, and sowed them in two different fields. She noticed that the plants which she grew from these seeds were larger in one field than the other.
  Explain why this can happen.

  MEG

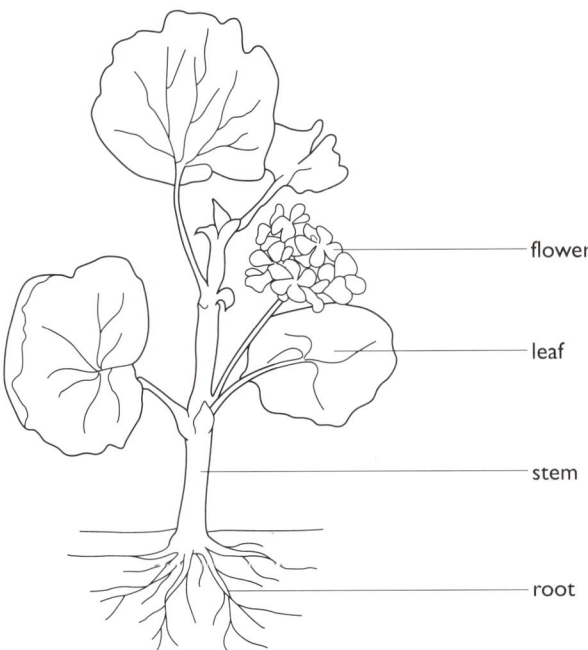

4 The diagram shows human body systems.

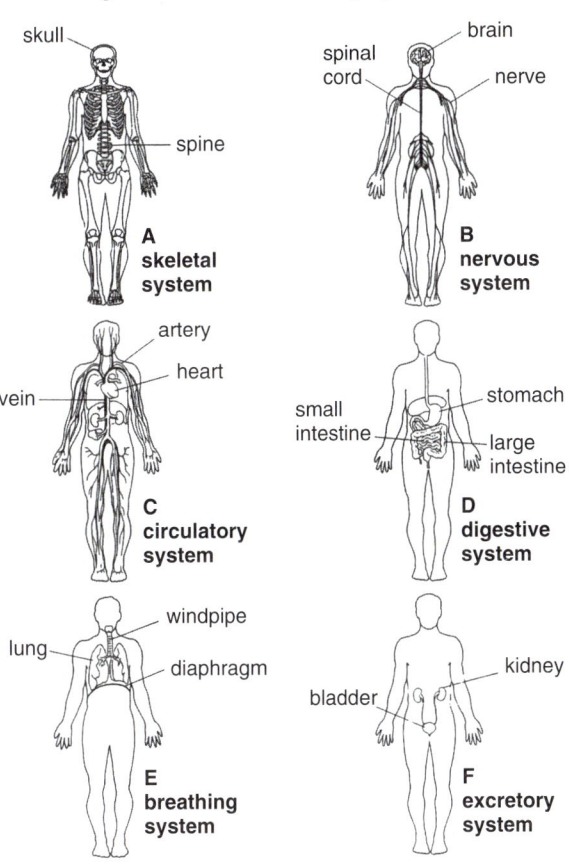

  a) Which diagram shows the system which
   i) filters the blood and removes poisonous waste
   ii) gets oxygen into the blood
   iii) supports the body
   iv) makes the body aware of its surroundings
   v) breaks down food
   vi) carries oxygen around the body?

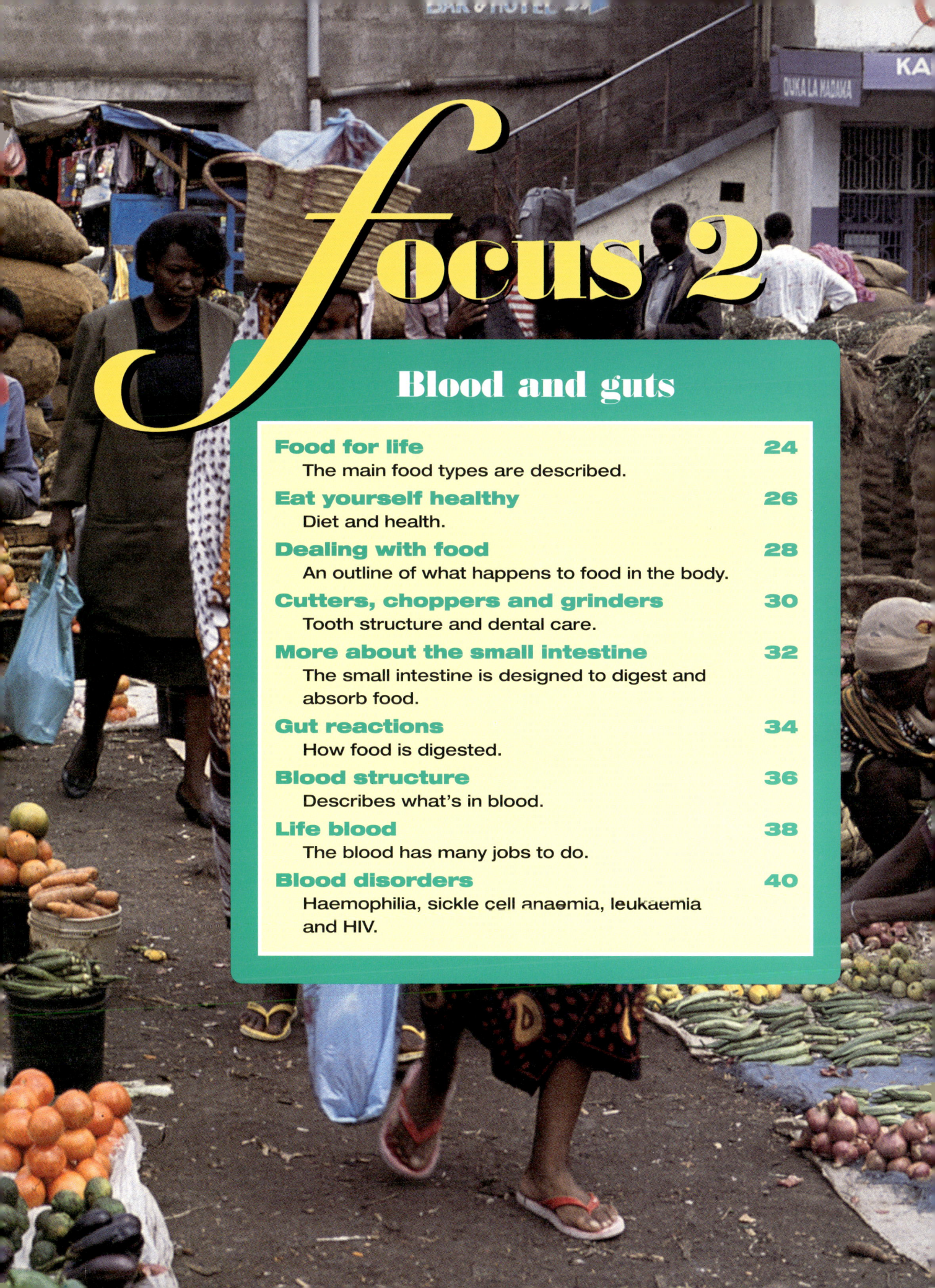

focus 2

Blood and guts

Food for life — 24
The main food types are described.

Eat yourself healthy — 26
Diet and health.

Dealing with food — 28
An outline of what happens to food in the body.

Cutters, choppers and grinders — 30
Tooth structure and dental care.

More about the small intestine — 32
The small intestine is designed to digest and absorb food.

Gut reactions — 34
How food is digested.

Blood structure — 36
Describes what's in blood.

Life blood — 38
The blood has many jobs to do.

Blood disorders — 40
Haemophilia, sickle cell anaemia, leukaemia and HIV.

Food for life

Food types

What type of food do you like? You can probably name several favourite foods. When the term **'food type'** is used in biology, it describes a substance in food, rather than a particular food such as chips.

The main food types are protein, carbohydrates and fats. All these are based on the element carbon and are called **organic** substances. Minerals and vitamins are very important too, even though we only need small amounts.

Some animals, such as a desert rat, get all the water they need from eating food. Humans drink a lot of extra liquid which is an important part of their diet.

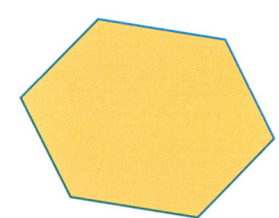

This is one sugar unit. It's often drawn as a simple ring. e.g. glucose

Carbohydrates

Carbohydrates are made from carbon, hydrogen and oxygen. Sugar, starch and cellulose are common carbohydrates made by plants. Cellulose is built from many long chains of glucose units. The result is a strong and tough material that helps to support plants. Cellulose in cereals, fruits and vegetables is called **fibre**. Fibre helps to keep food moving through the gut, and stops us getting constipated.

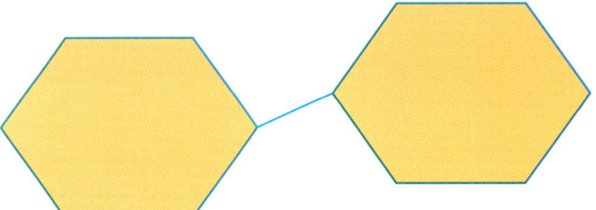

This sugar contains two units. e.g. sucrose

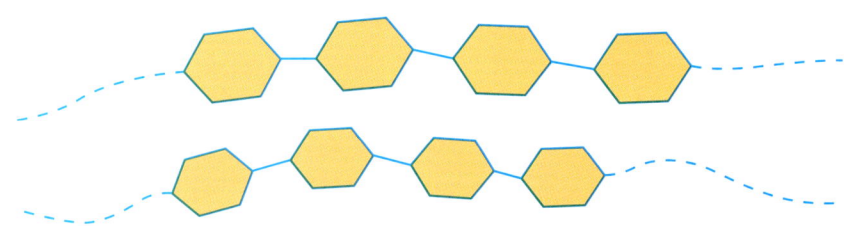

Many sugar units join in long branched chains. e.g. starch

Picture 1 The structure of some carbohydrates.

Food	Fibre content (%)
All-bran	30
apples	2
bananas	3
French beans	3
blackberries	7
Brazil nuts	9
wholemeal bread	7.5
white bread	4
raw cabbage	3
cornflakes	11
fruit cake	3
white rice	3

Source: Bender and Bender 'Food tables'

Table 1 Percentage of fibre in foods.

Glycogen is a carbohydrate made by animals. It is stored in the liver. Like sugar and starch, glycogen is an energy-rich food. The energy in food is transferred to cells during respiration.

Proteins

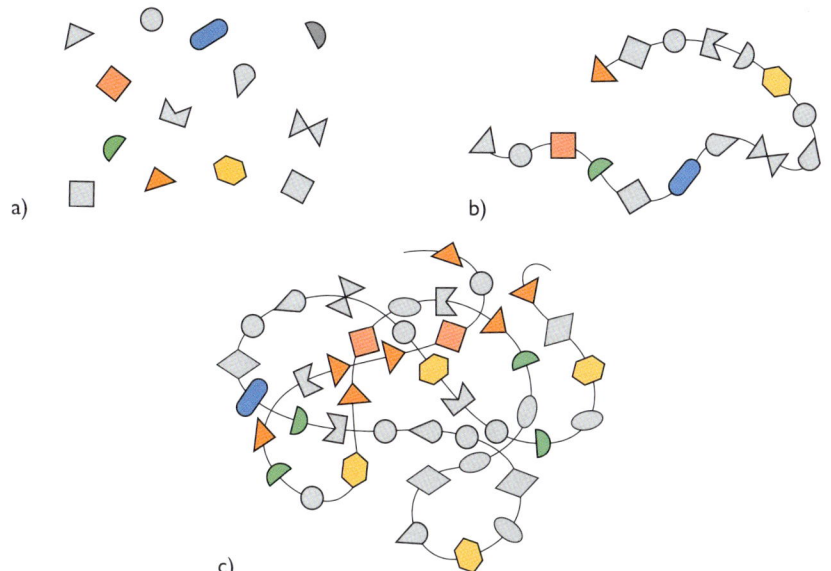

Picture 2 a) Amino acids. b) Amino acids join end-to-end in long chains. c) The chains are folded into a particular shape.

Proteins are also built from small units called **amino acids**. There are about 20 different amino acids. A protein may contain any combination of amino acids in any order, and so a huge variety of proteins is possible.

Proteins are needed to build new cells when living things grow. They make up important substances such as enzymes too. Enzymes are important in cells because they are catalysts (see pages 34–35 in this book).

Fats and oils

Fats and oils are high in energy, and may be stored in both plants and animals. Fats are solid at room temperature and usually come from an animal source, e.g. meat. Oils are liquid at room temperature and are usually stored by plants, e.g. in sunflower seeds. Apart from being an energy source, fats act as insulators and shock absorbers in animals. They are also important for building cell membranes.

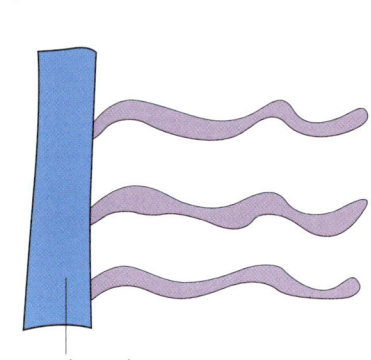

Picture 3 A fat is made of fatty acids. A fatty acid has an acid at one end. The fatty acids are joined by glycerol.

Questions

1. **a)** What is fibre?
   b) Why is fibre important in the diet?
   c) Name some foods that someone might choose to eat if they wanted to prevent constipation.

2. Which foods are high energy foods?

3. Which foods provide materials for cell growth?

4. Design a table to make a summary of information about food types. Here are some points to include:
   - name of food type
   - example of a food which is a source of the food type
   - chemical elements
   - how the food type is used.

Eat yourself healthy

Your diet is what you eat

Meals are usually a mixture of different types of food. A quick snack may contain mostly one type of food, e.g. a chocolate bar contains a lot of sugar. Eating a variety of foods helps to make sure that we get all the materials that the body needs. Fresh foods such as fruit and vegetables are very important. When vegetables are cooked they lose some of their mineral and vitamin content.

Humans may have a choice about what they eat, which leads to problems if they choose the wrong things. Wild animals (such as the song thrush in Picture 1) may reject some foods, but will generally eat whatever they can find. Other animals eat a limited range of foods, e.g. pandas rely on bamboo which is becoming scarce.

Picture 1 What's on the menu? A song thrush eats a variety of animal and plant foods.

What is a balanced diet?

A **balanced diet** contains all the types of food our bodies need, in the right amounts. Picture 2 shows a variety of foods. They are in groups according to the food type that they mostly contain.

Here are some points to consider about diet:
- how much energy a person needs depends on their lifestyle. Many people in developing countries don't get enough energy from food. This means people live for a shorter time and are more likely to become ill. On the other hand, many people in the UK and USA eat too much, and become overweight because their bodies store fat. This leads to heart disease which can be fatal.
- eating a lot of sugar can mean decayed teeth, as well as getting overweight.
- some amino acids, vitamins and minerals are essential for staying healthy (see *Materials* page 54 for information on diseases that result from a lack of these substances).

Picture 2 You can choose from many different foods to get a healthy diet, as long as you get the right balance.

Blood and guts

Special diets

Some people need special diets because of a medical condition. For example:

- a person with diabetes needs to control the amount of sugar they eat (see page 61)
- a person whose kidneys are not working properly should not eat a lot of protein (see page 81 and pages 88-89)
- some people are allergic to gluten (in wheat) so cannot eat bread or cakes made from wheat flour
- some people make more **cholesterol** in their bodies. This is a fatty substance that sticks on the inside of blood vessels and blocks them up, causing heart disease. Eating a low fat diet can help to reduce the amount of cholesterol made in the body
- some people have very high blood pressure and should not add salt to food or eat salty food.

	Baked potato	Potato crisps
Fibre (g/100g potato)	2	12
Energy (kj)	380	2200
Protein (g)	2	6
Fat (g)	0	35
Carbohydrate (g)	20	50
Water (g)	58	3
Vitamin C (mg)	10	15

Source: Bender and Bender; 'Food tables'

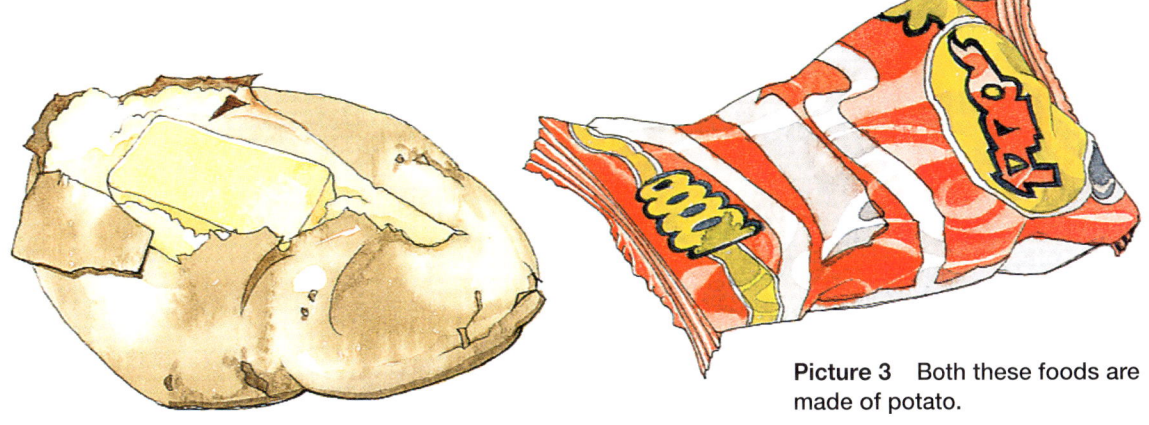

Picture 3 Both these foods are made of potato.

Questions

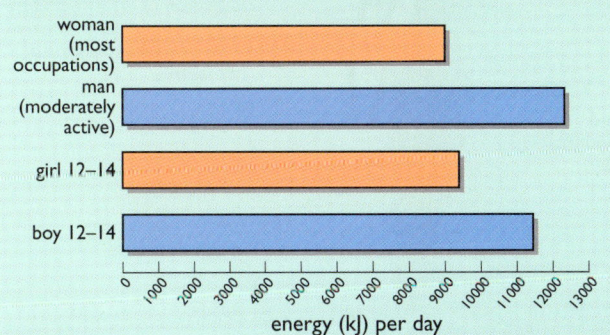

Table 1 Energy requirements for different people.

1 a) Which adults require most energy?

 b) Which young people require most energy?

 c) Suggest a reason why a woman who is breast-feeding needs 11 300 kJ per day, compared to 9200 kJ for other women.

2 a) Which form of potato shown in Picture 3 is mostly healthy? Give reasons why.

 b) Why are raw vegetables, such as salad, good for you?

3 a) Why do people go on slimming diets? Does dieting work?

 b) Find out about the 'slimming disease', anorexia nervosa.

4 a) Keep a diary of everything you eat and drink for a week. Which food types do you eat most of? You may be able to analyse your diet using computer software.

 b) Do you think your diet is healthy?

 c) Could you improve your diet?

Dealing with food

Processing food

Like most animals, we spend a lot of time feeding. It's a major activity in life – getting food, eating it and then dealing with it once it's inside our bodies.

The gut is the part of the body that processes the food we eat. It is really just a tube that stretches from the mouth to the anus. The structure of the tube changes along its length. Also, conditions such as pH (see the box opposite) change in different parts of the gut. This is because each part, such as the stomach or the small intestine, deals with food in a different way.

Food is first **digested**. This means that it is broken down into smaller particles. Then digested food is **absorbed** into the bloodstream. The inside surface of the gut is adapted to absorb water and digested materials easily (see pages 32–33).

Picture 1 describes how the digestive system works with the blood system to get food to all cells of the body. Picture 1 on page 12 in this book shows the layout of the digestive system.

Moving food through the gut

Muscles move food along the gut. Most of the gut has two sets of muscles in the wall. Circular muscles are arranged around the tube and longitudinal muscles run along the length. The stomach has a third set of muscles running at an angle to the other two.

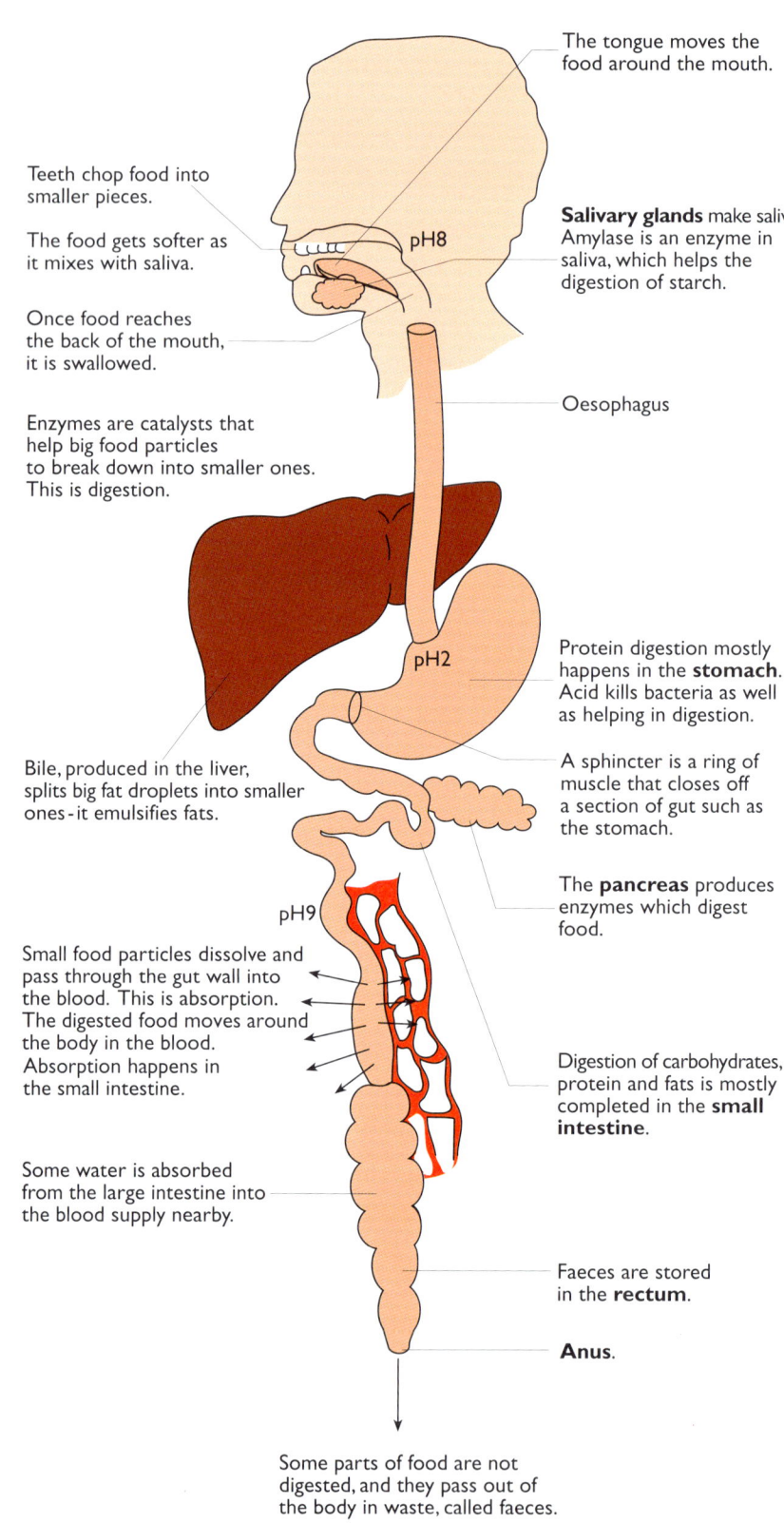

Picture 1 Process and deliver – fresh food gets to every cell in the body, carried by the blood.

Blood and guts

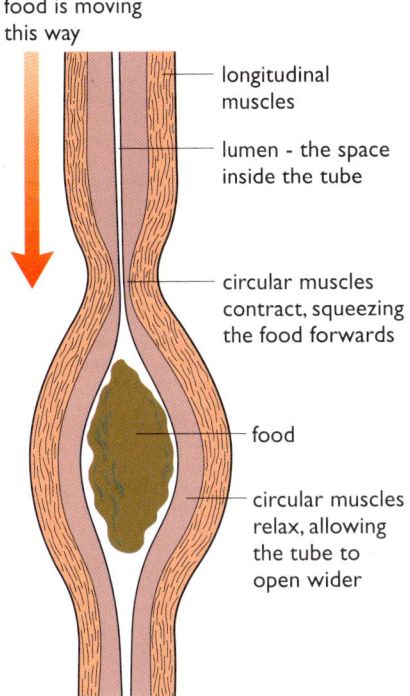

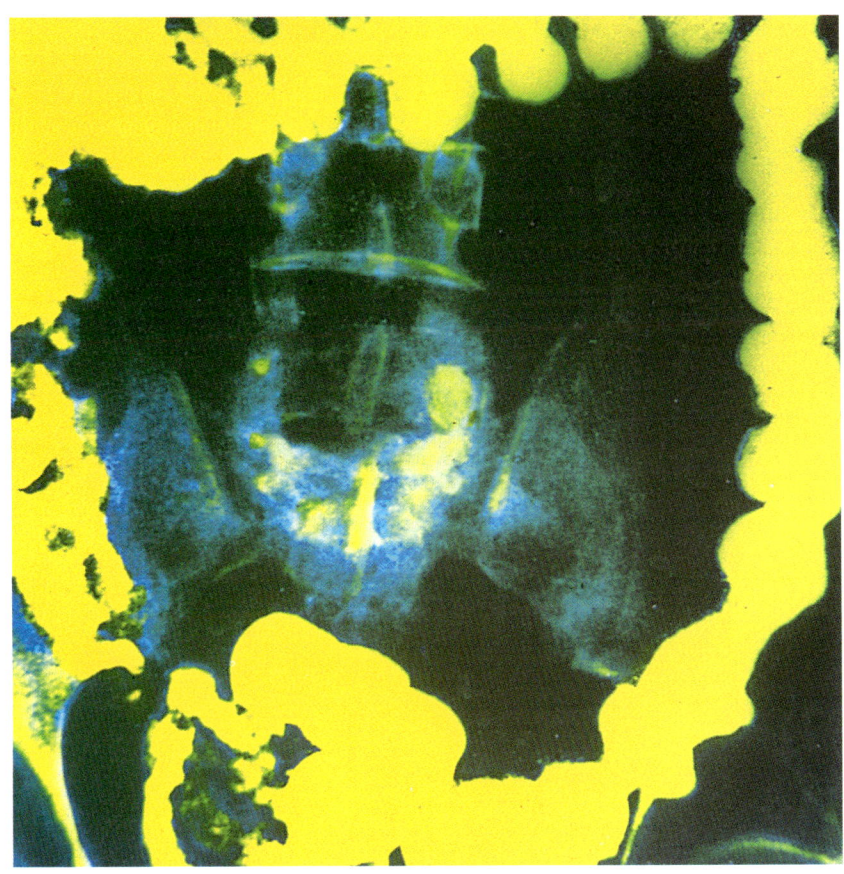

Picture 2 A ball of food is pushed by muscles through the gut.

When muscles contract they shorten in length. You can see from Picture 2 that when circular muscles contract they squeeze the gut, pushing food forward. When circular muscles relax the gut widens allowing food to move along. The longitudinal muscles can shorten sections of the gut, mixing up the food (see *Physical Processes*, Focus 1).

Acid or alkaline?

pH is a scale of acidity. pH 1–6 is acid, the lower the number the more acid. pH 7 is neutral – not acid or alkaline. pH 8–14 is alkaline, the higher the number the more alkaline. pH is important because it affects how enzymes work. Each enzyme will only work at a particular pH.

Questions

1. Why is a good blood supply needed in the digestive system?

2. Copy and complete this table:

Part of the digestive system	What it does
tongue	
saliva	
teeth	
stomach	
small intestine	
large intestine	
rectum	

3. In the stomach wall there are muscles running in three directions. While the ring muscles are closed, food stays in the stomach. What is the purpose of muscle movements while the food is in the stomach?

4. a) What is the pH
    i) in the stomach?
    ii) in the small intestine?

   b) What is the function of stomach acid, apart from helping to digest food?

Cutters, choppers and grinders

The arrangement of teeth

Eating food involves biting, nibbling and chewing. Picture 1 shows the types of teeth that help us eat food. Teeth aren't only used for eating – they're useful as tools and in defence too (see *Physical Processes* page 10).

Picture 2 shows the arrangement of teeth you're likely to have during your lifetime. The 'milk' teeth begin to fall out after the age of 5 years and are gradually replaced by permanent teeth. Teeth aren't necessarily permanent, of course – but they will last longer if you take care of them.

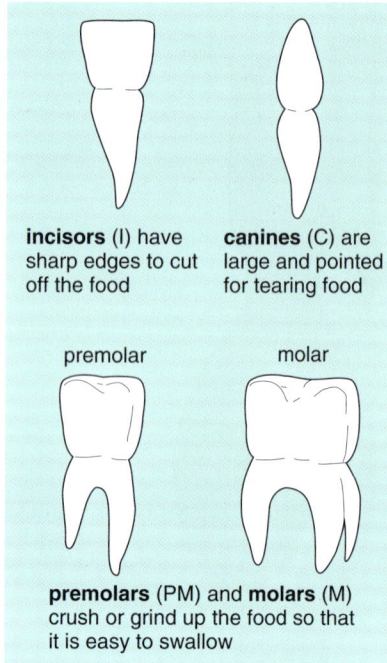

incisors (I) have sharp edges to cut off the food

canines (C) are large and pointed for tearing food

premolars (PM) and **molars** (M) crush or grind up the food so that it is easy to swallow

Picture 1 Each type of tooth is well designed for the job it performs. The shape is important. A molar tooth has a wide top surface for grinding. An incisor tooth has a narrow edge, which means that only small forces are enough to cut food.

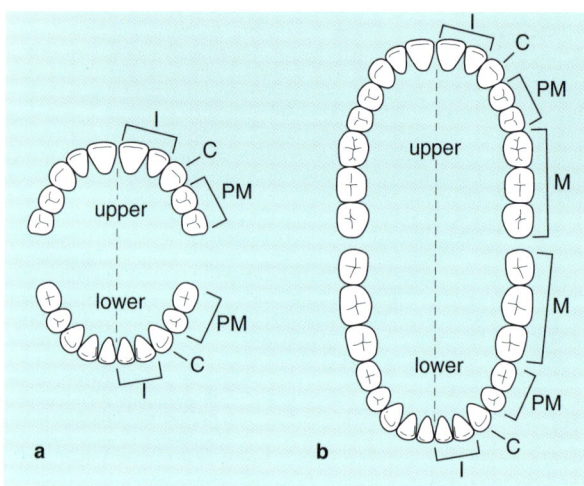

Picture 2 a) 'Milk' teeth in a 4 year old child. b) Teeth of an adult, also shown in the skull below.

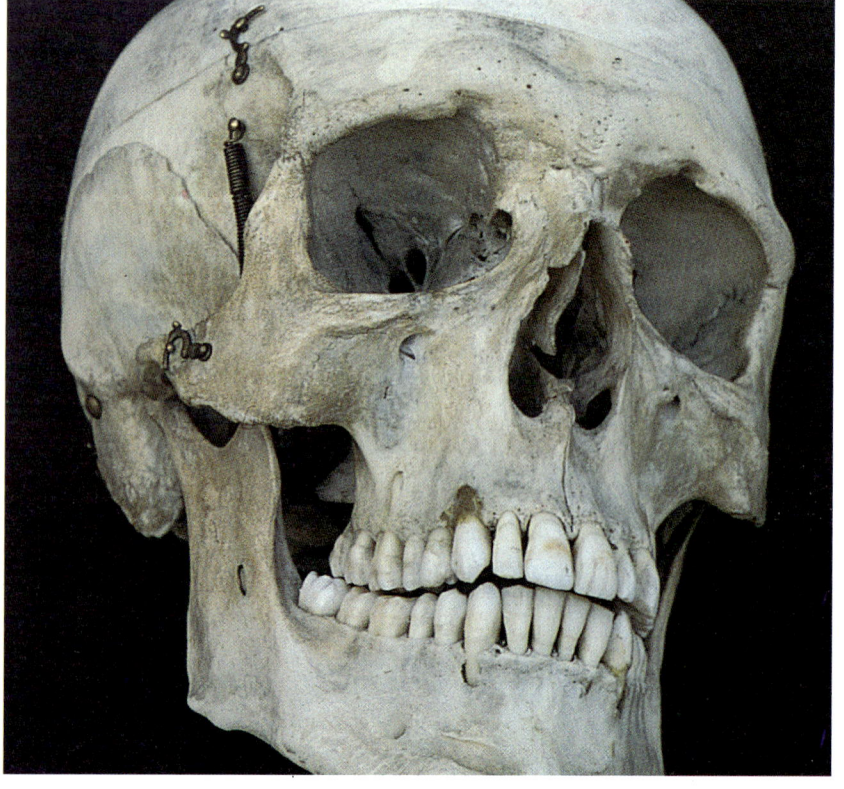

Tooth structure

Enamel is an extremely tough and hard-wearing material. It gives a sharp edge to cutting teeth and a tough surface to grinding teeth. Even so, enamel can be attacked by acid. Some acid is contained in foods we eat.

Take care and stop decay

Plaque is a sticky film which collects on teeth between meals. It contains food such as sugar, and also bacteria. The plaque becomes acidic when bacteria convert sugar to acid. The acid then attacks the enamel, making holes. This is called **decay**.

Blood and guts

Bacteria can get in through these holes, to the living part inside the tooth, called the **pulp cavity**. If bacteria multiply inside the tooth it becomes infected and may develop an **abscess**. The nerves in the pulp cavity take this information to the brain, and we feel pain.

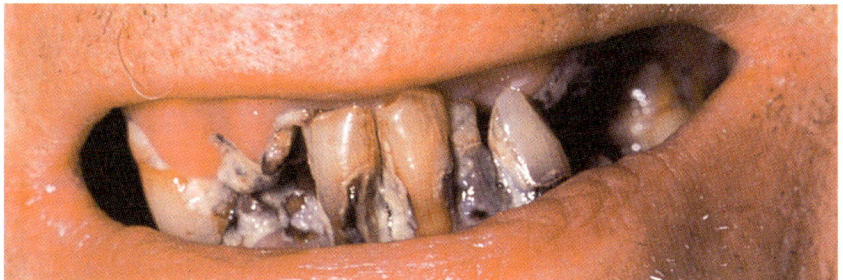

Picture 4 Advanced decay – unpleasant to look at and painful.

Cleaning teeth soon after a meal helps to remove food remains and so cuts down on decay.

Around 1970, a new active ingredient called fluoride was included in toothpaste. Fluoride actually gets built into tooth enamel and can help repair minor damage to teeth surfaces. In some parts of the UK, fluoride is added to drinking water to help protect peoples' teeth (particularly children's) living in an area. To stop decay spreading, some people paint teeth with a special fluoride gel. This treatment is used for young children who might be easily upset by the dentist filling their teeth (see *Materials* pages 50-51).

Picture 5 Incidence of dental decay.

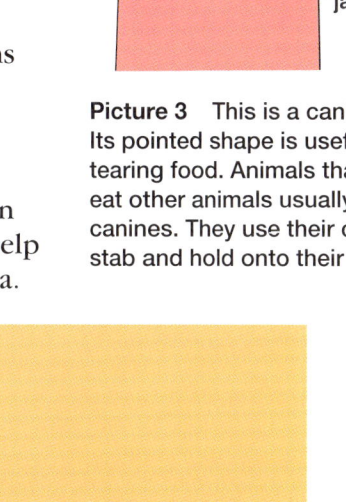

Picture 3 This is a canine tooth. Its pointed shape is useful for tearing food. Animals that catch and eat other animals usually have large canines. They use their canines to stab and hold onto their catch.

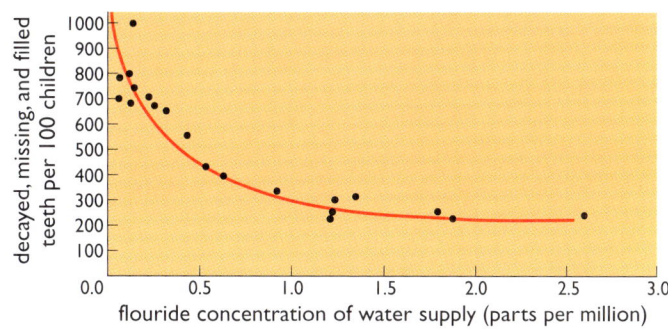

Questions

1. Copy and complete this summary table:

		Number of teeth on one side	Total number of teeth
		i c pm m	
milk set	upper		
	lower		
adult set	upper		
	lower		

i = incisors
c = canines
pm = premolars
m = molars

2. a) Which human teeth are involved in
   i) biting food?
   ii) chewing food?

   b) What are the differences in structure between incisors and molars? How are these differences related to function?

3. What do you notice about the pattern of decay shown by the data in Picture 5? What conclusions can you draw about the use of fluoride toothpaste?

4. Why can tooth decay lead to pain?

More about the small intestine

The small intestine is not really small

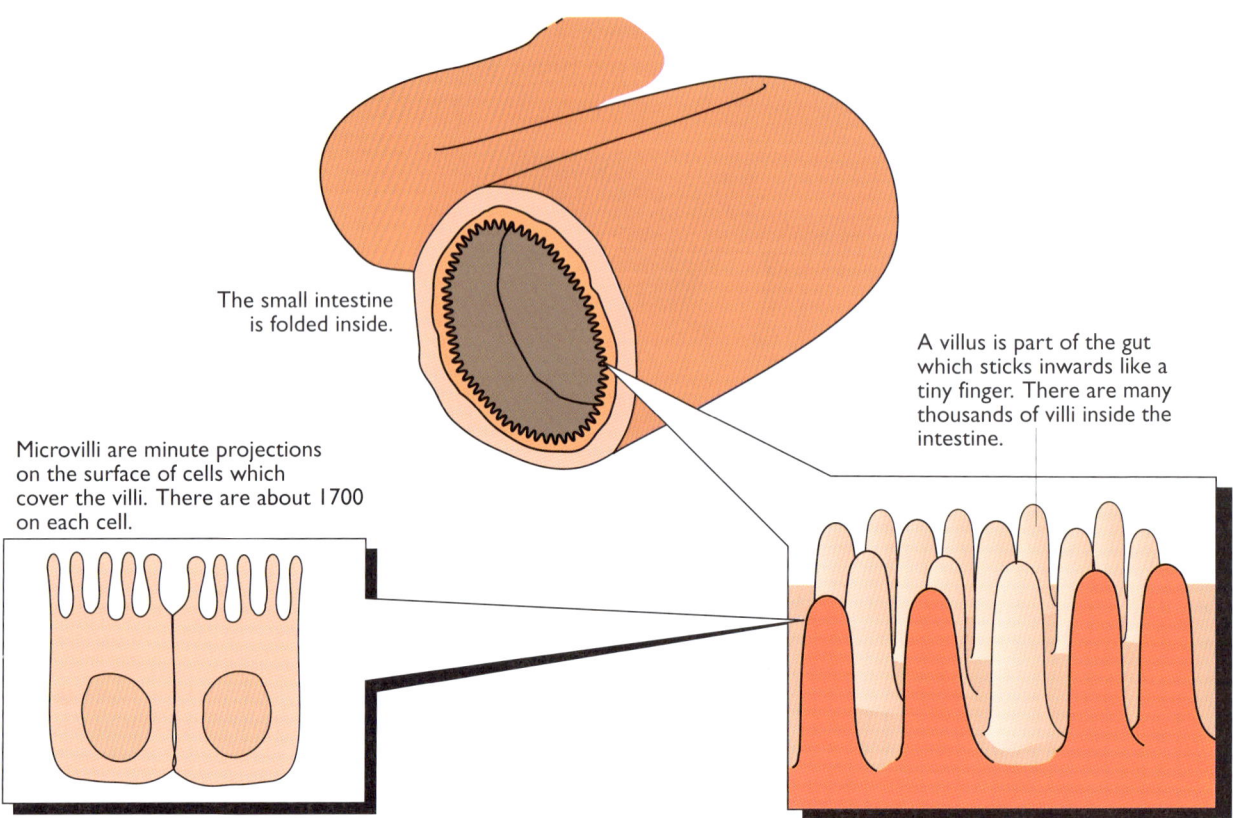

Picture 1 is a section of the small intestine. The inside of this part of the small intestine has an enormous surface area, about 200 m³ altogether. This is about the same size as two and a half tennis courts! The large surface area is achieved by folding, and special structures called **villi** and **microvilli**.

Picture 1 The structure of the small intestine.

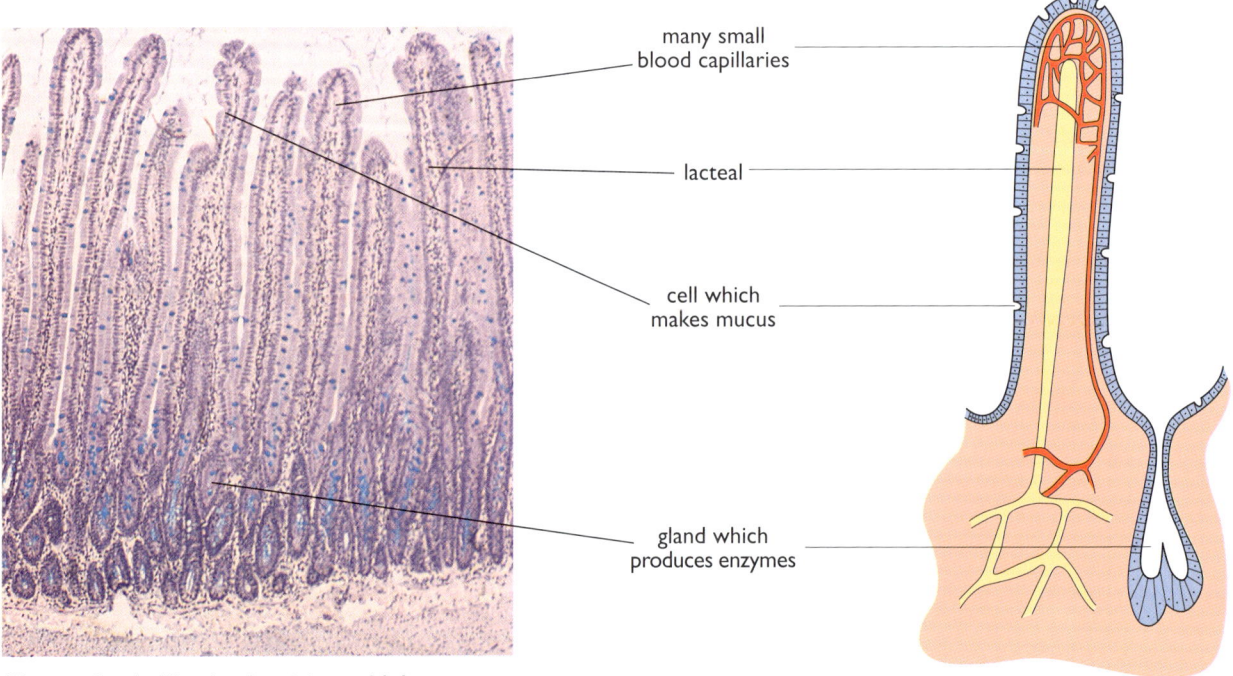

Picture 2 A villus is about 1 mm high.

Blood and guts

Many of the cells in the small intestine produce substances which pass into the gut. These substances are:
- a protective slime called **mucus**, which stops enzymes and stomach acid attacking cells which line the gut
- an alkaline liquid, which neutralises acid from the stomach so that enzymes from the small intestine work well
- digestive enzymes to break down the food.

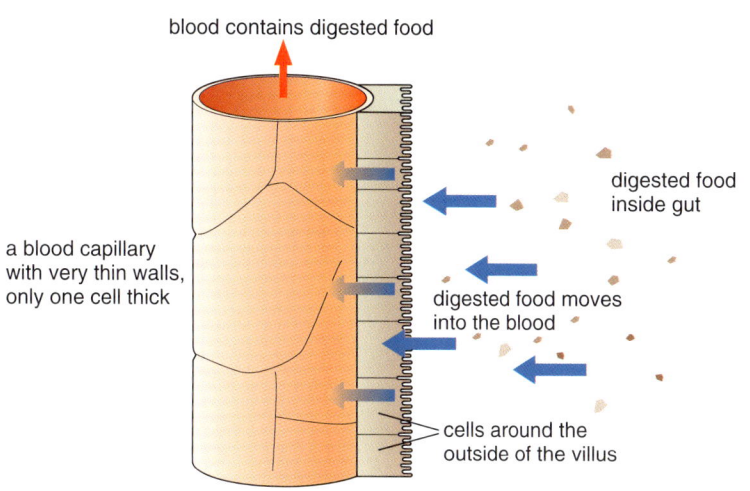

Picture 3 Soluble food has only a short distance to travel from the gut into the blood. This makes absorption very efficient.

Absorbing digested food

Once food is digested it is soluble. The soluble foods from carbohydrate and protein digestion move into the blood supply within each villus. The products of fat digestion move into other small tubes called **lacteals**.

Diffusion is due to the movement of particles in a gas or liquid (see *Materials* page 8). The more particles of a particular substance there are in one area, the more concentrated it is. When particles diffuse they spread out, from an area where they are more concentrated to an area where they are less concentrated. This difference in concentration is called a **diffusion gradient**.

A model to explain this idea is to imagine a ball at the top of a hill. If you let the ball go, it runs from the high point to lower ground.

Digested food diffuses from an area of higher concentration in the gut, to an area of lower concentration in the blood. Since the blood flows non-stop it carries away these soluble foods. This keeps a diffusion gradient between the inside of the gut and the bloodstream.

Questions

1. a) How is a large surface area achieved in the small intestine?
   b) How does a large surface area help in
      i) digestion?
      ii) absorption?

2. What are the reasons for the gut producing the following substances:
   a) mucus?
   b) an alkaline liquid?

3. a) Which layers of cells does the soluble food pass through, as it moves from inside the gut to the blood?
   b) How is the food absorbed from the gut into the blood?
   c) How does a diffusion gradient help to make absorption an efficient process?

Gut reactions

What are enzymes?

All living cells contain many enzymes. Enzymes are **catalysts** which speed up chemical reactions. This allows chemical reactions in living cells to happen at quite low temperatures. Cells are killed at high temperatures so this is important. In the gut, enzymes catalyse the breakdown of food particles (see *Materials* pages 106-107).

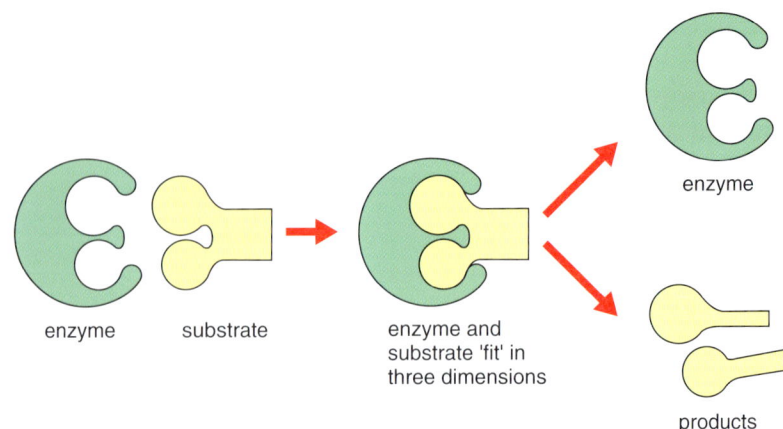

Picture 1 The 'lock and key' model of how an enzyme works.

Enzymes are made of protein. The main feature of an enzyme is its shape, in particular the shape of the **active site**. The active site is the place where reactions happen. The particles which are reacting are called the **substrate**. Since the active site has a particular shape, only certain substrate particles fit.

Picture 1 shows a substrate particle entering the active site. A breakdown reaction happens, forming new products. These products no longer fit the active site and so they move away, leaving the enzyme to work with new substrate particles.

This way of describing enzyme action is called the 'lock and key' mechanism. Substrates may change the shape of the active site slightly as they move in, making an even better fit – in the same way that a glove changes shape as a hand fits into it.

Although an enzyme speeds up a reaction, it is not actually altered by the reaction itself. What's more, tiny amounts of enzyme can deal with large amounts of substrate. For this reason, enzymes are often used as catalysts in industry (see *Materials* pages 104-105).

Digestive enzymes

Digestive enzymes are involved in breaking down big particles into smaller ones. The smaller particles are soluble and can diffuse from the gut into blood, and then into cells around the body. Table 1 gives a summary of the main types of enzymes that help you digest your food.

Picture 2 shows the breakdown of a protein. Protein is made of many smaller units called amino acids (see pages 24–25 for more information about different types of food).

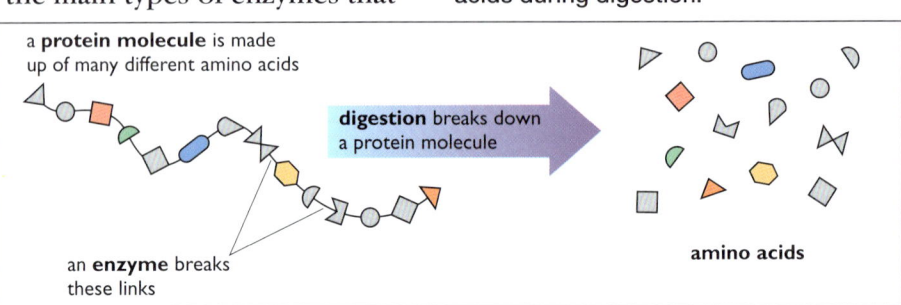

Picture 2 Proteins split into amino acids during digestion.

Blood and guts

During digestion a protein splits first into shorter chains of amino acids, and then into single amino acids.

Table 1 Enzymes involved in digestion.

Substrate	Enzyme	Products	Where it is made
starch	carbohydrates	sugar	salivary glands pancreas small intestine
proteins	protease	amino acids	pancreas small intestine
fats (lipids)	lipase	fatty acids and glycerol	pancreas small intestine

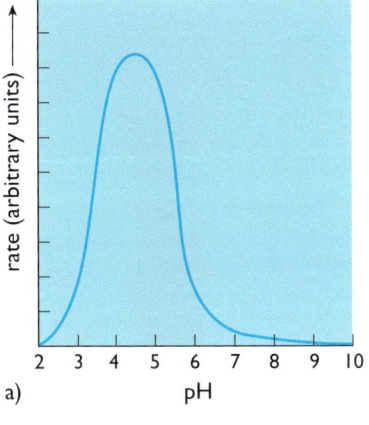

How fast do enzymes work?

The rate of a reaction is how fast it happens in a certain time. For a reaction catalysed by an enzyme, the rate can be estimated by finding out
- how many substrate molecules it can alter in a certain time
- how much product is made in a certain time.

Different enzymes work at their maximum rate in different conditions – in other words, they have their 'favourite' or **optimum** conditions. pH is particularly important since it affects the shape of the enzyme. Picture 3a shows the effect of changing pH on a carbohydrate enzyme.

Temperature affects how well an enzyme works (Picture 3b). At very low temperatures, particles react more slowly. High temperatures can change the shape of the enzyme molecule, so stop enzymes working altogether. Other substances such as salts or vitamins can make a difference to how well an enzyme works.

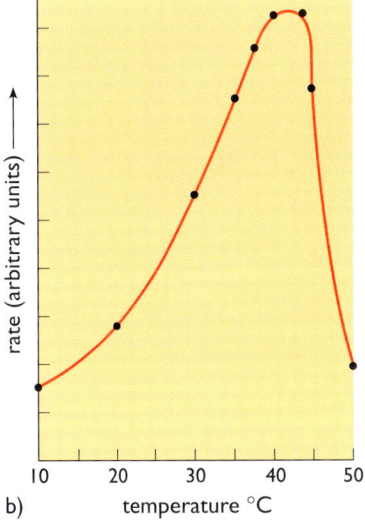

Picture 3 a) Effect of pH on how well an enzyme works. b) Effect of temperature on how well an enzyme works.

Questions

1. Make a list of key points about enzymes, e.g. very small amounts of enzyme are needed to speed up a reaction.

2. a) What is an active site of an enzyme?
   b) Why is the active site important?
   c) What affect might a change in pH have on the active site of an enzyme?
   d) The pH of the stomach is acid, but the small intestine is slightly alkaline. Would you expect enzymes from the stomach to work in the small intestine? Give reasons for your answer.

3. Use the 'lock and key' idea to explain why a carbohydrase enzyme does not help break down proteins.

4. a) For the enzyme shown in Picture 3a, what is the optimum pH?
   b) What is the effect of temperature increase for the enzyme shown in Picture 3b, between these temperatures:
   i) 20–40°C?
   ii) 40–60°C?

Blood structure and function

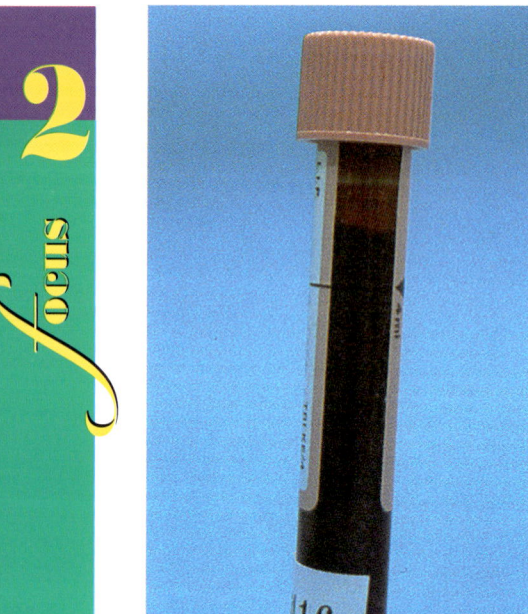

What's in blood?

Blood is a very special mixture. The liquid part of blood is called **plasma**, and it is mostly made of water. Substances such as sugar, salts and urea are dissolved in plasma.

Blood cells, platelets and plasma proteins are too big to dissolve, but are still carried around in plasma. **Platelets** are tiny particles made in the bone marrow. They are needed to help blood clot. **Plasma proteins** are substances such as hormones and enzymes.

Notice in Picture 1 how larger particles such as the blood cells settle after a few minutes in a centrifuge, leaving clear plasma above.

Blood cells

Blood cells are very tiny. A small drop of blood (about 1 mm^3) contains around 5 million red blood cells and about 7000 white blood cells of different types. Red blood cells and some white blood cells are made in the soft marrow at the centre of bones. Other white blood cells are made in glands that form part of the body's defence system.

Red blood cells look red because they are packed with haemoglobin. **Haemoglobin** is the compound in red blood cells which carries oxygen (see pages 38–39).

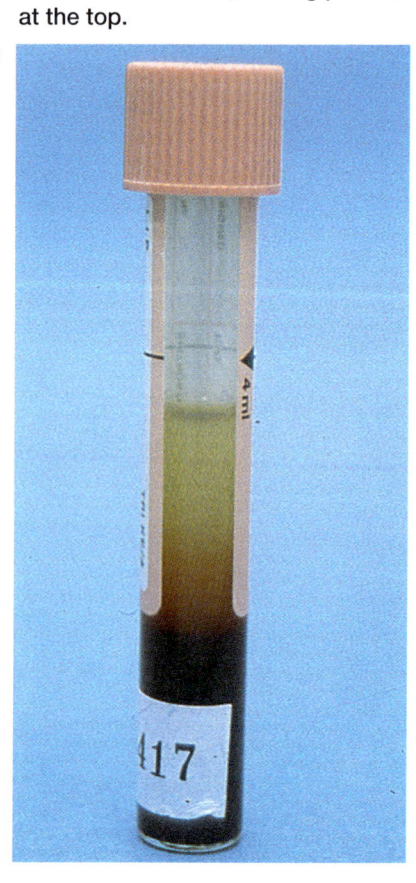

Picture 1 a) A fresh sample of blood. The blood is mixed. b) The same blood sample after centrifuging. Cells and platelets settle at the bottom, leaving plasma at the top.

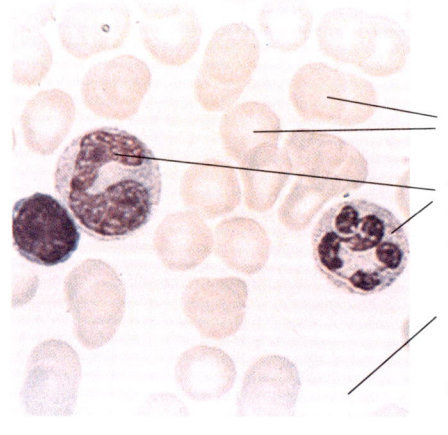

Picture 2 This is a smear of blood on a microscope slide, which has been stained.

- Red blood cells are disc-shaped and dented in the middle.
- There are several sorts of white blood cells, all containing nuclei, some of them can change shape and squeeze out of blood vessels.
- Plasma.
- Platelets are fragments of cells, there are about 0.25 million per 1 mm^3.

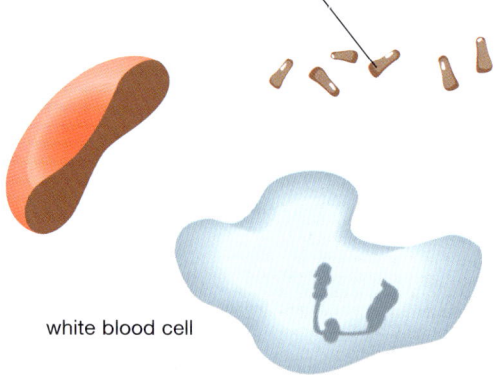

red blood cells

white blood cell

Blood and guts

What blood does

The main functions of blood are transport of many different substances, and defence against disease. Picture 3 describes how blood acts as a transport system.

Blood has an important part to play in defending the body against disease. If you cut yourself and bleed, the blood helps to clean the cut by washing germs out of it. The blood clots, later forming a dry scab over the wound.

Clotting stops the bleeding and prevents more germs getting in. New skin cells grow from below the surface and repair the damage. The scab dries up and drops off. Page 40 in this Focus gives more detail on clotting.

But the defence goes further than this. Any bacteria that do get in through skin are 'eaten' by some white blood cells. These special cells, called **phagocytes**, can change shape and flow around the bacteria. They surround bacteria and kill them by digesting them. Picture 4 shows an area that looks white because of the thousands of white cells collected there.

Other white blood cells are called **antibody** cells. They produce antibodies which make bacteria stick together in clumps, so it is easier for white blood cells to flow round them. Pages 38–39 give more information about antibodies and immunity.

Picture 3 As blood circulates it carries many substances with it.

- digested food moves from the intestines to where it is used or stored, and from stores to cells where it is needed
- hormones are chemical 'messages' carried from glands to the part of the body where they cause an action to happen
- warm blood can be diverted from the surface to the core of the body, or visa versa
- oxygen is taken from the lungs to all cells of the body in red blood cells
- waste products are moved from where they are formed to where they are removed, e.g. carbon dioxide is made in all cells and then carried back to the lungs to be excreted

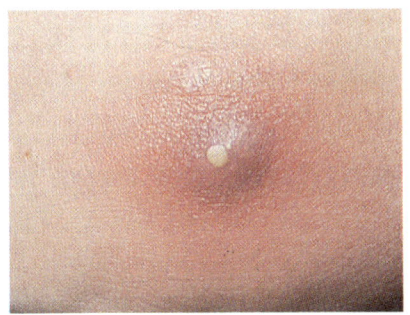

Picture 4 Within the pus in a spot there is a fight between white blood cells and bacteria. If the white blood cells win, the infection clears up and the spot goes away.

Questions

1. Why does blood contain water?
2. Draw up a table of information about the contents of blood. You could use headings like this (the first example is done for you):
3. List the ways in which the blood helps to defend the body against disease.
4. How does blood help a wound to heal?

Contents of blood	Description	What it does
red blood cells 5 million/mm^3 etc . . .	dented discs, contain haemoglobin	carries oxygen

Life blood

The oxygen carriers

Oxygen is needed by most living things for **respiration**. Respiration is a process that happens in all living cells. During respiration, energy is transferred from a food source to the cell. Red blood cells have the important job of supplying cells with oxygen.

Let's think again about the shape of red blood cells. They are circular in outline, but looked at from the side the middle is dented. Why? The answer is that these unusual cells don't contain a nucleus. This gives more space inside the cell for packing in haemoglobin (see Picture 1). It also means that the surface area of the cell is greater, so more oxygen can diffuse in and out of the cell.

$$Hb + 4O_2 \longrightarrow HbO_8$$
$$(\text{haemoglobin}) \qquad (\text{oxyhaemoglobin})$$

Haemoglobin takes up oxygen very easily. One interesting thing is that the first oxygen that combines with haemoglobin changes the shape of the molecule slightly, and this makes it easier for the next oxygen to fit in. This means that 'loading up' happens fast in places where there is lots of oxygen available.

The red blood cells move around the body to places that have a lower oxygen level. Here the oxygen leaves the haemoglobin, diffusing out of red blood cells into body cells. Some carbon dioxide is carried back to the lungs by red blood cells. But most of it is carried by the plasma.

Antibodies and immunity

There are several types of white blood cell. One type is the **antibody cell**. Antibody cells can detect that bacteria are foreign to the body. This is because the proteins on the surface of bacteria are different from proteins on the surface of human body cells. The proteins on the bacteria are called **antigens**.

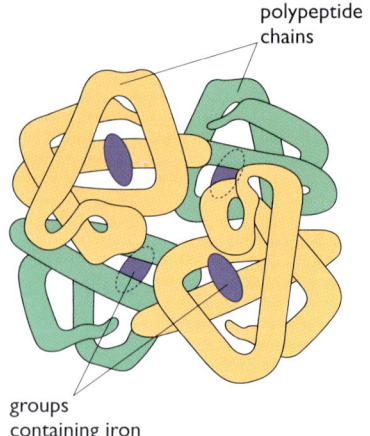

Picture 1 Haemoglobin (Hb) is a protein. It contains iron, which makes haemoglobin look red. It can hold up to four oxygen molecules (O_2).

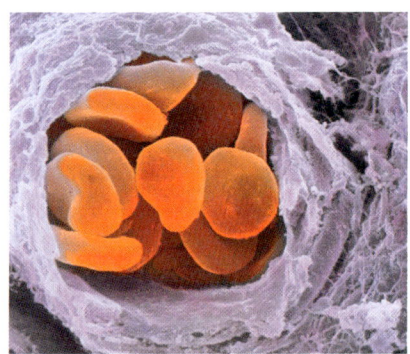

Picture 2 Oxygen can load into red blood cells and unload very rapidly, keeping body cells well supplied.

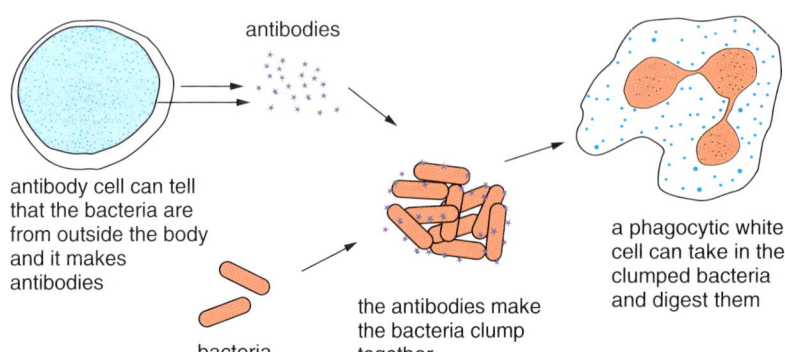

Picture 3 When the body is under attack from bacteria, antibody cells give a rapid response.

Blood and guts

The antibody cells act fast, producing antibodies that fit the shape of the antigens. Antibodies lock onto the antigens, causing bacteria to clump together. These clumps of bacteria are then destroyed by other white blood cells.

Once the bacteria are killed and the infection is gone, the white blood cells stop making antibodies. However, some of the white blood cells act like a memory. If the same sort of bacteria try to invade the body later, these antibody cells 'remember', and very quickly start making more antibodies. This is why you don't usually get diseases like chicken pox more than once. The antibody cells give you **immunity** – protection against further attacks.

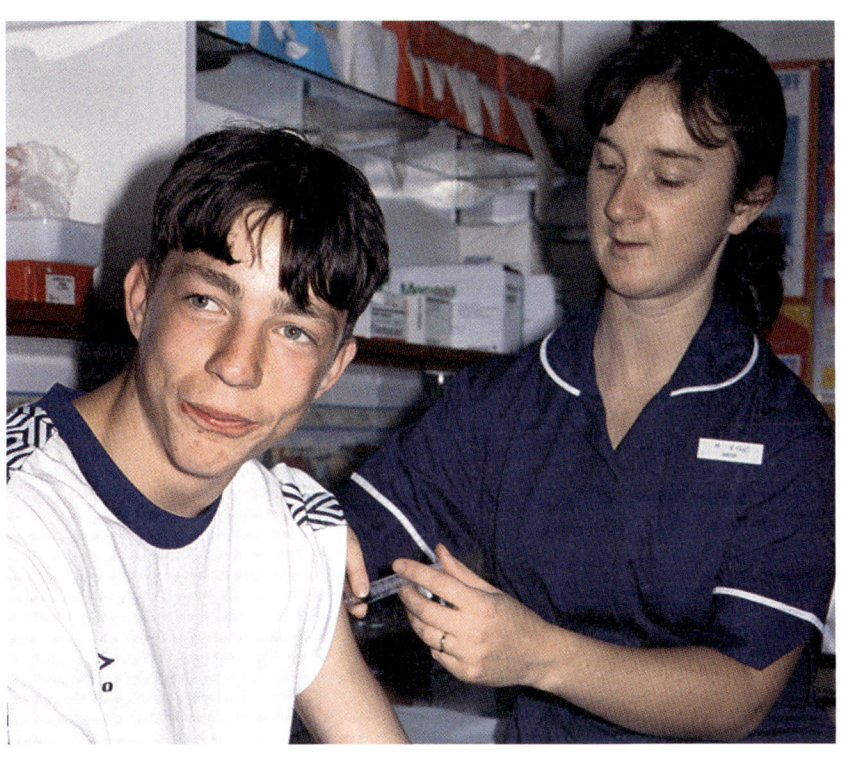

Picture 4 Immunisation saves millions of lives every year.

Scientists have used this idea of immune memory to develop immunisation. Some of the bacteria are treated so they can't cause disease. Even so, if they are injected into the body, the antibody cells respond and make antibodies.

Sometimes this makes children feel a little unwell for a couple of days. But in the long term the advantage is great. They now have immunity against that disease. If new bacteria of the same sort try to attack the body, the antibody cells can produce antibodies very quickly. Immunisation has had a huge effect on improving health and preventing death, particularly in children.

Questions

1 a) What is haemoglobin?

b) How much oxygen can a haemoglobin molecule carry?

c) Why is iron an important element in the diet?

d) Why is this feature important to how red blood cells function?

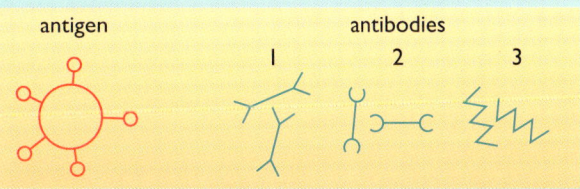

2 a) Picture A shows particles of an antigen. Which of the antibodies (1–3) will lock onto this antigen?

b) Sketch what the antibody and antigen complex might look like when they are together.

c) How does the clumping of bacterial cells help the body defend itself against disease?

Blood disorders

How blood clots – normally

Clotting is a complex process that involves lots of stages, and a dozen or so substances called **clotting factors**. This helps to make sure that blood doesn't clot too easily, for example when it's still circulating. If you cut yourself, cells in the skin are damaged. Clotting is triggered by clotting factors released from these damaged cells and platelets.

The final stage is that a protein called fibrinogen changes to insoluble fibrin threads. These threads make up a mesh. Platelets and red blood cells get caught in the mesh of fibrin threads. This is the basis of the scab, which then dries out and hardens. New skin cells grow under the scab to repair the damage.

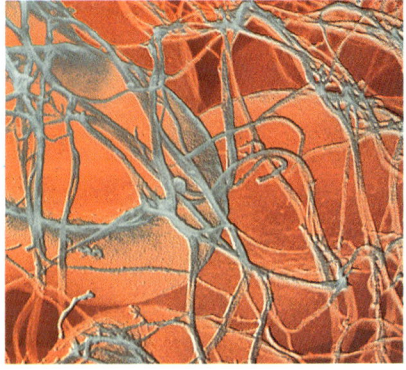

Picture 1   Platelets and blood cells get caught in a mesh of fibrin.

Haemophilia – a clotting problem

Have you ever noticed how quickly blood stops running out of a wound and how fast a scab forms? Imagine what happens if one of the clotting factors is not active. The whole process doesn't happen because of a lack of one factor. This means that bleeding continues with drastic effect – usually death. This condition is called **haemophilia** and it's inherited (see pages 104-105). It can't be cured, but it can be treated by giving the person the active factor they lack.

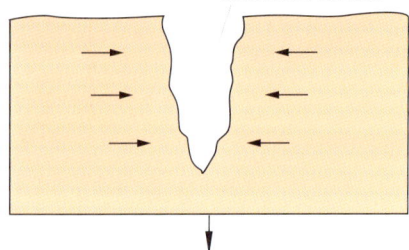
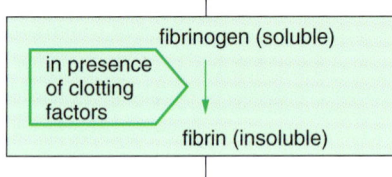
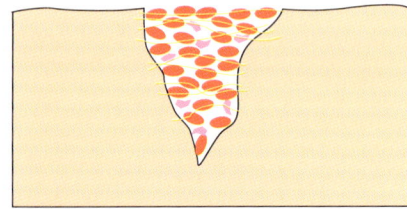

Picture 2   Stages in clotting.

Activity of factor as a % of normal activity	Number of people with haemophilia A	Number of people with haemophilia B
<2% (severe)	1981	348
2–29% (moderate)	1604	408
>30% (mild)	1505	270
(other)	316	72
Total	5406	1098

Source: The Haemophilia Society, 1993 data.

Anaemia – a problem with haemoglobin

Haemoglobin is the part of blood that carries oxygen. The body needs iron to make haemoglobin. If the body doesn't get enough iron from food, it may not be able to make enough haemoglobin. This condition is called **anaemia**, and it results in a poor supply of oxygen and tiredness.

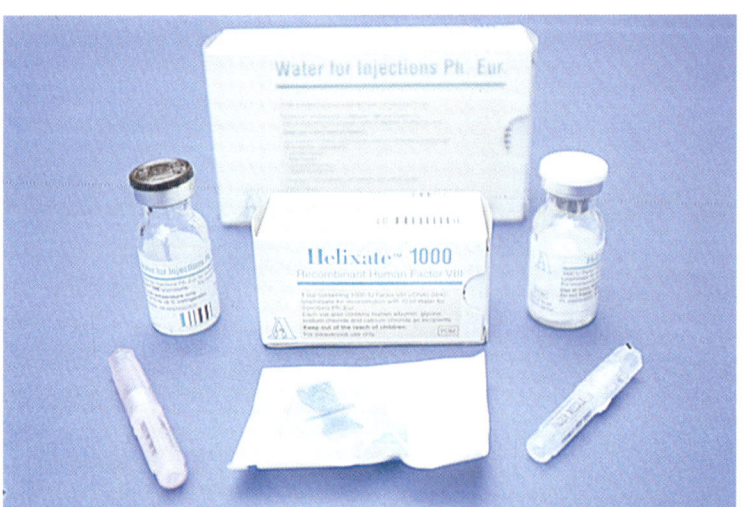

Picture 3   A clotting factor is taken from a donor's blood and given to a person with haemophilia.

Blood and guts

Sickle cell anaemia is an inherited type of anaemia. In this case the red blood cells have an abnormal shape, and contain less haemoglobin than normal cells. Pages 104–105 in this book describe how this condition is inherited.

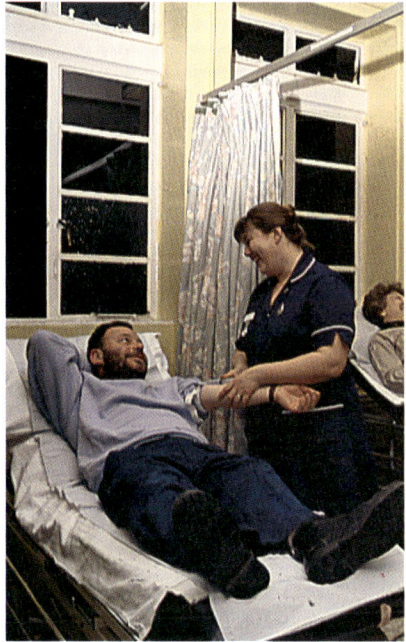

Picture 4 A drop of blood is tested to see that it contains enough haemoglobin, before someone can give blood.

Leukaemia – a problem with white blood cells

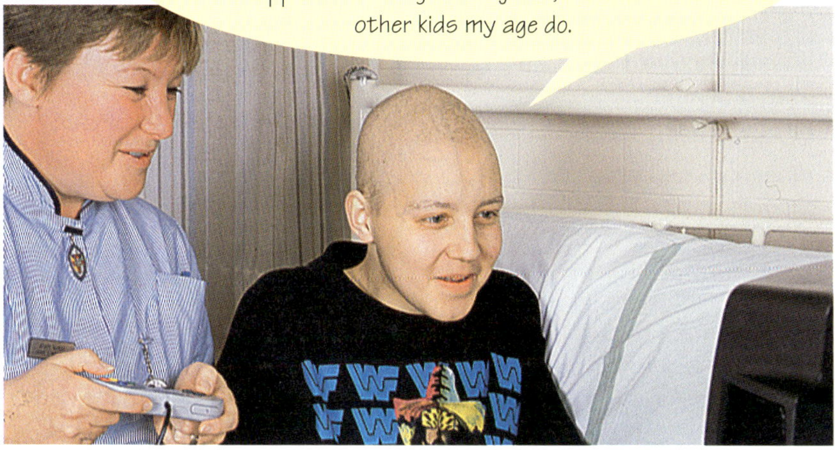

I'll admit that it was frightening being so ill with leukaemia. But the treatment is over and I've been given a clean bill of health. I really appreciate being healthy now, more than other kids my age do.

Picture 5 The treatment for leukaemia can cause temporary hair loss.

Leukaemia is a type of cancer involving the white blood cells. Many more white cells are produced than normal, but they are not properly developed. These white cells cannot help to protect the body against disease. Leukaemia often affects children, but many cases can be successfully treated.

HIV – also a blood disease

A person may become infected by **HIV** – a virus called **human immunodeficiency virus**. This virus may stay in the body for some years before any effects are noticed. Later, if the virus becomes active, white blood cells are destroyed. This means that the person's protection against disease is lowered.

A person infected with HIV may then develop **AIDS (acquired immune deficiency syndrome)**. This illness is caused by a variety of diseases that happen because the person cannot fight off infections.

Questions

1. Solubility is how soluble a substance is.

    a) What is the difference in solubility of fibrinogen and fibrin?

    b) Why is this solubility important in clotting?

2. Haemophilia used to be a fatal disease. Why isn't this true for the majority of cases today?

3. Both leukaemia and AIDS are blood disorders resulting from problems with white blood cells. In what ways are the white blood cells affected?

4. a) What are the two most common causes of anaemia?

    b) What are the effects of anaemia?

    c) Dianne said she felt very worn out. Would taking iron tablets help her?

Blood and guts

Activities

It takes guts

In simple terms the gut is a tube. Along the tube, different parts are designed for different functions. This means that the shape of the gut varies depending on the animal. Picture 1 shows the gut from 8 different animals.

Microbes help greatly in digestion, because they can provide enzymes that an animal may not be able to make. Many animals, called **herbivores**, eat mostly plant material which contains a lot of cellulose. Cellulose is a tough, fibrous material that resists digestion.

For this reason, cellulose must stay in the gut for longer. Parts of the gut, such as the stomach, caecum or large intestine, may be specially designed for this purpose, holding and digesting cellulose.

Table 1 The structure of the gut is related to diet.

Part of the gut	Function	Carnivorous animals (eat meat)	Herbivorous animals (eat plants)
overall size of gut	–	small	large
stomach	digestion	small	may be large or small
small intestine	digestion and absorption	–	–
caecum	digestion of cellulose and absorption	small	large
large intestine	digestion (sometimes) and absorption	short	long

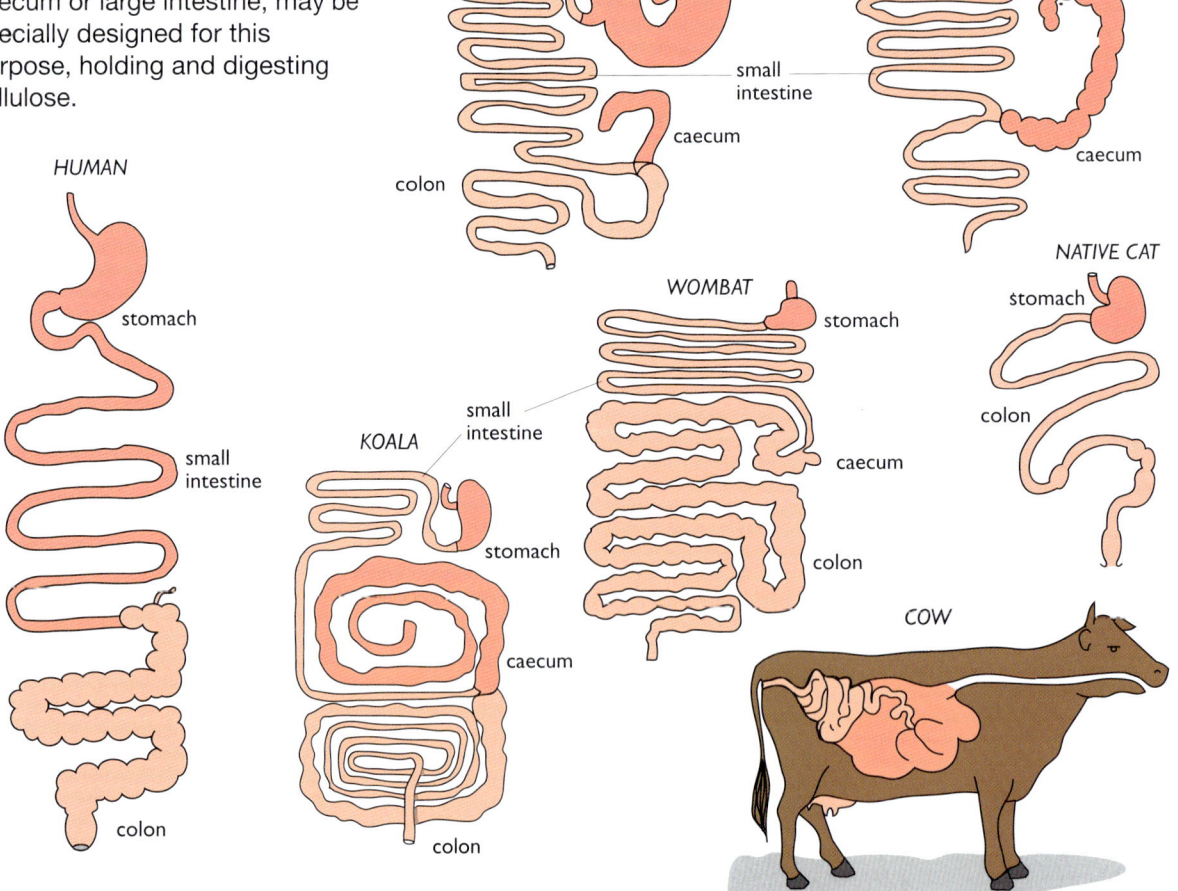

Picture 1 Source: Prof. Martin Connock *Biological Sciences Review*, Volume 5, Number 1, Sept. 1995

1. Describe the overall plan of a gut.
2. Why are the guts of different animals different in structure?
3. a) Suggest which of the guts in Picture 1 are from a herbivore.

   b) How can you tell from Picture 1 which of the guts belongs to herbivores?
4. a) A carnivore eats mostly meat. Which of the guts in Picture 1 comes from a carnivore?

   b) Why are the guts from carnivores smaller than the guts from herbivores?
5. Which of the animals holds food for digestion in its
   a) stomach?
   b) caecum?
   c) large intestine?
6. Most humans eat both meat and plants. How is human gut design similar to and different from gut design in herbivores and carnivores.

Teeth and diet

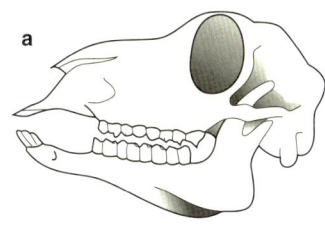

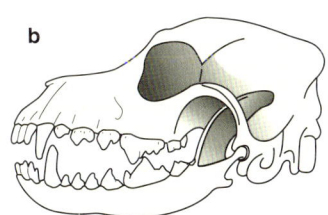

Picture 2 a) The lower jaw of this skull moves side to side, as food is ground between the ridged teeth. b) Some of the teeth in this jaw have sharp edges like blades, and others are pointed.

7. Picture 2 shows teeth in the jaws of a sheep and a dog.

   a) Which picture (a or b) shows dog teeth?

   b) Which animal eats plant material?

   c) Suggest a reason why animals such as sheep keep chewing their food for a long time before swallowing.

   d) How are the teeth of meat-eating animals well designed for the type of food they eat?

Looking at blood

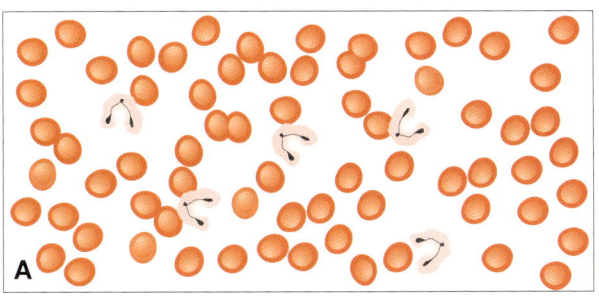

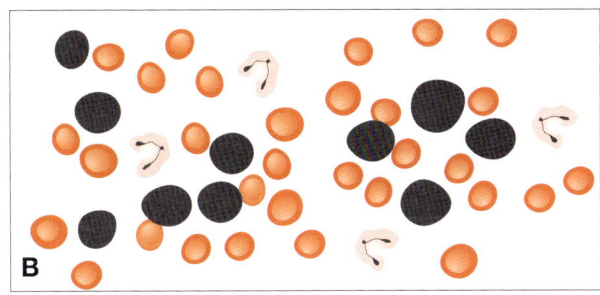

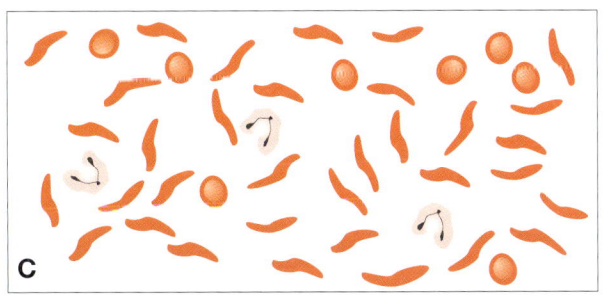

Picture 3 Three blood samples.

8. Picture 3 shows how three blood samples look through a microscope. One sample is normal blood, another is sickle cell blood and another is blood from someone with leukaemia.

   Predict which blood comes from which person. Use pages 40–41 to help you answer this.

BLOOD & GUTS EXPLORED

What makes us fat?

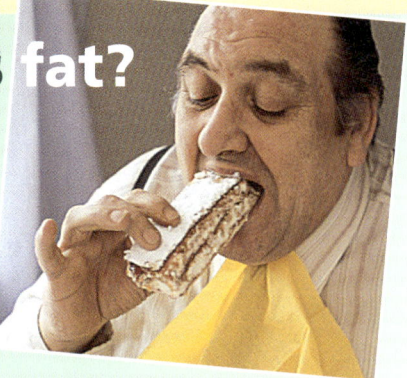

In many countries dieting is a growing industry. Thousands of women (and increasingly men) wish for a different body shape. Scientists are still unsure why some people get fatter than others. Randolph Leibel of the Rockerfeller University, New York, suggests that when we are young the body sets its own level of 'fatness', and tends to return to it. To change our body shape we probably need to be more active as well as change our eating habits.

In the 1990s, British children actually eat 20% less mass of food than children did in the 1960s. But they transfer less energy because they spend more time in front of a television or computer, and don't exercise as much.

Diet is important too. We do need some fat for the brain to develop, and for the body to work properly. But too much fat in the diet can make us overweight.

Train hard & train high

Mexico City stands at 2270 m above sea level. In the 1968 Mexico Olympics, Kip Keino and Naftali Temo were winners of the long distance races. They were athletes who lived and had trained at high altitudes. At high altitudes there is less oxygen in the air than at sea level. The body makes up for this by producing red blood cells containing more haemoglobin. This means that blood can carry plenty of oxygen to the muscles.

But there is a limit to how much benefit an athlete can gain by training at high altitude. This is because the extra red blood cells make the blood thicker, so it does not flow as easily and the heart has to work harder to push it around the body.

What's for tea?

A lot of people in the UK eat beef, pork or lamb for Sunday roast. Look out in your local supermarket for ostrich meat, a low-fat and protein-rich food source. If the idea doesn't appeal to you, remember that in some countries guinea pigs are a popular food, and in Europe frogs and snails make a tasty snack.

Down on the farm ostriches are roaming

A big bad tusk

At Whipsnade Wild Animal Park, dealing with teeth can be a big job. An elephant's tusk is really a modified tooth. And just like any other tooth it can develop problems. This photograph shows how keepers and the vet at Whipsnade set about dealing with Anna's painful gum.

Anna had cracked her tusk, leaving a small rough edge rubbing her gum. The gum became infected, so it was sensible to treat Anna, and examine the tusk to see if the infection had entered it. In the event there was no infection. The vet smoothed off the tusk, cleaned the gum and treated it with antibiotic cream.

Edmund Flach is the veterinary surgeon at Whipsnade Wild Animal Park

Anna is small as elephants go. She's a 13 year-old Burmese elephant, with a body mass of about 2 tonnes. Usually she's as good as gold, but we had to knock her out to deal with the tusk. A crane was at the ready in case she went down awkwardly. Elephants must lie on their sides, or the weight of the intestines can damage the heart and lungs.

Chewing for clean teeth

Is chewing gum good for your teeth? Sugar-free chewing gum certainly doesn't cause decay. Chewing in fact causes you to make more saliva. An enzyme in the saliva breaks down carbohydrate food that is stuck around the teeth, helping to clean up the surfaces. How might you test out this idea, to see if chewing gum after each meal can reduce tooth decay?

Why is blood group important?

If someone loses blood during an operation or because of injury, they may need to replace it with blood from someone else. The blood must be matched correctly, or it could mean the difference between life and death.

Notice that if the blood is not matched correctly, the red blood cells stick together in clumps. This blocks up blood vessels and can cause death. Which person can receive blood from any blood group? Which person can give blood to any blood group?

Blood group of person giving blood	Blood group of person receiving blood			
	O	A	B	AB
O				
A				
B				
AB				

Matching blood groups

Blood and guts

Summary

- The main food groups are carbohydrates, fats, proteins, minerals and vitamins. Fibre and water are also important in the diet.
- Fats and carbohydrates are high energy foods.
- Protein is needed for the body to make new cells during growth.
- A balanced diet contains all the food materials the body needs in the right amounts.
- Teeth are needed to bite, chew, tear and grind food into smaller pieces.
- Food is digested partly in the mouth and the stomach, but mostly in the small intestine.
- Digested food is absorbed into the blood from the small intestine.
- Enzymes are catalysts which help to digest food. They are affected by pH and by temperature.
- Blood is a mixture containing:
  - water which is a liquid and can flow through blood vessels
  - dissolved substances such as sugar, salts and urea
  - plasma proteins such as hormones and clotting factors
  - red and white blood cells
  - platelets.
- The main functions of blood are transporting substances, and defending the body against disease.
- Haemoglobin in red blood cells carries oxygen around the body.
- White blood cells make antibodies. Antibodies lock onto antigens, making them clump together.
- White blood cells can surround bacteria, killing them.
- Immunisation is a way of protecting people against disease.
- Haemophilia is a disease in which blood doesn't clot.
- Anaemia is due to a lack of haemoglobin caused by not absorbing enough iron from food.
- Leukaemia is a type of cancer, which causes many immature white blood cells to form.
- HIV is a virus that infects cells in the body, especially white blood cells.

Questions

1. To keep healthy it is important to have a balanced diet which includes carbohydrates, proteins, vitamins and some fat.
   The amount of carbohydrate a person needs to stay healthy may depend on their weight.
   Suggest **one** other factor which affects how much carbohydrate a person needs. Explain your choice.
   MEG

2. Experiments were carried out to investigate the action of two enzymes at different pH values. The enzymes were amylase and pepsin (a protease). All experiments were carried out at 37°C for 20 minutes. The results are shown on the graph.

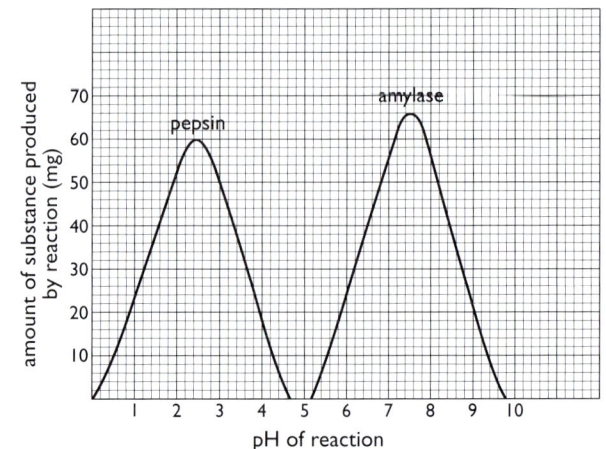

Questions continued

a) How much substance was produced in the pepsin-controlled reaction at pH 3?
b) At which pH values were 60 mg of substance produced by:
 i) pepsin?
 ii) amylase?
c) Which substance is produced when:
 i) pepsin acts on protein?
 ii) amylase acts on starch?

London

3 a) The chart shows an analysis of four food samples.

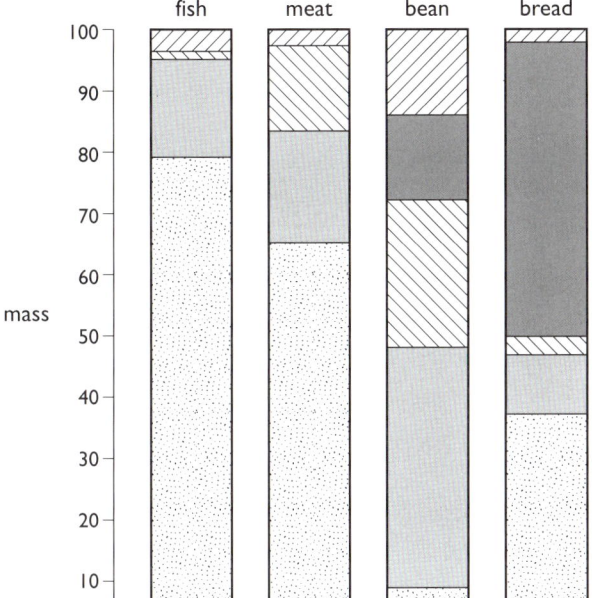

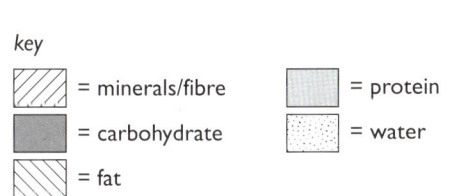

key
- ▨ = minerals/fibre
- ▩ = carbohydrate
- ▨ = fat
- ░ = protein
- □ = water

i) What is meant by a balanced diet?
ii) Is it possible to provide a balanced diet using only the foods included in the chart? Explain your answer.

b) i) Earlier this century it was thought unnecessary to have roughage (fibre) in a healthy diet. Why was it **not** thought necessary to include roughage in a healthy diet?
ii) We now believe that fibre is an important part of the diet. What useful purpose does fibre have in the diet?

c) State **one** illness caused by a dietary deficiency other than a shortage of fibre.
What is the cause of the illness?
Suggest **one** way of preventing this illness.

d) i) Some people will not eat any animal (including fish and poultry) or any animal product. What is a possible dietary requirement that they could be deficient in?
ii) Suggest how this deficiency could be avoided.

MEG

4) Bronchitis is an infection of the bronchial tubes which lead to the lungs.

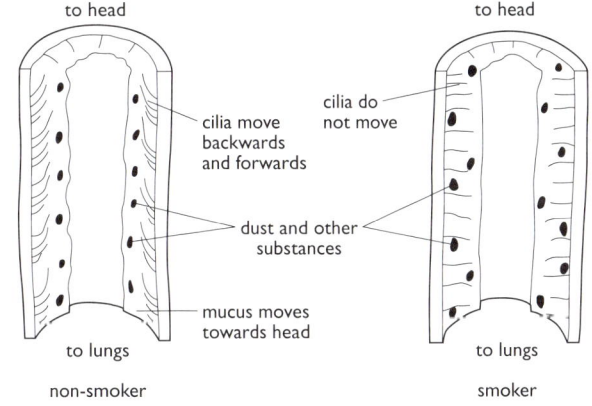

a) What general pattern is shown by this information?

b) The diagram below shows the effects of cigarette smoke on small hairs called cilia in the bronchial tubes.

i) What effect does cigarette smoke have on the movement of mucus?
ii) Suggest why smokers tend to cough more than non-smokers.

MEG

focus 3

Coordinating life processes

Sensitivity — 50
Being sensitive is unique to living things, and it helps survival.

A closer look at nerve cells — 52
The nervous system helps to coordinate the body's activities.

Reacting and learning — 54
About reflex actions, and how learning influences our responses.

A sensitive eye — 56
Sight is a very well developed and important sense for humans.

Drugs and sensitivity — 58
A drug is any substance that alters some aspect of how the body works.

Chemical coordinators in animals — 60
Hormones are chemicals that help to coordinate the body's activities.

Becoming an adult — 62
Sex hormones, puberty and the menstrual cycle.

Human reproduction — 64
The facts about how humans reproduce.

Hormones and fertility — 66
Hormones affect fertility, and may be used to change how likely it is that a baby is conceived.

Chemical coordinators in plants — 68
This section gives information on plant hormones and how they are used by commercial plant growers.

Sensitivity

Detecting change

Sensitivity is to do with detecting changes both inside and outside the body. Imagine what happens when the phone rings – you may hear it and decide to answer. As you move to deal with the call, you can detect the movement in your muscles. In those few moments the body has been constantly checking changes within the body and in the surroundings.

Picture 1 If the moth had detected the bat sooner, it may have escaped capture.

Survival often depends on detecting changes that happen in the environment. The reason may not be as dramatic as shown in Picture 1. Being aware that it's freezing outside and that you need to wrap up warmly, can be just as important to health.

The body works best if the conditions within it remain fairly constant. To do so, there needs to be a way of detecting changes as they happen. Focus 4, *Controlling change*, explains how humans control body conditions.

Detecting and responding

The nervous system is the part of the body that *detects* changes. Both the nervous system and chemical coordinators, called **hormones**, are involved in *responding* to changes. The action of hormones is described on pages 60-61.

The nervous system

Picture 2 shows a simple model of the nervous system. A **stimulus** is a condition which is detected by the body, e.g. light (detected by eyes) or pain (detected by the skin). A **receptor** is the part of the body that detects a stimulus, e.g. the eye, or pain receptor in the skin. An **effector** is the part of the body that carries out an action or responds, because of the stimulus that the body detected.

Information moves through the nervous system as electrical signals called **nerve impulses**. The brain interprets or works out what to do about the information it receives constantly.

How does this model work? All around the body there are receptors picking up information. Some receptors are individual cells. Others are whole organs, such as the ear. The information we detect may be about changes that are happening inside the body, or outside it.

Coordinating life processes

Most of the information goes to the brain, which works out what response (if any) is needed. As a result, effector organs carry out some actions which help us to survive. Picture 3 gives the main ways in which we detect and respond.

The receptors are sensitive cells that give us our senses such as taste, smell, sight and hearing. There are many other receptors that are not mentioned in Picture 3. For example, parts of the body are able to detect blood pressure, or the amount of sugar or oxygen in the blood.

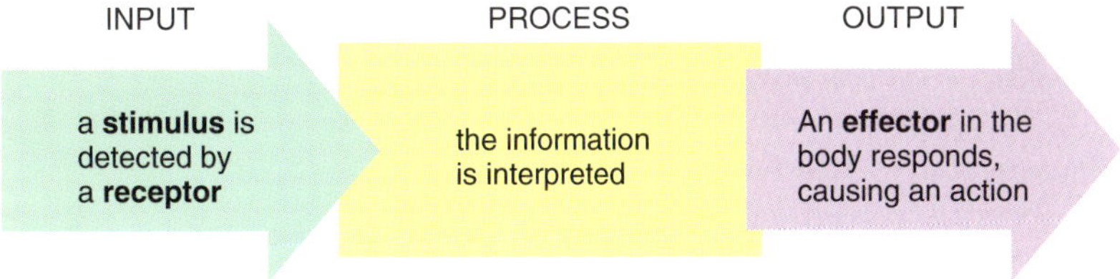

Picture 2 Inputs, processing and outputs of the nervous system.

INPUT → a **stimulus** is detected by a **receptor**

PROCESS → the information is interpreted

OUTPUT → An **effector** in the body responds, causing an action

Picture 3 A model of the nervous system.

Receptors/sense organ	Stimulus detected	Process	Effectors	Response
eye 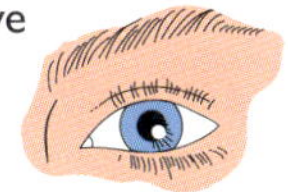	ligt	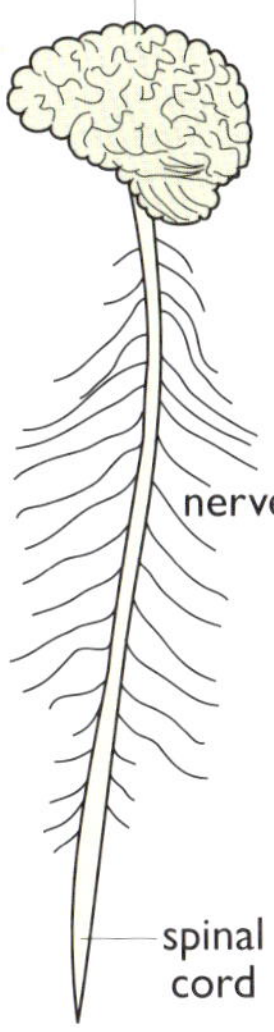 brain	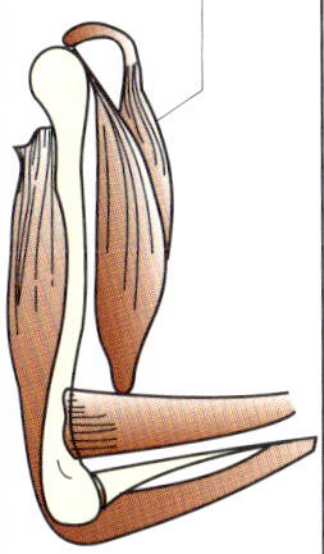 muscles	contract and move
ear 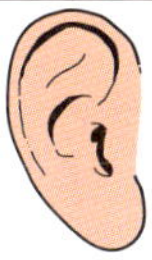	sound, gravity and motion			
skin receptors 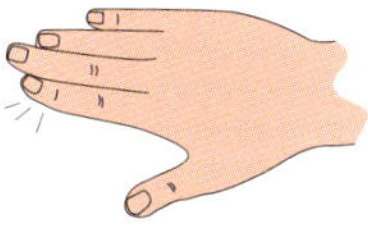	pressure, pain and temperature	nerves		
stretch receptors 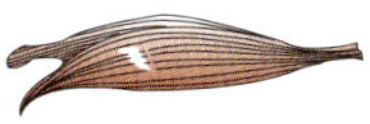	stretch in muscle cells			
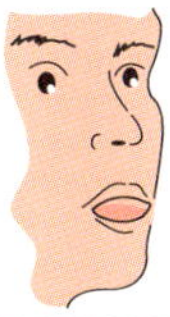 chemo-receptors in nose and on tongue	tastes and smells	spinal cord	glands 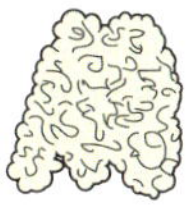	make hormones, enzymes, bile and acid

Picture 4 Plants have receptors, too, sensitive to light, water and gravity. These sunflowers track the sun as the Earth turns during the day.

Questions

1. Why is it important for a living thing to detect changes
   a) inside the body?
   b) outside the body?

2. Try using the model of the nervous system shown in Picture 2 to draw a flow chart of the events that happen
   a) when you choose an ice cream from a freezer in a shop
   b) when the fire bell is rung at school
   c) when you select a ring the right size
   d) when you knock a snooker ball into a pocket.

3. a) The ear can detect motion and gravity, giving us an awareness of position and allowing us to balance. Suggest some activities that need good balance.
   b) What activities sometimes confuse our sense of balance? Why?

4. Suggest a reason why having a blocked nose can make food seem very tasteless.

A closer look at nerve cells

Nerve cells

Cells are the basic units that living things are made of and there are many different types. The nervous system is built mostly of nerve cells, called **neurones**. Neurones have a specific job to do, so the structure is different from other cells. In fact there are three main types of neurone (Picture 1).

Like all cells, neurones have living contents called cytoplasm, nuclei and a cell membrane (see pages 8–9). Much of the cytoplasm is in the **cell body**. But since neurones carry information over a long distance, some of the cytoplasm is in a long, thin thread called the **axon**.

Some axons have a fatty covering that stops nerve impulses passing through. This means that nerve impulses from one neurone can't 'short circuit' with another neurone. The fatty covering also helps to speed up how fast the nerve impulses travel.

One end of a sensory neurone is a receptor. Picture 1 shows a receptor cell from the eye. The other end of the cell connects with other neurones, and has tiny branches to do this.

Notice that relay neurones have branches at both ends. In the spinal cord and brain the relay neurones connect sensory neurones with motor neurones. Motor neurones pick up impulses at one end and transfer them to an effector organ. It has nerve endings that connect with the effector organ, e.g. a muscle.

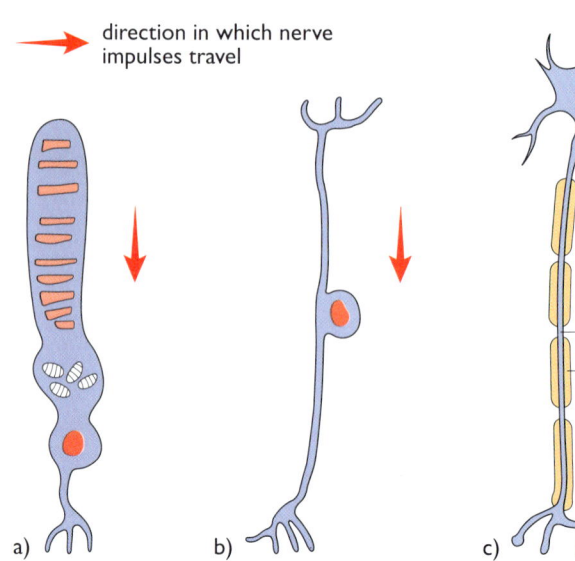

Picture 1 a) Sensory neurone from the eye. b) Relay neurone. c) Motor neurone. Neurones vary in structure depending on which part of the nervous system they belong to. The arrow shows the direction that nerve impulses move along each neurone.

Linking up

A **pathway** is the route taken by nerve impulses. For example chemoreceptors in a person's nose and mouth detect the taste and smell of food. Nerve impulses move along a sensory neurone, through a relay neurone in the spinal cord, to the brain. The brain interprets the information – delicious! As a result, nerve impulses travel from the brain, through a motor neurone to muscles in the jaw. The muscles move and chew food, salivary glands make saliva, and the intestines make enzymes.

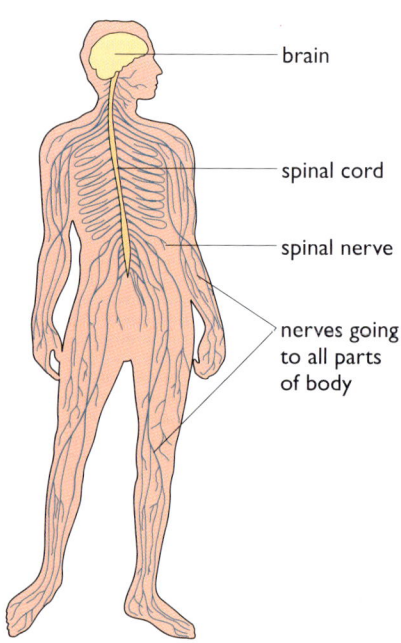

Picture 2 The main parts of the nervous system.

Coordinating life processes

So how are nerve cells arranged in the nervous system? Many nerve cells are found in groups with their axons bundled up inside a protective coat. These bundles of axons make up a nerve. Nerves enter and leave the spine at various points. Within the spine and brain there are many relay neurones.

Crossing the gap

Although two nerve cells are close together, there is still a small gap between them. This gap is called the **synapse**, and the nerve impulse needs to move across it. Picture 4 shows how this happens.

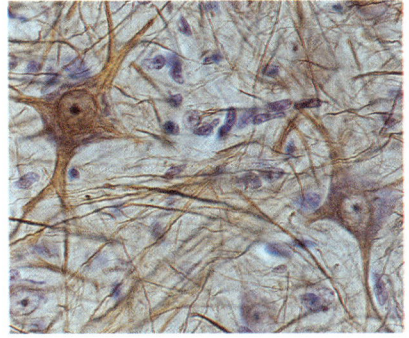

Picture 3 Very close contact between two neurones in the brain.

Chemicals made by the end of a neurone move across the gap. They fit into receptor sites on the next cell, and trigger an impulse. Drugs can affect the synapse, slowing down or speeding up the movement of nerve impulses across the synapse (see pages 58–59).

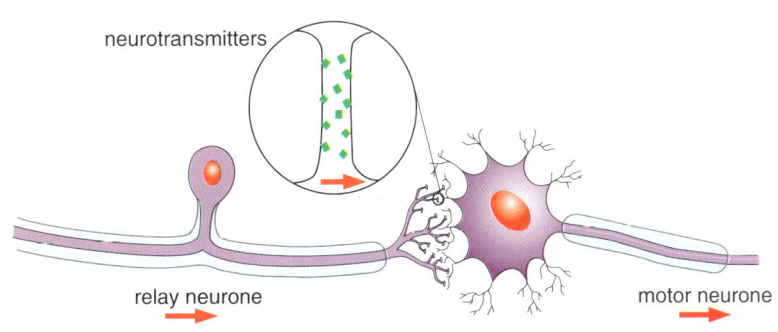

Picture 4 Chemicals bridge the synapse.

Sometimes nerve impulses don't get through the system or part of it. There is a gap very like the synapse between a motor neurone and a muscle. If the motor neurones stop sending electrical signals across the gap, the muscle doesn't work. This is what happens to someone with motor neurone disease. The muscles gradually waste away and stop working.

Questions

1 Copy and complete a table like this one, putting in information on neurones. Use ticks to fill in the table:

Feature	Type of neurone		
	sensory	relay	motor
receptor at one end			
effector at one end			
part of a sensory nerve			
part of a motor nerve			
connect with other neurones (at one end)			
connect with other neurones (at both ends)			
lead away from the brain			
lead towards the brain			

2 Suggest a reason why the brain and spinal cord are surrounded by bone.

3 Multiple sclerosis (MS) is a disease in which the fatty sheath around neurones breaks down, and the neurones are damaged. What effects might this have, if the damage was to

a) sensory cells?
b) motor cells?

4 Suggest a reason why ambulance paramedics often place a firm collar around someone's neck before moving them, if the person has had an accident or fallen awkwardly.

Reacting and learning

Quick reactions

How fast are your reactions? It's simple to test your reactions using a ruler as shown in Picture 1. This will only give a rough estimate, and you need to repeat the test at least ten times. Practising will probably help to speed up your reactions. You can try testing out this idea.

Sometimes we react very quickly without even thinking about it. This type of reaction is called a **reflex action**. An example of a reflex is blinking if something flies towards your eyes unexpectedly.

Picture 2 shows an example of a pathway that nerve impulses move through in a reflex action. Let's imagine that Brook has been feeding his pet parrot with seeds. In his hurry to grab a seed, the parrot catches Brook's finger with his sharp beak. In about 0.2 seconds Brook has pulled his finger away.

The reflex pathway is the shortest pathway the nerve impulses can take.
It may involve only three neurones:
- the sensory neurone detects pain
- the relay neurone connects sensory and motor neurone in the spine
- the motor neurone causes the muscle to contract.

This reflex action has not involved the brain directly, since Brook reacted without thinking. But even so Brook knew what had happened because his brain was informed.

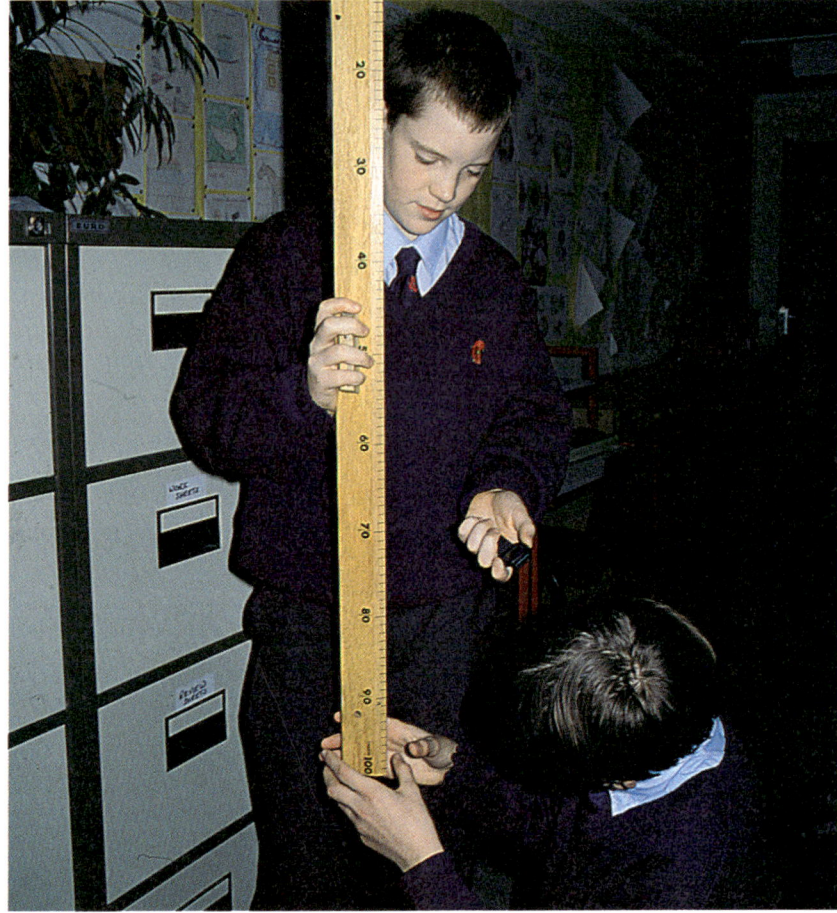

Picture 1 These students are testing their reactions.

One person holds the ruler close to the other's fingertips, and then drops it without warning.

The other person catches the ruler. Read the scale where their thumb crosses it.

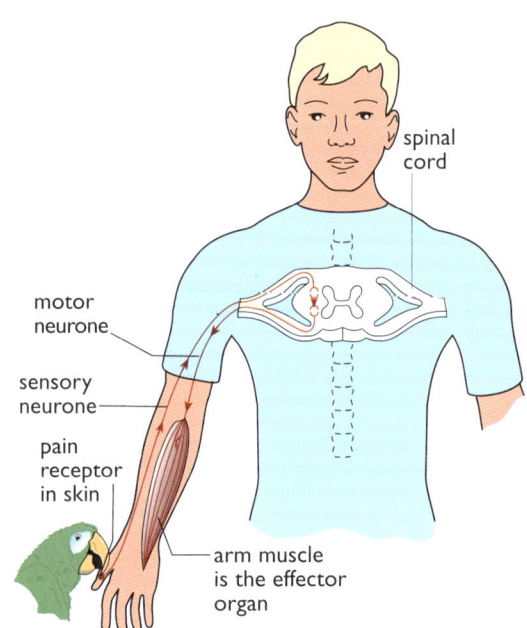

Picture 2 The fast track for impulses gives a quick reaction time.

Coordinating life processes

Learning from experience

It can be a great advantage to react really fast, as long as the reaction is the right one. Imagine picking up a bowl of food that is burning hot. If you drop it without thinking you might hurt yourself more, by spilling hot food over your legs.

The link to the brain is important here, because it means you can choose how to react, even though there is a strong urge to drop the hot dish. You have learned not to drop the dish immediately from past experience. This is an example of a **conditioned reflex**, because learning has changed how you react.

The human brain

No-one has discovered exactly how the brain works, although scientists have found out a lot about it. The brain is made up of hundreds of millions of neurones. 'Centres' in the brain, such as the one concerned with speech, mostly contain cell bodies. There are many synapses between them, so that information can pass quickly between thousands of cells. The established pathways between neurones in the brain allow us to remember things – they give us memory.

The folded part of the brain is an outer layer only a few millimetres thick. Yet this remarkable part of the brain makes us what we are as people. It is responsible for memory and learning, intelligence and decision-making. It controls our senses and speech too. The things that we think to ourselves (our conscious thoughts) happen in this area too.

Other parts of the brain are involved in controlling how the body works without us having to think about it, e.g. breathing and heart rate. One interesting thing shown in Picture 4 is that information that comes from the right side of the body is dealt with by the left side of the brain, and vice versa.

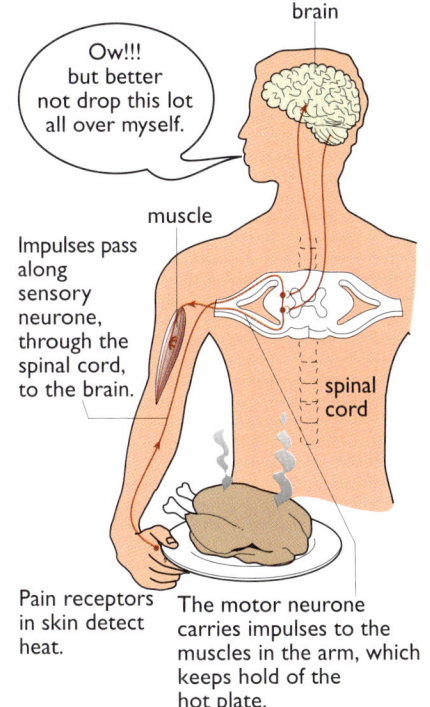

Picture 3 What we have learned in the past can override reflexes.

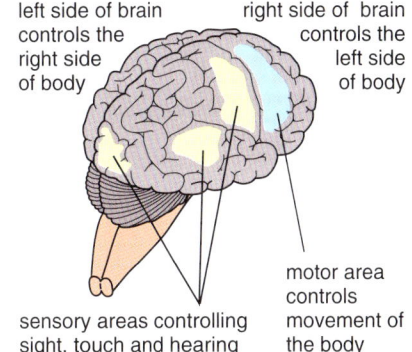

Picture 4 Different parts of the brain control different activities.

Questions

1. **a)** What is a reflex action?
   b) Why are reflex actions fast?
   c) Why are reflex actions useful for survival?
   d) What reflex action happens when you get pepper up your nose?
   e) Are these reactions a reflex?
      i) braking suddenly when riding a bike?
      ii) returning a very fast shot in tennis?
      iii) catching a glass before it falls over?

2. A baby passes urine at any time without thinking about it, yet a toddler becomes 'potty trained'.
   a) What reflex reaction happens when the bladder is fairly full with urine?
   b) How can learning change this reflex?

A sensitive eye

What is vision?

Some simple, one-celled animals have particles in their cytoplasm that alter in light. These particles may be concentrated as an 'eye-spot'. This is the first stage in developing sensitivity to light. More complex animals have individual cells which are sensitive to light, sometimes grouped together, e.g. starfish have light sensitive cells inside tiny, cup-shaped pits. This means that they can detect the direction the light comes from.

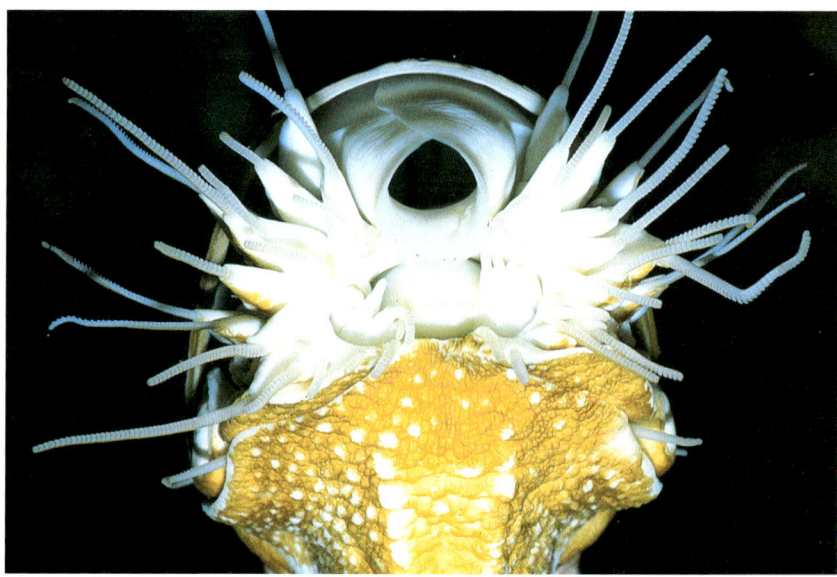

Insects have simple eyes that use many tiny lenses (30 000 in the eye of a dragonfly) to concentrate the light. But the eyes of birds and mammals are more developed and gather enough information to give a coloured and 3-dimensional picture. In other words, we can detect shape and distance.

What you can see of the eye when you look at someone, is only a small part of the whole structure. Sunk in the bony socket, the eyes are also covered by flaps of skin. These eyelids with eyelashes are a further line of defence against damage, partly because they trap dust, but also because of the blinking reflex mentioned on page 54 in this book.

Picture 1 This shelled creature lives deep in the sea. It is called Nautilus, and has not changed much over the last 400 million years since it first appeared. It has an eye with a hole at the front which can change in size. With the hole at its smallest, it can probably see a clear image. The eye does not have a lens.

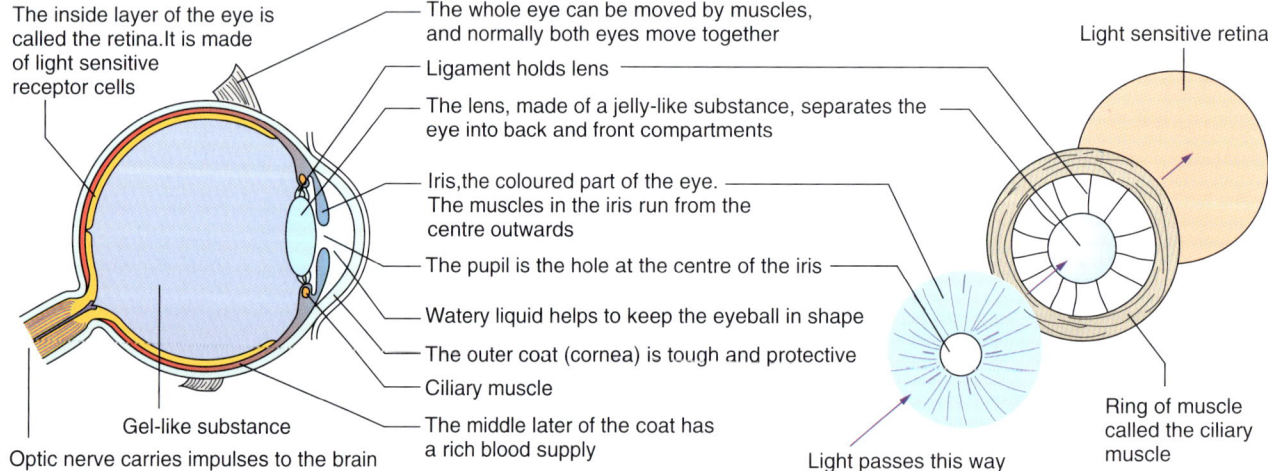

Picture 2 The structure of the human eye.

The **retina** is the inside layer of the eye. It is made of light sensitive receptor cells. There are two types, called **rods** and **cones**. The rods and cones produce nerve impulses when light strikes them (see *Physical Processes* pages 58-59).

Light is scattered by objects around us. The amount of light entering the eye depends on how much light there is outside, the size of the pupil and whether the eyelid is open.

Coordinating life processes

Getting things in focus

Light scattered from a point on an object must be focused to a point on the retina. The direction of light rays is changed, bringing them together. Both the cornea and the lens help in focusing light (Picture 3).

The shape of the lens is convex since it is fatter at the centre than at the edges. A fat, convex lens converges light more than a thin, convex lens. The size of the lens in an eye can be adjusted, so that the light can be converged just the right amount, making the point of focus exactly on the retina. This gives a crisp image and sharp eyesight.

A ring of muscle called the **ciliary** muscle adjusts the shape of the lens. Picture 4 shows that the lens is held in place by tiny ligaments, which are attached to the ring of muscle. If the muscle contracts, the ring gets smaller and the ligaments go slack. This lets the lens flop into a fat shape. If the ring relaxes it is larger and stretches the ligaments. These pull on the lens and make it thinner. Table 1 is a summary of this idea.

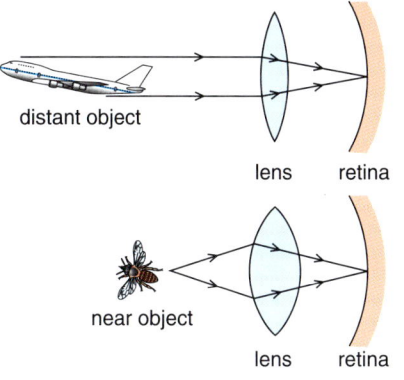

Picture 3 Light rays converge a) from a distant object, b) from a near object.

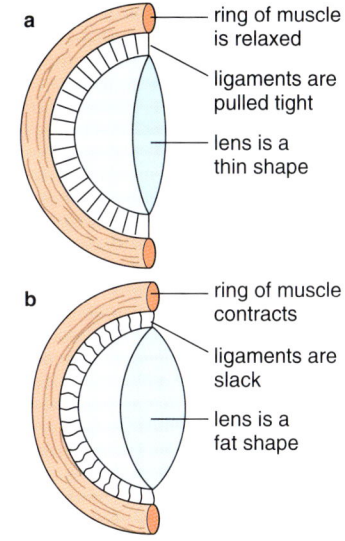

Feature	Distant object	Near object
reflected rays	enter eye almost parallel	enter eye diverging
ciliary muscle	relaxed	contracted
ligaments	pulling on lens	slack
lens shape	thin	fat
light converged	to a smaller extent	to a greater extent
image	focused on the retina	focused on the retina

Table 1 Adjusting the focus.

Picture 3 Light rays converge a) from a distant object, b) from a near object.

Questions

1. a) Why can't you see anything when you're in total darkness?

   b) Why does light make it possible for you to see?

   c) Why is accurate sight useful?

2. How is the eye protected?

3. Which parts of the eye are concerned with

   a) controlling how much light enters the eye

   b) changing the shape of the lens

   c) focusing light

   d) detecting light

   e) passing nerve impulses to the brain?

4. a) How does the eye focus light from a close object?

   b) A watchmaker works with many very tiny parts. Why

      i) is it best to do close work in a bright light?

      ii) does it make the eyes feel tired after a long while?

Drugs and sensitivity

What are drugs?

Drugs are chemical substances which alter the way that the body works. Some drugs are used in medicines, but others are substances of abuse. People usually mean **substance of abuse** when they talk about drugs, and that is how the word drug is used in this book. The word **medicine** is used to mean a substance that improves health. However, even medicines can be abused if too much is taken, or the dose is repeated too often, or it's used unnecessarily.

Medicines

If you look on the label of a medicine container, you will probably see the words *active ingredient*. The active ingredient is the part that affects the body, stopping pain, preventing illness or treating disease. Table 1 shows some types of medicines that have improved health for many people in recent years.

Table 1   Examples of medicines.

Type of medicine	Effect	What it does
analgesic	painkiller	blocks pain receptors in nervous system
germicide (antiseptic)	kills bacteria e.g. on skin	toxic to bacteria, stops infection
antibiotic	kills bacteria inside body	prevents bacteria growing and infection
anaesthetic	relaxes muscles and takes away sensation of pain	blocks nerve impulses to muscles, and from pain receptors to brain
immunisation	prevents infection	causes antibody production, prevents infection (see pages 38-39)

Drugs

People take a drug because it causes a change of mood or feeling. Table 2 is a summary of information about some drugs. The main types are:

- Sedatives, which tend to slow down the nervous system and a person's reactions
- Stimulants, which speed up body reactions
- Hallucinogens, which make people 'see things' that are not really there.

A drug user may **depend physically** on the drug (or be **addicted**). This happens if the body gets used to chemical changes that the drug causes. Giving up is not so easy because the drug user may feel awful because they suffer **withdrawal symptoms**. These may include sweating and diarrhoea, shaking, weakness and muscle pains.

But in fact the withdrawal symptoms last only a matter of days. Probably a greater challenge is facing life without the drug, because it's a habit – and part of a whole lifestyle. This is called **psychological dependence**. You'll see from Table 2 that not all drugs are illegal.

How do drugs and medicines change how the body works?

One way that both medicines and substances of abuse can affect how the body works, is by affecting synapses between nerve cells. The synapse is described on pages 52–53.

Alcohol 'blocks' the synapses, which is why it slows reactions and is a sedative. Other drugs increase the number of impulses at a synapse, making reactions even faster. This is the case with stimulants which speed up body reactions.

Picture 1   Alcohol slows down nerve impulses. The result can be unconsciousness.

Coordinating life processes

Table 2 Information about drugs.

Type of drug	Examples	Legal status in the UK
sedatives	alcohol (also called 'booze')	may be bought at pub from 18 years, drunk at home from 5 years, need licence to sell
	tranquillisers (also called 'tranx'), sleeping pills	POM
	solvents/glue/lighter fuel	illegal as a drug of abuse
	cannabis (also called 'pot', 'dope', 'ganja', 'hash', 'grass')	illegal
stimulants	amphetamines (also called 'uppers', 'speed', 'whizz')	POM, controlled drug, but also sold illegally
	tobacco/cigarettes	legal from 16 years
	cocaine (also called 'coke', 'snow')	POM (rarely prescribed) controlled drug, also sold illegally
	cocaine freebase (also called 'crack')	illegal
	caffeine (in coffee, tea, chocolate, soft drinks)	legal
hallucinogens	cannabis [see sedatives]	illegal
	LSD (also called 'acid')	illegal
	hallucinogenic amphetamines ('ecstasy', 'E')	illegal
painkillers	opium	POM (rarely prescribed), controlled drug, also sold illegally
	heroin (also called 'H', 'smack')	POM, controlled drug, but also sold illegally
	medicines which contain codeine	controlled drug but legal to possess without a prescription

POM = prescription only medicine
Controlled drug = contains substances included in the Misuse of Drugs Act 1971 and Regulations.
Source: 'Medicines and Drugs', ABPI.

Questions

1. Suggest some reasons why people use
   a) medicines
   b) drugs.

2. Jon drinks 2 pints of beer each night on the way home from work, and usually has two doubles of whisky during the evening. He feels he needs the drinks to relax after a stressful day at work. Over the weekend he drinks about 10 glasses of wine with friends.

   a) How many units of alcohol is Jon drinking regularly?
   b) Why does he find alcohol relaxing?
   c) Do you think he is using drink as a substance of abuse?

3. Suggest why amphetamines are also called 'speed', and how they might alter the way in which the body works.

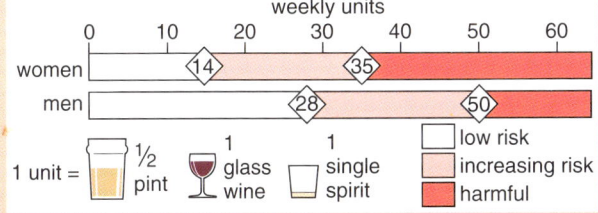

Picture 2 Units of alcohol in some drinks.

Chemical coordinators in animals

What are chemical coordinators?

The word **coordination** means that 'all parts of a system work together'. This is what hormones help the body to do. **Hormones** are chemicals that coordinate body processes. They act continuously, responding to changes that happen in the body. Unlike the nervous system, chemical coordinators act in a more general way over a period of time, e.g. affecting growth.

Glands and hormones

Picture 2 shows the main glands which produce hormones in humans. Hormones circulate throughout the body in blood. But where do they act? Most hormones have certain **target organs**, and don't affect other parts of the body. They lock into receptor sites on the surface of cells in the target organs, causing chemical changes within them. Other hormones such as insulin affect most body cells.

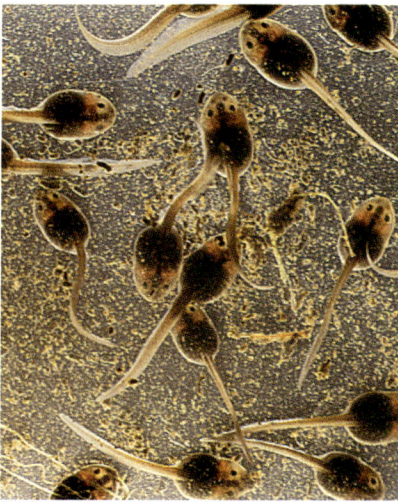

Picture 1 These tadpoles have been kept in an aquarium for some months. Their diet is limited and lacks iodine. Iodine is needed for the tadpoles' thyroid gland to make growth hormone. Despite their age, these tadpoles have not developed into frogs.

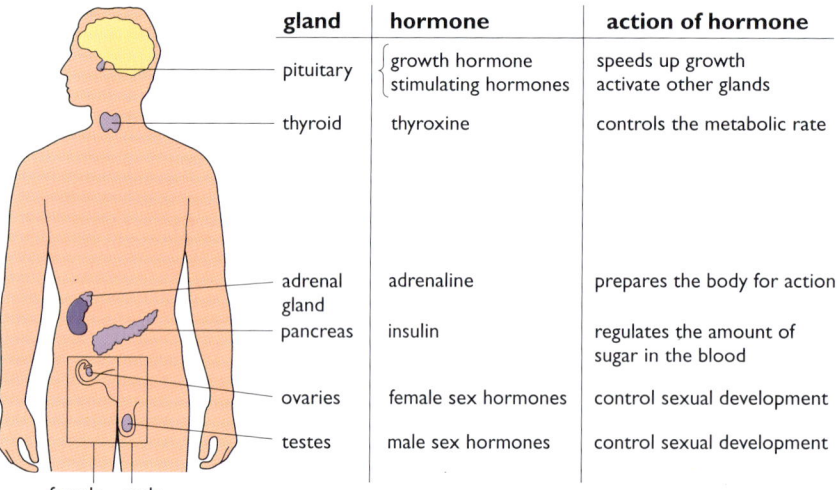

gland	hormone	action of hormone
pituitary	growth hormone	speeds up growth
	stimulating hormones	activate other glands
thyroid	thyroxine	controls the metabolic rate
adrenal gland	adrenaline	prepares the body for action
pancreas	insulin	regulates the amount of sugar in the blood
ovaries	female sex hormones	control sexual development
testes	male sex hormones	control sexual development

Picture 2 Some human hormones and their action.

Transport of hormones

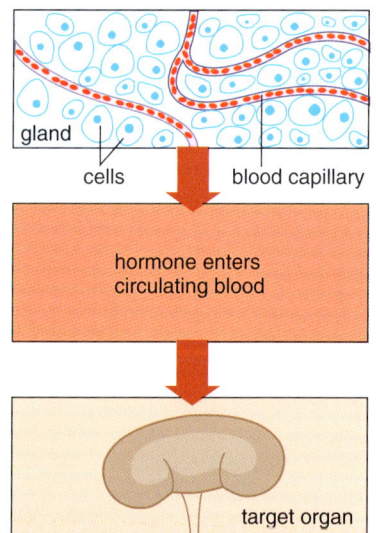

Picture 3 Hormones are made in glands, and move directly into the bloodstream. You can see blood capillaries between cells of the gland. Blood capillaries are tiny blood vessels. Hormones move from the gland into the bloodstream, and then circulate around the body.

Case study

Hormones and control of sugar level

Blood sugar level is critical, because too much or too little can damage cells. A constant sugar level in the blood is best, because it helps cells to work at a steady rate.

In practice, keeping a balance is a bit like trying to keep a see-saw flat when children are jumping on and off all the time. At one end of the 'see-saw', the body gets sugar by consuming food and drink. We tend to eat a variety of foods at different times, and in different amounts, daily. At the same time, we use up sugar at different rates because our activity varies. Even so, the level stays constant.

Coordinating life processes

So how does the body cope? As the sugar level changes, a hormone is released. **Insulin** and **glucagon** are the two hormones mainly involved.
- insulin converts sugar in the blood to a store of glycogen, and makes cells more permeable to sugar (so sugar moves out of the blood and into cells)
- glucagon converts stored glycogen to sugar, and makes cells less permeable to glucose (so sugar remains in the blood for longer).

The effect of insulin is to lower blood sugar level. Glucagon, on the other hand, raises blood sugar level. So together these hormones stop sugar level getting too far from the correct level. This type of control is called **negative feedback**, because the hormone has a negative effect on the change in level, returning it to the optimum.

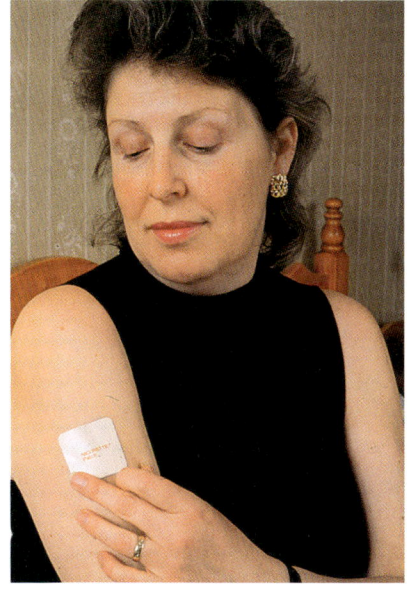

Picture 4 If skin patches are successful, diabetics may not need daily insulin injections.

A lack of insulin

Some people don't make enough insulin. This is a condition called **diabetes**, which is usually inherited. The main effect of diabetes is that the blood sugar level is not controlled, which can be fatal if not treated.

Nowadays diabetics can treat themselves by injecting human insulin. It may soon be possible to use skin patches to get insulin into the body. The human insulin is made by bacteria, which have the human gene for insulin production.

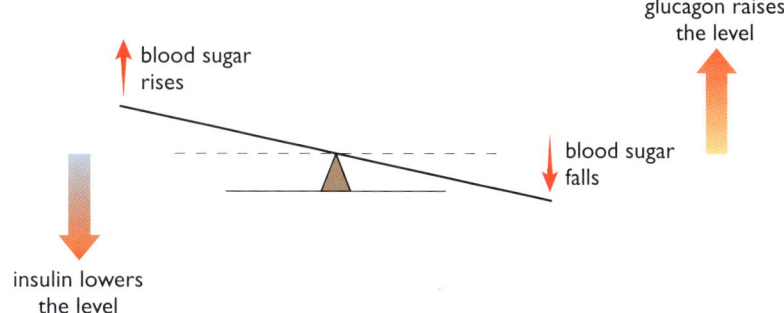

Picture 5 Hormones help the body to cope with changing sugar levels.

Questions

1. **a)** How does hormone get from a gland into the bloodstream?

   b) What are the advantages of hormones circulating in blood?

2. **a)** Suggest a reason why the pituitary is sometimes called the 'master gland'.

   b) What are the effects of adrenaline? Why are these effects useful in dangerous situations?

3. Suggest the effect of the following activities on blood sugar level and hormone production:

   a) eating a meal, including a sugary dessert

   b) missing a meal

   c) going to sports club after school, before getting home for tea

   d) having a lazy day lying in the sun.

Becoming an adult

Lifestages

There is a general pattern to life. It begins at the moment a sperm cell fertilises an egg cell. Childhood is a stage when young people grow and develop new skills. The **reproductive stage** of life is when you can produce children. This starts in early adulthood and continues to middle age. Retirement and old age follow, and finally death.

Picture 1 Four generations of the Ledger family.

Changing from a child

Adolescence can be an exciting stage in life, because it is the first step on the ladder to maturity and independence. The set of physical changes that happen between childhood and adulthood are called **puberty**. The changes are necessary because a young person is entering the reproductive stage of life. So what are the changes during puberty?

The **secondary sexual characteristics** are physical changes that happen at puberty (see Picture 2). The exact age that these changes happen to each person varies, but for girls it's generally between the ages of 11 and 13 years. For boys, puberty usually happens between 14 and 16 years.

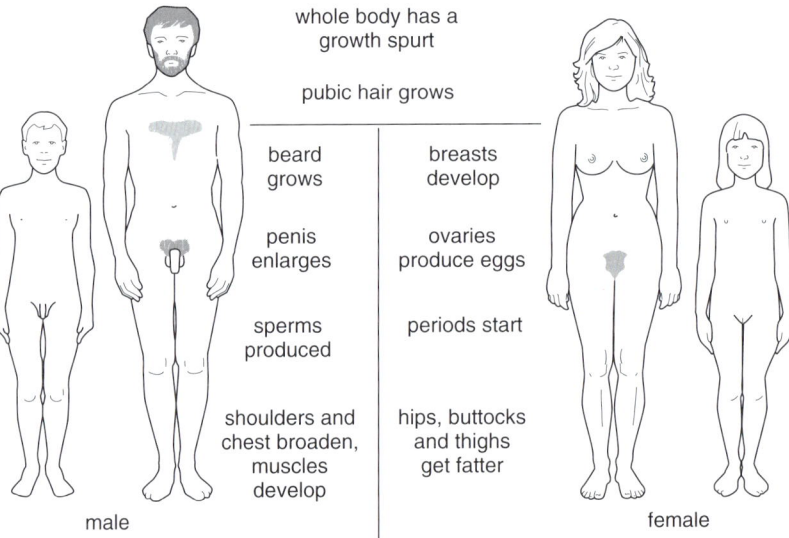

Picture 2 Physical changes that happen at puberty are called the secondary sexual characteristics.

Sex hormones cause the changes at puberty. The main sex hormones in girls are oestrogen and progesterone. Testosterone is the main male sex hormone.

Sometimes youngsters feel self-conscious about these changes. A common concern is whether the changes you experience are the same as everyone else's. But in fact it's natural for there to be a lot of variation, for example in the amount of pubic hair that people develop, or in penis size or breast size. Also the change in hormones can cause mood swings which is why adults may find teenagers 'difficult'.

Coordinating life processes

The menstrual cycle

For most women, the reproductive years begin around the ages of 11 to 13 years, and continue to around 45 or 50 years. This spans the time between puberty, when periods start, and the **menopause** when periods stop. Having a period is called **menstruation**. The diagram below shows the cycle which is repeated throughout these years.

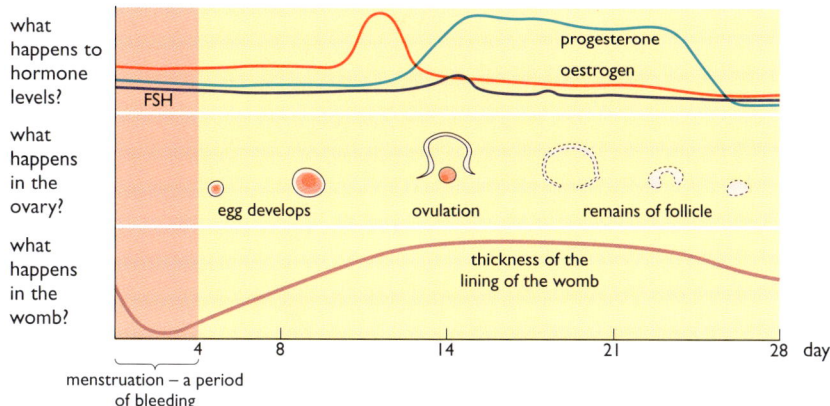

Many different hormones are important in the menstrual cycle, and only a few are mentioned here:
- Follicle stimulating hormone (FSH), from the pituitary gland, causes an egg to mature.
- The follicle in the ovary makes oestrogen, which causes the lining of the womb to thicken.
- After day 14, progesterone keeps the lining of the womb thick until the period starts.

At around day 14, an egg leaves the ovary. It may be fertilised by a sperm as it moves along the oviducts. If so, the woman does not have a period. Instead the fertilised egg sticks on the lining of the womb and develops into a baby.

If an egg is not fertilised, the level of progesterone drops. By 28 days a period starts as the lining of the womb is shed. Usually a period lasts around four days.

Sex cells

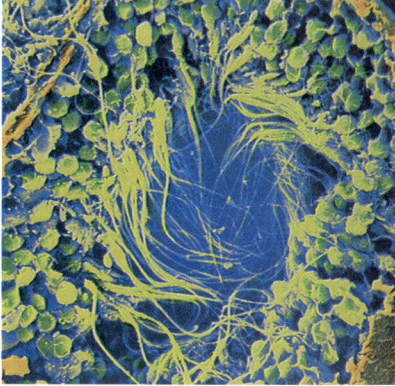

Picture 3 a) Millions of sperm cells develop inside the testis.

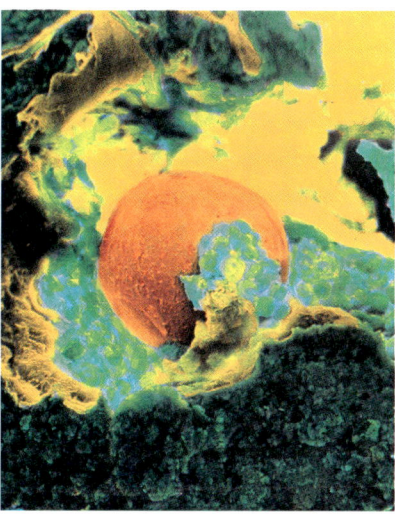

b) An ovary contains thousands of immature egg cells called follicles. As an egg matures, it bursts through the surface of the ovary. Usually one egg is produced each month, from one or other of the ovaries.

Questions

1. In which of the lifestages shown in Picture 1, is
   a) growth most active
   b) pregnancy most likely
   c) the working phase of life
   d) rest and retirement?

2. Many body changes happen during puberty. Suggest reasons why these changes are important:
   a) breast development
   b) testes begin sperm development
   c) muscles develop in males
   d) hips widen in females.

3. Use Picture 4 to help you answer this question.
   a) If a woman's period started on November 10th, what day is it likely to finish?
   b) On what date is the same woman likely to ovulate?
   c) Between which dates is the woman most likely to conceive a baby?

Human reproduction

How humans reproduce

Most humans produce very few offspring. However, reproduction is a very successful process. What features make it so successful? The fact is that reproduction happens inside the body, protected from hazards in the environment:

- eggs are fertilised by sperm cells *inside* the oviducts
- offspring develop *inside* the uterus.

The female reproductive system

Most female humans produce one egg each month, from one or other of the two ovaries. An egg travels along an oviduct, where it may be fertilised by a sperm. The womb or uterus has special features that mean a baby can develop inside. For example, it can expand hugely during pregnancy.

The placenta only develops during pregnancy and has a vital job to do. The **placenta** is a way of bringing the mother's blood and the baby's blood very close together, without the blood actually mixing. The placenta can filter out some toxic substances, but not all. Drugs, for example, pass through into the baby's blood, and it can be born addicted.

Picture 2 shows twins in the uterus. Each has its own placenta and sac. The baby in Picture 3 is in position ready for birth through the vagina.

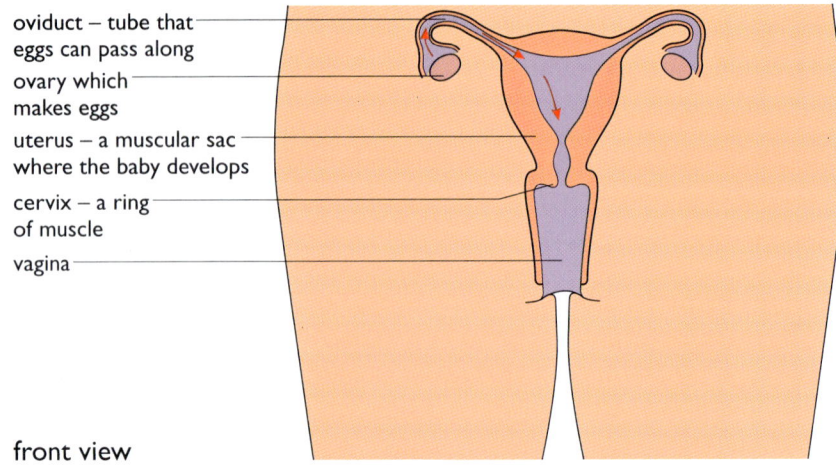
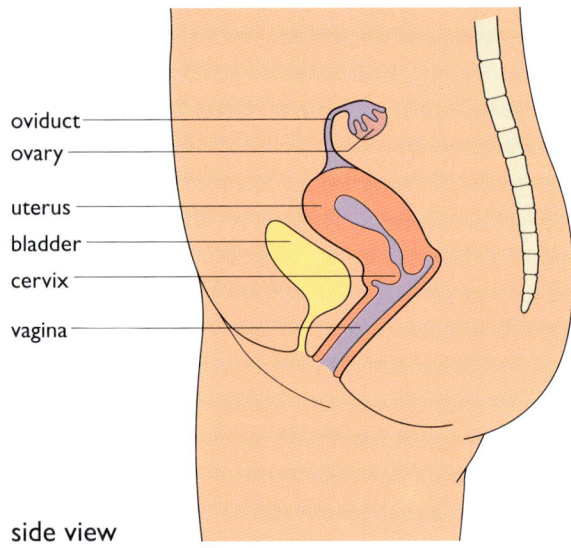

Picture 1 In humans, the egg is fertilised and a baby develops inside the body.

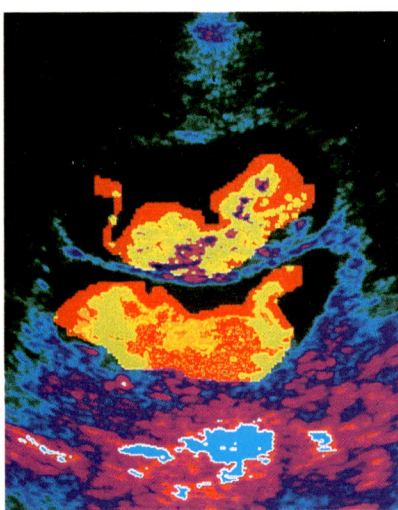

Picture 2 This scan shows twins in their mother's uterus.

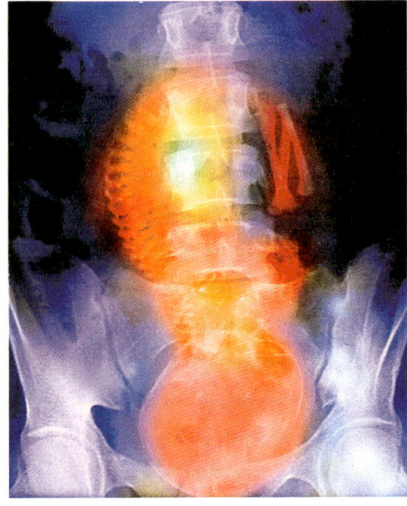

Picture 3 A developing baby just before birth.

Coordinating life processes

The male reproductive system

Millions of sperm cells are continually made in each testis. During **ejaculation**, they are pushed out of the body by muscles in the sperm tubes. Sperms that are ejaculated into a woman's vagina swim towards the uterus by vigorously wiggling their tails. Some sperms reach the oviducts where fertilisation may happen.

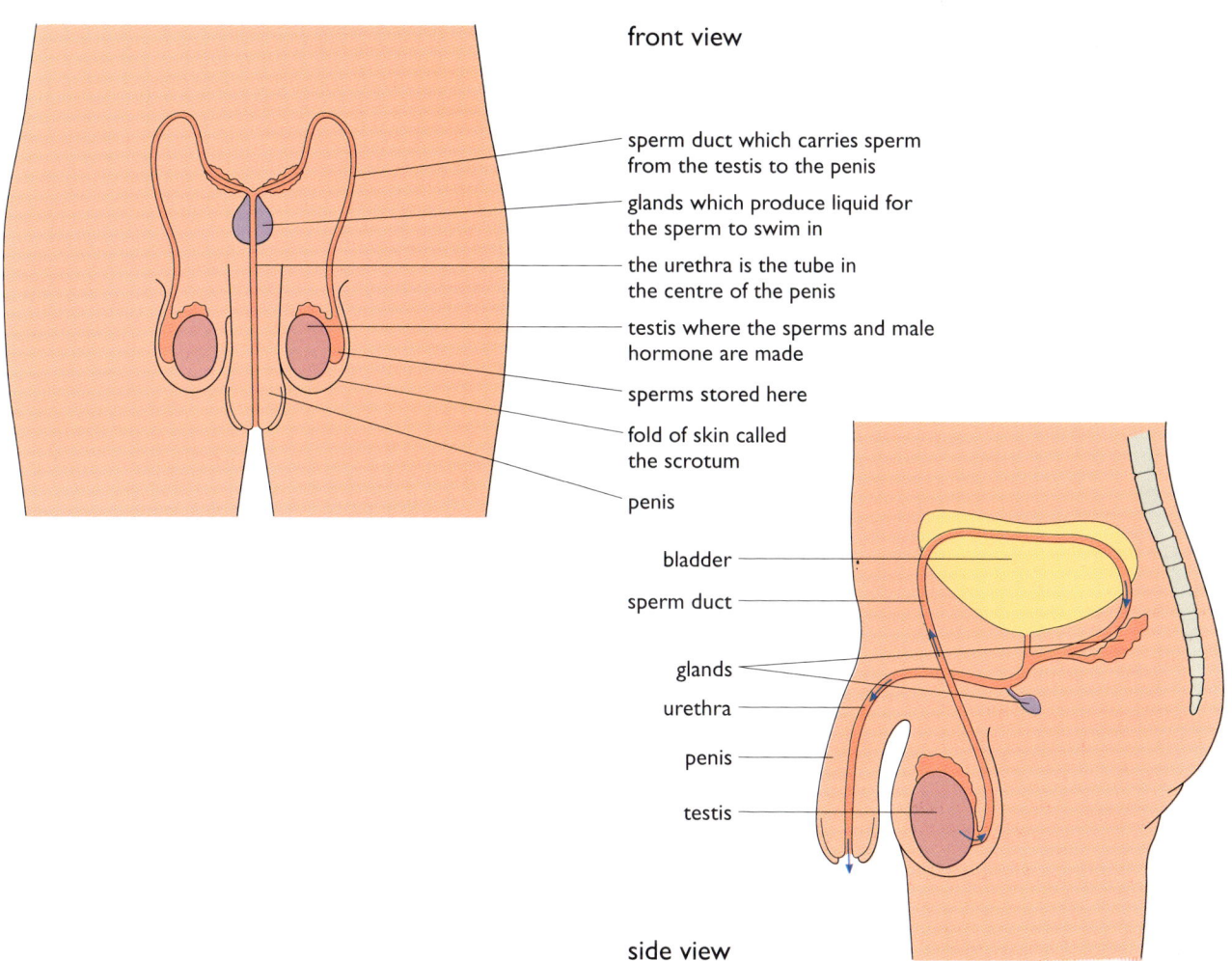

Picture 4 The job of the male reproductive system is to produce sperms, and transfer them to the female.

Questions

1. Look at Picture 3 on page 101.

   a) Where does fertilisation happen when frogs reproduce?

   b) What hazards in the environment might frogs' eggs be destroyed by?

   c) Suggest a reason why human females produce less eggs than frogs.

   d) Suggest a reason why human females produce much smaller numbers of eggs, compared to the number of sperms produced by males.

2. Doctors advise a woman who is pregnant not to smoke or to drink alcohol. Why?

3. One common reason for women not being able to have a baby is if the oviducts are blocked. Why does that cut down the chance of fertilisation?

4. What is the job of

   a) the placenta

   b) the sac

   c) the umbilical cord?

Hormones and fertility

Altering body processes

Hormones affect both growth during childhood, and development at puberty. Table 1 shows the results of using hormones and similar chemicals to influence growth and milk production.

Table 1 A dairy farmer can use hormones to increase yields. *Source*: SATIS 16–19 Unit 9 'Cattle and chemicals'.

Hormone	Untreated cattle	Treated cattle
BST (the hormone that causes milk production)	food → cow → milk	food → cow → milk (more)
steroid growth hormone	food → cow → meat	food → cow → meat (more)

Altering fertility

Sometimes people have problems which are like the opposite sides of a coin. For example, a couple may plan not to start a family at present, because their situation isn't right. Another couple might be trying to conceive a baby, without success. The use of hormones might provide an option for both couples.

Increasing fertility

Treatment with hormones is only one approach to increasing fertility, and is not the answer in every case. However, women with infertility problems may be treated with hormones, including FSH, to increase the chance of egg production. Eggs can be taken from the ovary and fertilised by sperms in a dish. The fertilised egg can then be placed into the uterus. Despite the fact that a new life is started outside the body, the pregnancy continues in the normal way (Picture 1). This is called IVF (*in vitro* fertilisation).

Decreasing fertility

The main basis of **contraception** is stopping fertilisation, by preventing sperms meeting eggs. Table 2 is a summary of contraceptive methods. The 'Pill' is a contraceptive method used by women which involves using hormones.

Picture 1 Hannah, Sophie and Natalie are triplets, but they are not identical. They developed from three separate eggs which were put back into their mother's womb, after fertilisation *outside* her body.

Coordinating life processes

Method of contraception		How it works
Rhythm (natural) method		Keep a check of dates during the menstrual cycle; around ovulation there is a slight rise in body temperature. Avoid intercourse a few days before and after ovulation.
Condom		A thin rubber sheath is placed over the penis to collect sperms.
Diaphragm or cap		A thin rubber cap is placed in the vagina, to stop sperms getting past.
Female condom		Fitted inside the vagina, and collects sperms.
Intrauterine device		Fitted into the womb, and stops any fertilised eggs staying there.
Contraceptive pill		The combined pill prevents an egg being released from the ovary.
Sterilisation		The oviducts or the sperm tubes are cut, so that egg cells do not reach the uterus, and sperm cells do not pass out of the body.

Table 2 Summary of contraceptive methods.

Source: 'Medicines and Drugs', Wellcome Foundation.

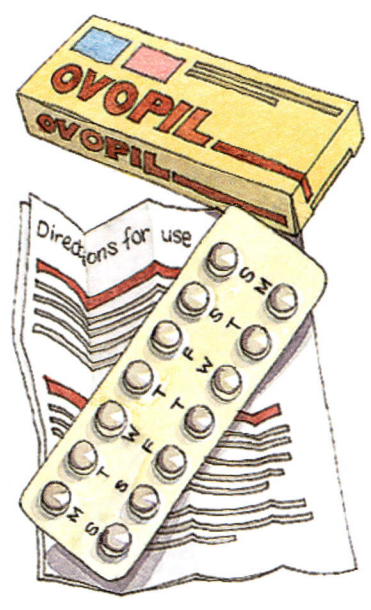

Picture 2 'The Pill' contains chemicals similar to hormones. A doctor has to prescribe the Pill, and can give advice about its use.

A combined Pill contains two types of hormones. The hormones may stop eggs being released from the ovaries. Also the Pill can make the conditions inside the vagina more difficult for sperms to survive, as well as making the mucus thicker. Sperms find it more difficult to swim through the mucus to reach an egg in the oviducts.

Questions

1. Table 1 gives data on using hormones in farming.

   a) What is the effect of using BST hormone on milk production?

   b) Why is it cheaper for a dairy farmer to use hormones, despite the cost of the hormone treatment such as vet's bills?

   c) What is the effect of using growth hormone on cattle which are farmed for meat?

   d) Some people buy meat that has been produced without giving hormones to animals. The meat costs more, so why do they think it's worth it?

2. **a)** Why is FSH used in fertility treatment?

   b) Suggest a reason why multiple births (several babies in one pregnancy) tend to happen more frequently when a woman has had fertility treatment.

   c) Why is hormone treatment not the answer for all childless couples?

3. Suggest reasons why it's important for a woman to take the Pill exactly as instructed.

Chemical coordinators in plants

Plants respond by growing

Whole plants don't make sudden movements in the way that animals do. In fact most plant movements aren't detectable by the human eye. Even so, parts of a plant move because of cell growth. This happens when cells divide and then increase in size. The increase can be fairly rapid, because of water entering a cell while the wall is still stretchy.

Sometimes the response to touch can be more rapid than that shown in Picture 1. Picture 2 shows a very rapid response. But what makes it happen? Scientists have recently found proteins that can contract, similar in some ways to muscle proteins. They have detected electrical signals in cells too, leading to the idea that these fast responses may be like animal responses.

Picture 1 Plants move by growing, in this case around a support. They grow more quickly in the dark, which might be one reason why it's easy to miss it happening.

Tropisms

Growth movements are called **tropisms** if a plant is responding to a change in the environment, e.g. an increase in light.

Picture 2 What makes a Venus Fly Trap snap shut?

Picture 4 Roots grow towards a water source at the bottom of the pot.

The part of the plant above the soil is the **shoot system**. The shoot system is sensitive to gravity and light, and sometimes to touch. All or some of these conditions can influence at the same time the way a plant grows.

The plant in Picture 3 is growing towards light, so this is called positive phototropism. At the same time, gravity is acting on the plant. Since the shoot is growing in the opposite direction to the force of gravity, this is a negative response called negative **geotropism**.

Picture 3 Stems grow in the direction of light. This is called **phototropism**.

Coordinating life processes

The plant in Picture 4 has roots growing in the direction of water. This is a positive response called positive **hydrotropism**. Gravity is acting on the roots too. The roots grow in the same direction as the force of gravity, so this is positive geotropism. Some roots are not affected by light, while others actively grow away from it.

The effects of plant hormones

Tropisms are controlled by plant hormones. Like animal hormones, they may be made in one part but act in another. Picture 5 shows some simple experiments carried out by a Dutch scientist called Fritz Went. After setting them up, he left them in the dark.

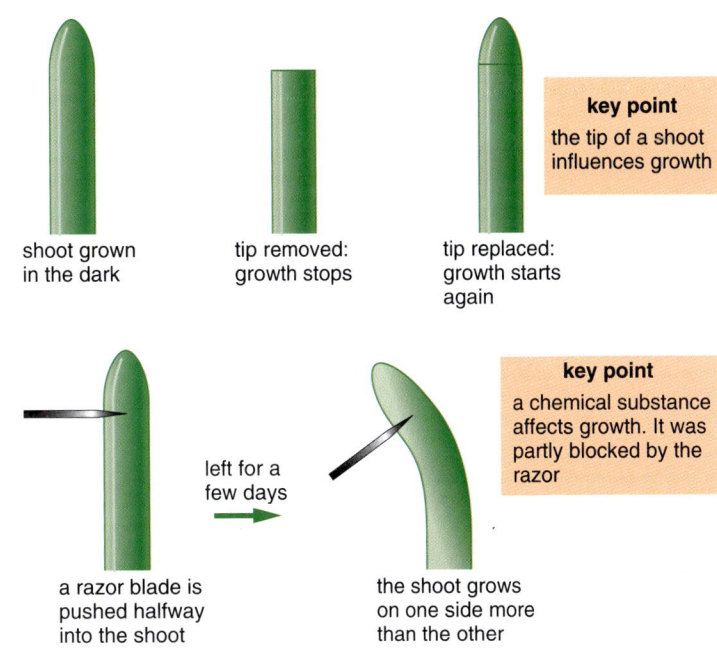

Picture 5 Experiments with shoot tips.

Questions

1. What are the advantages for a plant of the shoot clinging to a support?
2. Copy the summary table below, of information about tropisms. Then complete the table.

Tropism	Part of the plant responding	Conditions in the environment that cause the tropism
positive phototropism		
positive geotropism		
negative geotropism		
positive haptotropism		touch

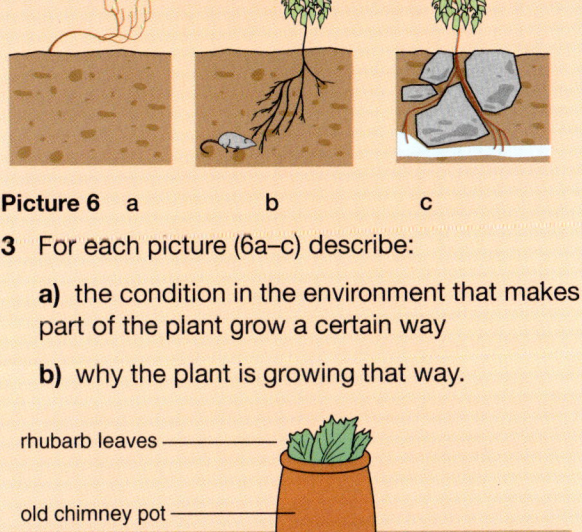

Picture 6   a   b   c

3. For each picture (6a–c) describe:

   a) the condition in the environment that makes part of the plant grow a certain way

   b) why the plant is growing that way.

Picture 7 Rhubarb stems are 'forced' to grow in a dark tube.

4. Suggest a reason why gardeners put a dark tube around the first shoots of rhubarb, to get an early crop.

Coordinating life processes

Activities

Coordinating the human body

Table 1 Features of the nervous system and the hormone system.

	Nervous system	Hormone system
speed of response	rapid	usually slower, over a period of time
part of the body involved	nerve cells	glands
type of communication	nerve impulses	chemicals called hormones
how message travels	through nerves	in the bloodstream

1. Suggest why it is useful to have two systems controlling the body.

2. Look at Table 1.

    a) Which system usually produces a slow change?

    b) Where are hormones made in the hormone system?

    c) Which system is mainly involved in:
    i) growth?
    ii) hearing an alarm bell?
    iii) feeling the sun's warmth?
    iv) developing hair under the arms at puberty?
    v) making muscles move?

3. A nerve runs from the tip of Tom's toe to his spine. If he stubs his toe, an impulse moves to the spine at 100 metres/second. How long will it take the impulse to get to the spine? Work out your answer using the formula below.

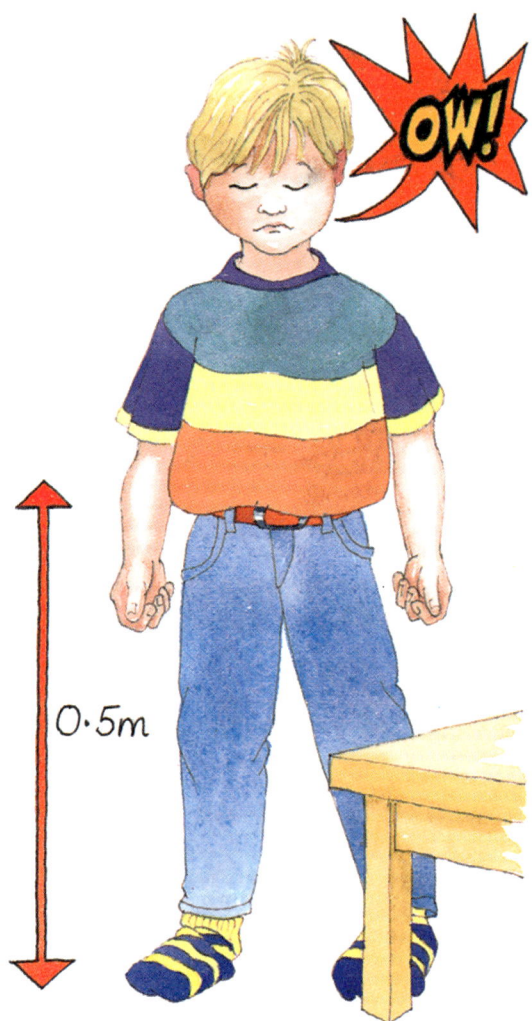

$$\text{speed (m/s)} = \frac{\text{distance (m)}}{\text{time (s)}}$$

Plant hormones

Table 2 Information about plant hormones.

Hormone	Effect
auxin	makes stems grow faster, particularly at the tip; makes cells get longer; low concentrations stimulate root growth
giberellin	increases stem growth between the places where leaves are attached; makes fruit grow bigger; helps seeds germinate
abcissic acid	slows down the growth of cells in roots and stems and causes leaf fall
ethylene	slows root and stem growth; causes fruit to ripen

Use Table 2 to help you answer these questions.

4 Which hormone might be used:

a) to get more success with germinating seeds?

b) to ripen bananas during their journey to the UK?

c) in rooting powder for cuttings?

d) to get a bigger fruit crop?

e) to strip a wooded area of leaves?

What is a stroke?

If blood clots inside a blood vessel in the brain, it can cause a blockage. Part of the brain may not get enough blood and so won't be supplied with enough oxygen. As a result, cells in this area of the brain may die. This is called 'having a stroke'.

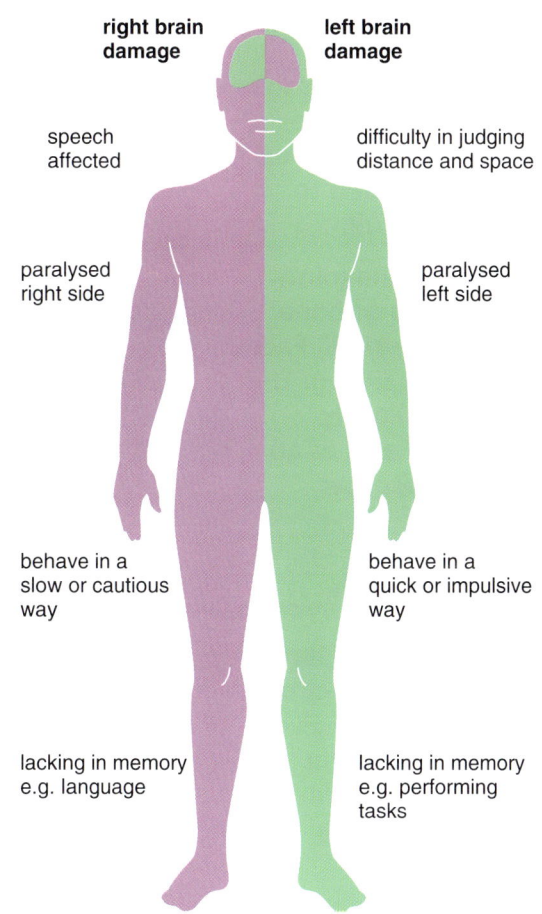

Picture 3 The effects of a stroke.

1 Why is the brain damaged when someone has a stroke?

2 Suggest why a stroke can vary from being very mild to very serious, even fatal.

3 After Mary had a stroke, she was not able to talk. Which side of her body was likely to be paralysed?

4 Look at Picture 4 on page 55. Why does a stroke on one side of the brain have effects on the opposite side of the body?

5 Is it likely that someone will recover after a stroke?

A COORDINATED APPROACH TO LIFE

Brain box? It needs to be strong for head-bangers

Scientists have confirmed what seems obvious – head-banging is bad for you: it literally shakes the brain apart. So what's different about the ibex? Why don't their brains get damaged when they use their skulls in head-to-head combat? The impacts can involve forces up to 60 times that needed to fracture a human skull.

The answer lies in the joints between the plates of bone which make up the skull. Each joint is like a wide zigzag. The zigzag can move slightly under impact, and acts as an excellent shock absorber.

Ibex use their skulls as bony crash helmets

Bionic eyes

Scientists in the United States believe that a micro-electronic 'chip' will help them to give sight back to people who become blind later in life because their retinas are damaged.

The light sensitive chip would be put into the retina at the back of the eyeball. The chip does the job of damaged rods and cones, allowing impulses to travel to the brain. It is too early to say what visual images someone might see, and how the brain would deal with them.

Will artificial eyes turn out to be just tiny electronic chips?

- Silicone capsule
- Microchip
- Electrode array
- Retina
- Optic nerve
- Lens
- Vitreous humour

Are your senses 'mixed up'?

In April 1995, a survey of students and the general public was carried out in Cambridge. Some people who took part in the survey saw letters, words or numbers in colour, and four of them heard coloured music. More complex cases than this have been reported. For one woman, a smell such as grass has a colour too – purple. And roses smell grey.

It seems that more females experience sensory mix-up than males, and that the condition may be inherited. Exactly what happens in the brain when the senses 'mix', is still not known. Some scientists believe it is to do with the way that nerve cells are linked, but there are no clear answers yet.

Drugged spiders weave crooked webs

Scientists think that with a little help from a computer program (and a few spiders), they may be able to tell how toxic a drug is. It seems that spiders weave their webs according to set patterns. The pictures show how four drugs affect the patterns that spiders weave.

Chloral hydrate and marijuana are both sedatives. The spider gets so laid back it doesn't complete the task. Benzedrine (or speed) and caffeine (from coffee) are stimulants. On benzedrine, the spider sets about its task with great gusto but appears to ignore the planning.

Caffeine affects the spider so much that it only strings a few threads together.

Scientists investigating this think that spiders could be used for testing how toxic a drug is. After giving a spider a drug, scientists would estimate how well it made its web. The more out of shape a web is, the more toxic the drug must be.

Health Warning!
Scientists have found out the rave drug, Ecstasy, causes brain cells to lose their axons. Axons can grow back, but in studies on rats and squirrels, the axons grew back abnormally. The effects may well be the same in humans.

Web-weaving takes some skill

Marijuana | Benzedrine | Caffeine | Chloral hydrate

Male sea birds lose interest in sex

Some chemicals such as pesticides act on the body in the same way as a female sex hormone, oestrogen. Michael Fry is a bird scientist at the University of California. Since the 1970s he has studied the effects on bird life, of chemicals that mimic oestrogen. In some places, the chemicals are present in sea water, and so get into the sea birds' food source.

Fry discovered that these chemicals can cause chicks to develop abnormally, along both male and female lines. These 'intersex' chicks do not show normal mating behaviour. He noticed that males fail to turn up at the breeding sites. Faced with a lack of males, Fry found that many nests were shared by two females.

Chemicals affect the development of chicks. What might the long-term effects be on a population of gulls?

Coordinating life processes

Summary

- Sensitivity makes living things aware of what's happening around them, and within their own bodies.

- The nervous system consists of nerve cells, nerves, the spinal cord and the brain. In a nerve pathway, a receptor detects a stimulus and is connected to a sensory neurone. A motor neurone carries nerve impulses to an effector organ, e.g. a muscle.

- A reflex action is an automatic response which happens very quickly. A conditioned reflex has been learned.

- The eye is a sense organ. The lens inside the eye focuses light onto the retina. The retina contains rods and cones which are sensitive to light.

- Drugs alter some aspect of how the body works. Medicines contain drugs which improve health. Drugs of abuse are used because they produce a change in mood or feeling.

- Hormones are made by glands. Hormones are chemical coordinators. They cause more general changes in the body than the nervous system does.

- Puberty is a set of changes which happen to the body as a person grows from a child into a young adult.

- Menstruation is controlled by several hormones including oestrogen. An important male sex hormone is testosterone.

- In humans, fertilisation happens when the nucleus of a sperm cell joins with the nucleus of an egg cell. Fertilisation happens in the oviducts.

- Contraception generally works by preventing fertilisation.

Questions

1 a) A spectacle lens was placed over some writing.

i) What does the lens do to rays of light?
ii) Which type of lens is it?

b) An optician was explaining to a young person why he needed to wear spectacles. The optician drew this diagram of an eye to show normal vision.

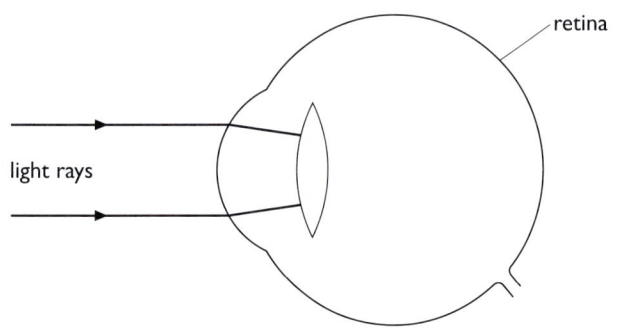

i) Two light rays are drawn up to the lens of the eye. Copy the diagram. Using a sharp pencil and ruler continue these lines to show how they are focused on the retina.
ii) Describe the sort of image formed on the retina.
iii) Describe how information is transmitted from the retina to the brain.

c) The optician had an ornamental light which used optical fibres. The young person could not understand how the light appeared at the ends of the fibres. Explain how it works. Use a diagram if it helps your answer. Look at *Physical Processes* to help you.

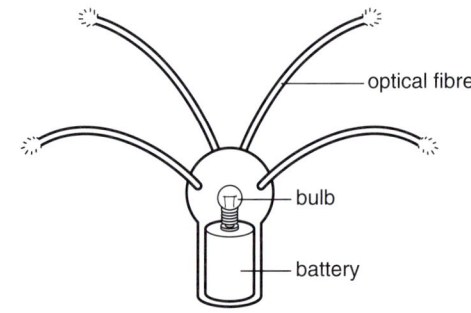

Questions continued

d) The young person went to hospital to have some dirt removed from the surface of one eye. The nurse placed a large bandage over the eye and told the person not do drive a car.
Why was this instruction given?

MEG

2 Dr Jones was concerned about the number of smoking related problems suffered by his patients and he decided to keep a record of the deaths per year in smokers and non-smokers. His findings were as follows:-

Average number of cigarettes smoked per day	0	5	10	15	20	25	30	35
Number of deaths per year	2	5	8	12	15	18	24	26

a) What does the table tell you about the effects of smoking?
b) Give **two** causes of death in smokers.

WJEC

3 The table shows the water and glucose content of the blood plasma and the urine of three people.
A and C are not diabetic. B is diabetic. C had been given a small drink containing 10 g of glucose 30 minutes before the information was collected.

Substance (g/dm³)	A (non-diabetic) Blood plasma	Urine	B (diabetic) Blood plasma	Urine	C (non-diabetic) Blood plasma	Urine
Water	911	960	912	958	910	961
Glucose	1	0	1.8	0.4	1.9	0

a) Explain why the glucose content of the blood plasma and urine are different in A and B.
b) Explain why A and C had the **same** amounts of glucose in their urine but **different** amounts of glucose in their blood plasma.
c) What causes diabetes?

MEG

4 a) The diagram shows the human male reproductive system.

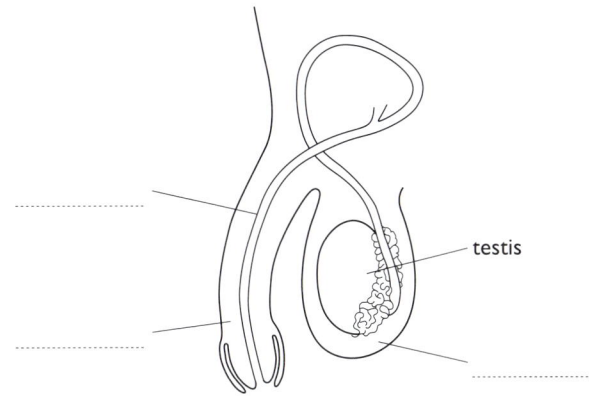

i) Copy the diagram. Use the **correct** words from the list to finish labelling the diagram.
**anus   bladder   penis
scrotum   sperm duct   urethra**
ii) What is the job of the testes?

MEG

5 There are two systems in our bodies for controlling how we react to changes around us – the nervous system and the endocrine system. The nervous system carries messages as electrical signals. The endocrine system carries messages using chemicals in the bloodstream.
a) i) If you tread on a pin, you will probably move your foot very quickly. The reaction is controlled by the nerves in the spine rather than the brain.
ii) Why is it an advantage to control responses like this by the nerves in the spine rather than in the brain?
b) i) What name is given to the chemical messengers produced by the endocrine system?
ii) Name the fast-acting chemical messenger which prepares the body for action.

focus 4

The body in balance

Controlling change — 78
A steady state is best for living cells.

Regulating water — 80
Water makes up most of living tissues and it has to be regulated.

About body temperature — 82
Why are some bodies hotter than others?

Controlling body temperature — 84
Some ways in which living things control body temperature.

Controlling change

Coping with change

The vending machine in Picture 1 stores and gives out drinks. People put money in, the machine processes their choices and they get drinks out. But what might happen if the cash box wasn't emptied? Or if the store of drinks wasn't replaced? To work properly, the vending machine has to be reset regularly.

What goes into and comes out of the machine keeps changing. Some days people buy more drinks, or more of one type of drink. Like the vending machine, a human body is changing all the time. To keep a steady supply of energy, the body needs oxygen and food. But what we eat changes from day to day, and so do our activities.

Picture 2 shows someone being very energetic. She needs more oxygen and so her breathing rate has increased to cope with this.

Picture 1 The inputs and outputs of a vending machine change moment to moment.

Picture 2 Sometimes we breathe faster than at other times, to get more oxygen. At the same time, the air we breathe out contains more carbon dioxide.

Just think how you'd feel if you'd been skating like the person in Picture 2. Boiling hot, probably! But your body doesn't actually boil, and its temperature stays about the same. In fact we can cope with most temperature changes that happen inside and outside our bodies. This is because we can control our body temperature, except in extreme conditions.

Some types of illness, such as infections, raise the body temperature, because they interfere with the body's temperature controls. The body still regulates temperature, but at a higher level.

Picture 3 This ski-suit is made of a light insulating material. It helps the skier to stay warm despite the freezing conditions outside.

The body in balance

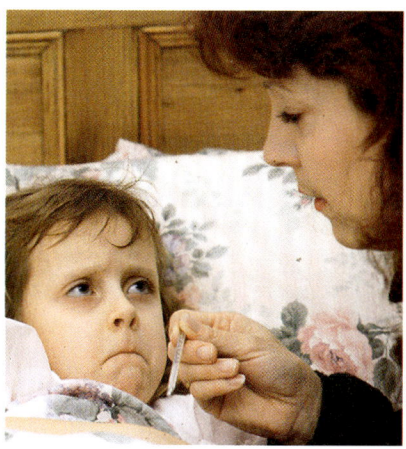

Picture 4 Having flu can cause a 'high temperature'.

Keeping conditions constant

The word **homeostasis** means keeping conditions constant. Homeostasis involves many ways of controlling conditions inside the body, despite changing inputs or changing conditions outside.

Many chemical changes happen in living things. Only some of the products of these reactions are useful. Other products are toxic if they build up in the body. What's more, we may take in more of a substance than we need. Table 1 shows some of the conditions that need to be controlled in humans.

Condition	Reason why the level must be controlled	Organ/system that controls the level
sugar in the blood (from digested food)	affects water movement in and out of cells; too little can make you unconscious	two hormones, insulin and glucagon, are involved, and the liver has overall control
oxygen in the blood	too little means death; too much can damage nerve cells	centres in the brain control how fast we breathe and how fast the heart beats
pH	blood plasma and the fluid around cells is pH 7, a change in pH might stop enzymes working	kidney
temperature	human body 37°C; high temperature causes fits, sweating and makes you unconscious, low temperature causes body to slow down, and makes you unconscious	the skin, including the blood system
water and salts	affects all cell processes and cell structure	kidney
toxins, including some wastes	various effects, often on nervous system	liver mostly

Table 1 Controlling conditions inside the body.

Questions

1 a) Why do conditions within the body change all the time?

b) Suggest some of the main inputs to the human body.

c) Which waste substances leave the body?

2 a) What is homeostasis?

b) Why do our bodies work best if the level of sugar remains constant?

c) Why is water level important in tissue fluid and blood?

d) Which organ deals with toxic substances in the body?

3 When Sam was nearly two years old he was teething and sometimes got a high temperature. Suggest why his mother gave him medicine to lower his temperature.

Regulating water

Balancing water

Living things need to be able to balance water intake and water loss. This balance is called **osmoregulation**. For animals that live on land, the challenge is usually keeping enough water in the body.

Some animals such as snails, slugs and worms use slime coverings to help keep water in. Others, such as woodlice, have a hard outer covering which is waterproof.

Plants have ways of conserving water too. Picture 2 shows a cactus which is well adapted to surviving a dry climate. When there is a brief rainstorm, the cactus roots rapidly absorb water, which is stored in the fleshy stem. Other plants such as pine trees have a thick, waxy layer called the **cuticle** on the surface. The waxy layer is waterproof.

Water gain and water loss

Table 1 shows how humans gain and lose most water. You can see that the most important ways we lose water are through urine and sweating.

We have a waterproof skin, which helps cut down on evaporation at the body surface. Even so, we still lose about 0.5 litres of water per day because of sweating. If weather conditions are hot, the amount of sweat produced will be greater – but the amount of urine is likely to be less, to make up for this.

Water gain (%)		Water loss (%)	
drinks } food	86	tears	(very little)
		sweat (evaporation)	20
made in the body	14	breathing out	16
		urine	60
		faeces	4

Table 1 Water gain and loss in humans (ml). *Source: Revised Nuffield Biology.*

Picture 1 A thick slime covering helps to keep this snail moist, and helps it to glide along.

The inside of the lungs is not waterproof. It's wet, because the surface membranes of cells in the lung let water pass through. This means we can't avoid losing some water at the same time as we breathe out.

Picture 2 This saguaro cactus can store water in its stem. The leaves are tiny prickles that lose very little water by evaporation.

The body in balance

The human kidney

Osmoregulation is a very important process for all living things. In humans, the kidneys carry out this process. They keep a balance in the body's water needs, and correct the levels of dissolved salts and acidity. At the same time, kidneys **excrete** a waste product called urea.

A human kidney is dark red in colour because of its rich blood supply. The kidneys are held at the back of the body. Blood circulates so rapidly around the body that all of it goes through the kidneys during a six minute period. As blood passes through it is filtered and balanced.

Some of the filtered water, salts, and a waste substance called urea leave the kidneys and make up urine. Urine collects in the bladder, which empties every now and then. We learn bladder control at around the age of 2 years.

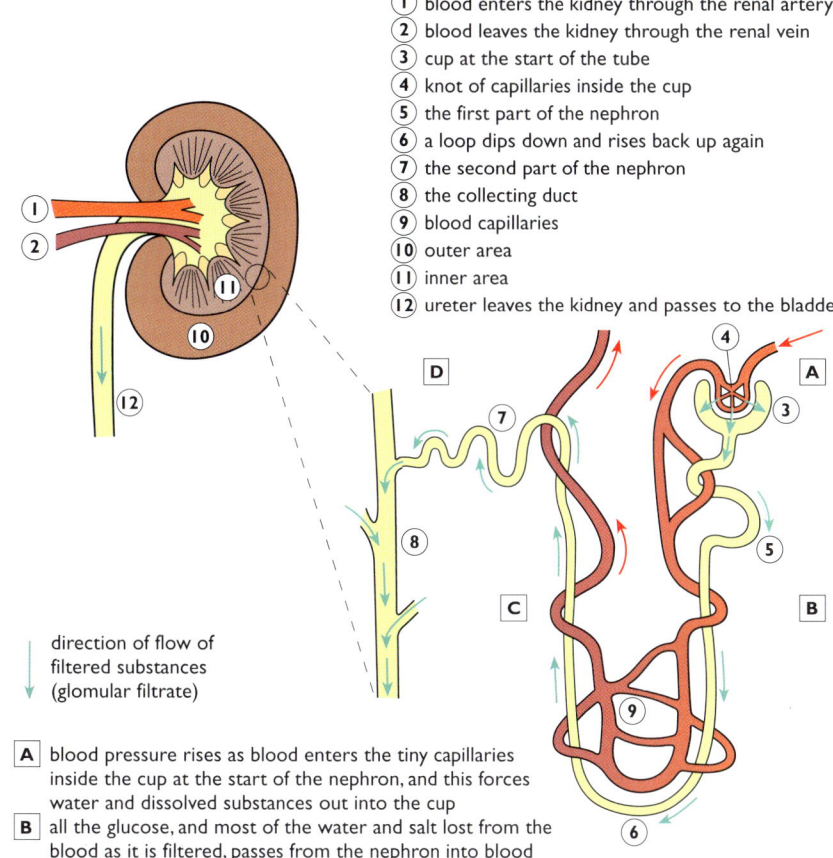

① blood enters the kidney through the renal artery
② blood leaves the kidney through the renal vein
③ cup at the start of the tube
④ knot of capillaries inside the cup
⑤ the first part of the nephron
⑥ a loop dips down and rises back up again
⑦ the second part of the nephron
⑧ the collecting duct
⑨ blood capillaries
⑩ outer area
⑪ inner area
⑫ ureter leaves the kidney and passes to the bladder

direction of flow of filtered substances (glomular filtrate)

A blood pressure rises as blood enters the tiny capillaries inside the cup at the start of the nephron, and this forces water and dissolved substances out into the cup
B all the glucose, and most of the water and salt lost from the blood as it is filtered, passes from the nephron into blood capillaries nearby
C the second part of the nephron can actively take up unwanted substances from blood, and can also put substances into blood, e.g. to control pH
D the second part of the nephron and collecting duct "fine tune" water balance, water moves out of the tubule and back into the blood

Picture 3 The urine system.

Questions

1 Why is keeping enough water in the body a challenge for

   a) a small land animal such as an insect
   b) for animals that live in salt water?

2 The table below shows water gain and water loss in a kangaroo rat that lives in the deserts of North America.

Water gain (%)		Water loss (%)	
made in body	45	urine	11
eaten/drunk	5	faeces	2
		evaporation	37

Source: *Biological Sciences* Green, Stout and Taylor

a) Compare these figures with the amounts shown for humans in Table 1. How are the amounts different for humans in terms of:
   i) water taken in as food and drink
   ii) water lost as urine?

b) Suggest reasons why the data for humans and kangaroo rats is different.

c) Suggest how the kidney might be adapted to help an animal survive in dry conditions.

3 List some ways in which water loss is prevented

   a) in animals.   b) in plants.

4 On a hot day most people sweat more than on a cool day. How might this affect

   a) their thirst
   b) the amount of urine they produce?

About body temperature

Body temperatures

The coldest natural temperature recorded on Earth so far is -68°C, and the hottest is 58°C. These are extremes, but many places change temperature over a wide range as the seasons come and go. Picture 1 shows what happens to the body temperature of some animals, as the temperature around them changes.

You can see from Picture 1 that the pattern is different for mammals and birds, compared to fish. The reason is that mammals and birds belong to animal groups that can control their body temperature. They are called **endotherms**, because they rely mostly on heating from within the body. The 'endo-' part of the word means 'from inside'. Endotherms often have a body temperature above that of the surroundings.

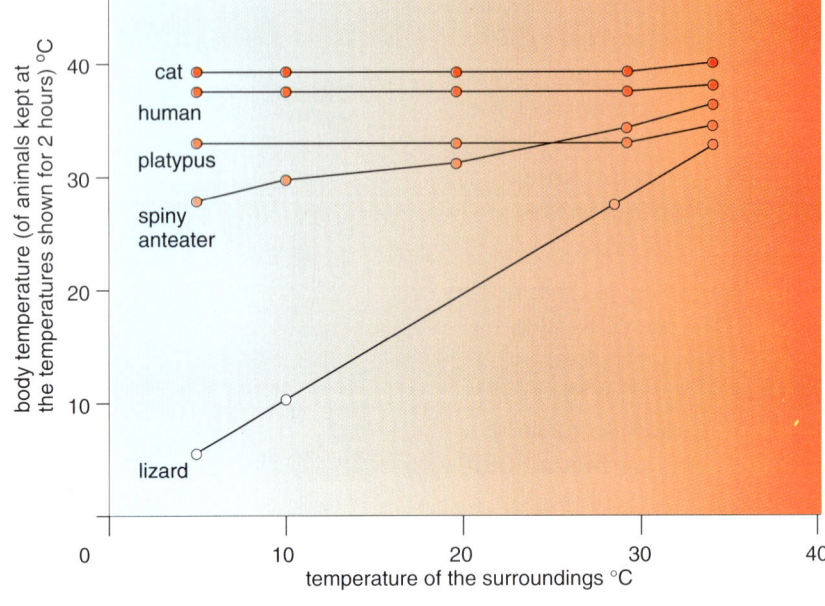

Picture 1 A graph to show change in body temperature as external temperature varies.

There are few climates that endotherms cannot survive, which makes them successful at living in most environments. But to keep warm enough to survive in cold conditions, endotherms use up a lot of food. They have a high rate of transferring energy stored in food to body cells. This means they can be very active.

The lizard in Picture 2 can't fully control body temperature. Animals like this are called **ectotherms**, since their heating is mostly from outside the body. The 'ecto-' part of the word means 'from outside'. Their body temperature varies more than an endotherm's, according to the temperature of the surroundings.

Behaviour and temperature control

Ectotherms and endotherms behave in ways that help them to keep their body temperature steady. Ectotherms such as lizards lie on hot surfaces to warm up, or move into water or mud to cool down. They tend to be active during the daytime, when it's warmer.

Picture 2 A lizard – an ectotherm.

The body in balance

In hot climates endotherms may face the challenge of overheating. Panting helps to cool the dog in Picture 3. This is because the saliva evaporates, cooling the blood supplying the inside surfaces of the nose and mouth. Since the blood going to the brain passes close to this cooled blood, it is cooled too. Cooling the brain in this way is very important for a lot of mammals.

In cold climates, an endotherm, such as a tiny dormouse, may not be able to find enough food to survive the winter. Hibernation is a way of avoiding cold temperatures, and shorter days. The dormouse in Picture 4 has gone into a very deep sleep. It can survive by using fat stores in the body, since its activity level is very low.

Picture 4 This dormouse takes a winter break by sleeping.

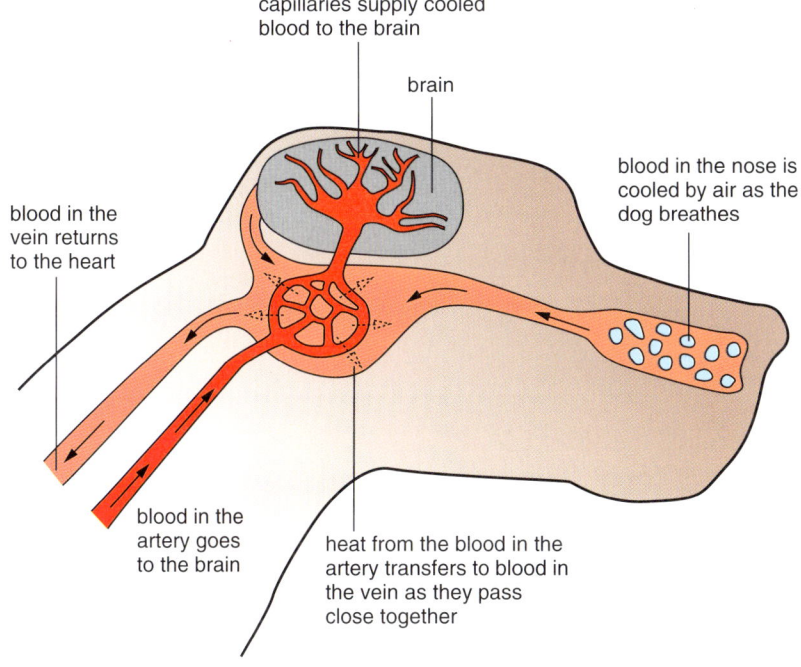

Picture 3 Panting is cool behaviour for dogs.

Questions

1. Which of the animals in list A are
   a) ectotherms
   b) endotherms?

   List A: bee, rat, bear, trout, owl, snake, frog.

2. How is the graph for a camel's body temperature slightly different from that of other mammals?

3. What is the main energy source for endotherms?

4. Suggest a reason why these animals might behave in the following ways:
   a) hippopotamuses wallow in mud
   b) penguins huddle together.

5. a) Why are the shorter, colder days in winter a disadvantage to a field mouse?

6. Suggest some advantages of being an endotherm.

Controlling body temperature

Keeping warm and keeping cool

Keeping at a steady temperature is important for living things. Regulating temperature is called **thermoregulation**. A thermostat in an oven is a thermoregulator. If the oven temperature drops, the sensors in the oven detect the drop, and the heating source switches back on. The heating switches off as temperature rises over the set level.

You can see from Picture 1 that humans have several ways of controlling body temperature. The most important ways are blood flow in the skin, and sweating.

Blood flow in the skin

The skin covers the surface of the body. It is made of several tissues, including a rich supply of blood (see pages 14–15). We get cooler when we radiate heat energy from skin surfaces. We also cool when sweat evaporates (see *Physical Processes*, page 123).

Picture 2 shows that the amount of blood getting close to the skin surface can be varied. If the tiny blood vessels near the surface are wider, more blood flows through them. The blood is cooled at the surface, and the more that reaches the surface the more we cool down.

If the blood moves deeper into the body away from the skin surface, it cools down less. This is why fingers and toes (and the end of your nose!), tend to feel coldest in chilly weather.

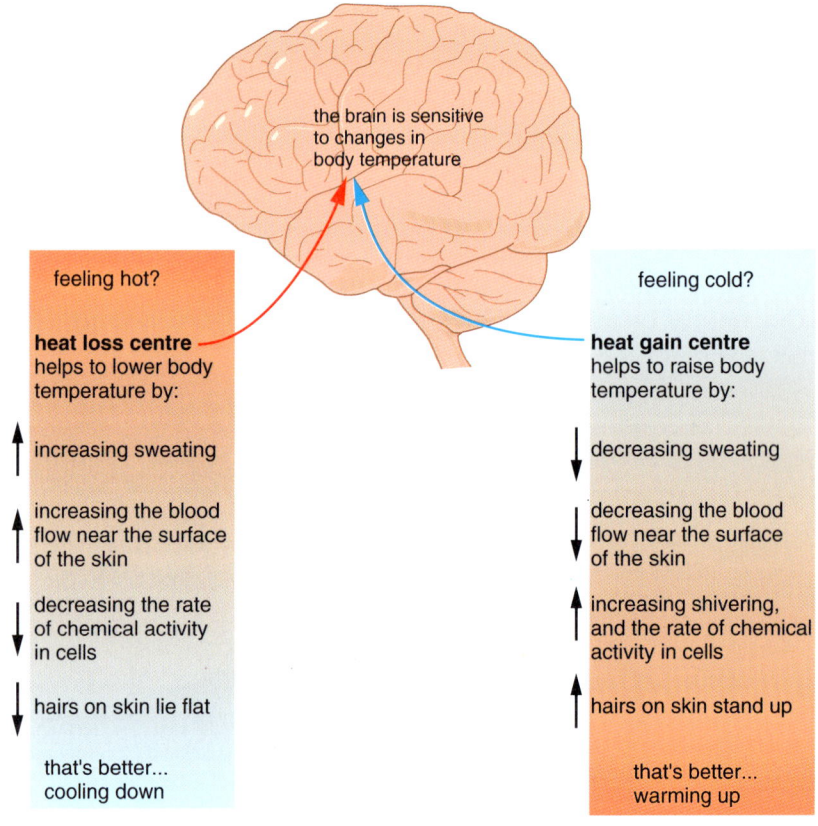

Picture 1 The brain acts like a thermostat, switching the body's temperature controls up or down.

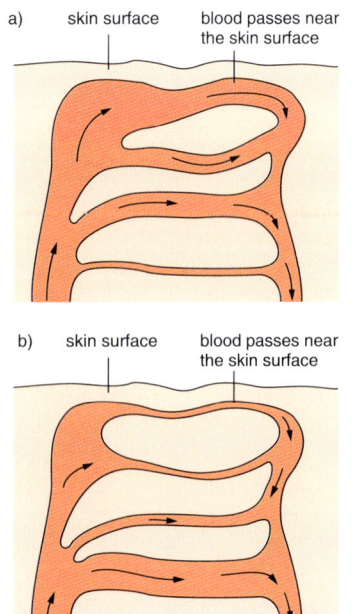

Picture 2 a) More blood passes near the body surface. b) Less blood passes near the body surface.

The body in balance

Sweating

Sweat is liquid containing water, salts, amino acids and urea. Sweat particles need energy to escape from the liquid and become a vapour. They take this energy from the skin, making it feel cooler. Choosing suitable clothing for hot weather is important, because some fabrics stop sweat escaping easily from the body surface.

Insulation

In the winter, insulating clothing is an advantage as it stops us losing heat. Fat underneath the skin has this effect too. What's more, animals with hair, fur or feathers can fluff them up to get a deeper covering. This means that more warm air is trapped, so the body doesn't cool as much.

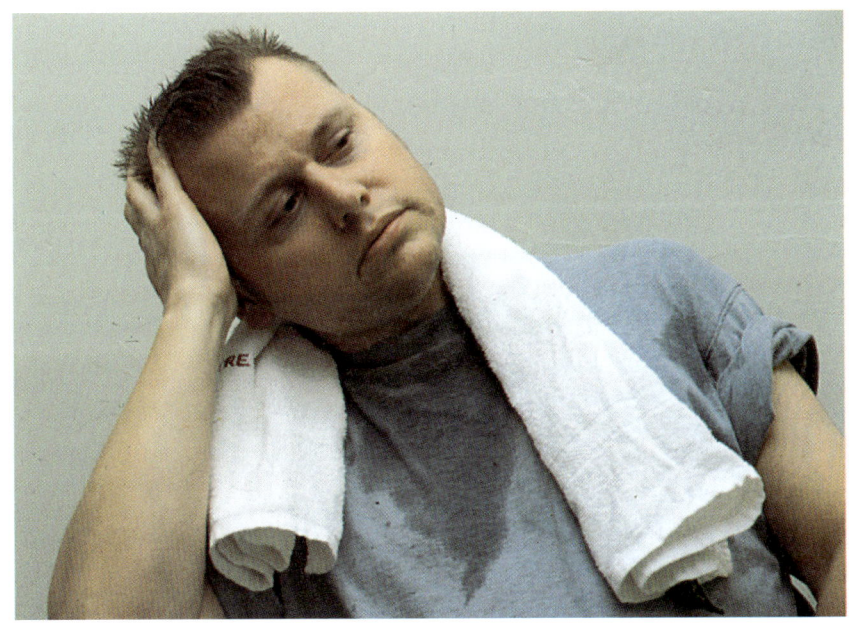

Picture 3 Hot weather makes people sweat more, which can be very uncomfortable.

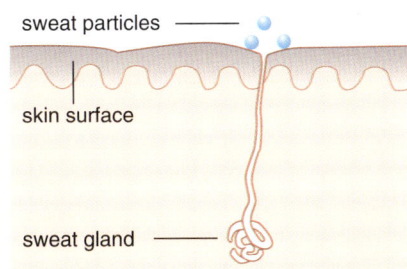

Picture 4 Sweat particles evaporate at the skin surface.

Questions

1. How does the brain detect that body temperature is changing?

2. **a)** If people have pale skin, their cheeks may get 'flushed' when they are hot. Why does this happen?

   b) Alcohol tends to widen blood vessels so that more blood flows near the skin surface. How would this affect skin temperature?

   c) Pete is a hill walker. After setting up his tent for the night he felt cold, and had a small drink of brandy. Brandy contains alcohol.

   i) Why did the brandy make Pete feel warmer at first?

   ii) Why might the alcohol cause cooling overall?

3. Which of the birds in Picture 5 shows
   a) a bird in winter
   b) a bird in summer?

   Give reasons for your choices.

4. Picture 6 shows an elephant. The numbers are average body temperature at that place in the elephant.

   Average temperature of surroundings = 19.15°C
   Average temperature deep inside the body = 36.4°C

   Picture 6

   a) What is the difference between the average temperature of the elephant and its surroundings?

   b) Is the elephant an endotherm or an ectotherm?

   c) Which parts of the elephant are coolest?

   d) Suggest reasons why these parts are coolest.

Picture 5

The body in balance

Activities

The kidneys and water balance

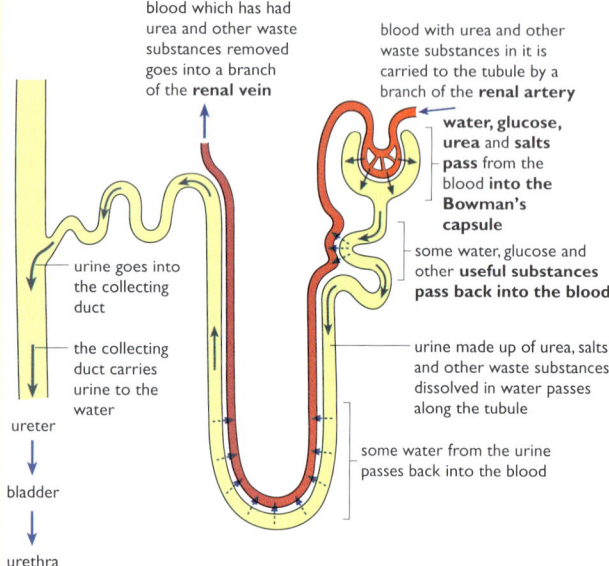

Picture 1 Each kidney contains about one and a half million nephrons. Each nephron is a tiny tube about 12–14 millimetres long.

Study Picture 1 carefully, reading all the labels and numbered notes. The kidney is made of millions of tiny tubes called nephrons, packed closely together. The start of each tube is in the outer area, which is called the cortex. At the end of the nephrons are collecting ducts, which empty close to the start of the ureter. Urine moves down the ureter to the bladder.

The key points about what a nephron does are:
- pressure pushes water and dissolved substances out of the blood into the tubule: this is **filtration**
- the first part of the tubule actively moves useful substances back into the blood: this is **absorption**
- the fine tuning of water balance happens in the second part of the tubule and the collecting ducts: this is **regulation**.

What you eat and drink will affect how the kidney balances water and salts. If you drink lots in a short time, the kidney makes a lot of dilute urine. On the other hand, less urine is made if you drink less, or eat lots of salty food, or lose more water by sweating.

1. **a)** Which substances are filtered out of the blood into the cup at the start of the nephron?

   b) Which of the substances filtered into the tubule, are later absorbed back into the blood? Suggest a reason why.

   c) Suggest a reason why blood cells are not filtered out of blood.

   d) In which part of the kidney are salts and water balanced to the correct level?

   e) What is the main substance that is excreted by the kidney?

What happens if the kidneys don't work properly?

Sometimes people get kidney failure, because of illness or because the kidneys get damaged. Pages 88–89 describe dialysis, which involves using a machine to do the job for the kidneys that don't work.

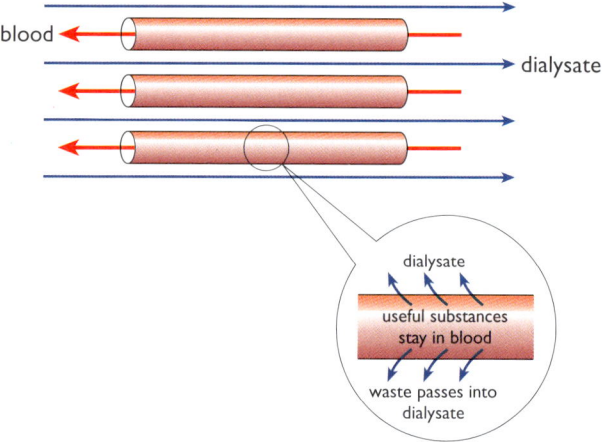

Picture 2

Since the human body can manage with one kidney rather than two, another option is to transplant a healthy kidney from someone else. This may be a person from within the family, or perhaps from someone who died in an accident. The person who gives the kidney is called the **donor**.

2. **a)** Suggest some reasons for kidney failure.

   b) What are the options for treating kidney failure? Pages 88–89 will help you answer this question. Think about the advantages and disadvantages for each option, from the patient's point of view.

Controlling body temperature

Read pages 86-87 before attempting this activity.

How much can animals control their body temperature? Mammals and birds control their body temperatures to within a few degrees Celsius. This is mostly achieved by controlling how much blood circulates near the skin surface, and by sweating.

Fish and reptiles have little control over their body temperatures, which vary according to their surroundings. They may change their body temperatures to some extent by behaving in certain ways, e.g. moving into the shade or into deeper water.

3   Here is some information about animals. Complete the table by filling in the column called 'Effect on body temperature'.

Table 1 Controlling body temperature in animals.

Animal	Feature	Effect on body temperature
whale	thick layer of fat under the skin	
dog	pants when it is hot	
crocodile	lies in the sun	
elephant	ears with large surface area	
goat	loses its winter fur in the spring	

4   **a)** Why does blood cool when it passes near to the surface of an animal's skin?

b) What difference can you see between the size of an Arctic fox's ears and a desert fox's ears?

c) Which of the foxes will experience more cooling effect through its ears?

d) Suggest a reason why Arctic foxes have smaller ears then desert foxes.

e) The climate in Europe is cooler than in Africa but warmer than in the Arctic.

Copy Picture 3c and draw some ears onto the fox. Show what size you think the ears will be in comparison to the ears of an Arctic fox and a desert fox.

Picture 3   a) An Arctic fox. b) A desert fox from Africa. c) A European red fox.

THE BODY IN CONTROL

Kidneys, dialysis and water balance

The kidneys filter the blood that passes through them. Water, salts and waste substances are filtered out from the blood and into the kidney tubes. These tubes control how much of each substance the body holds on to, and what goes into urine. If someone's kidneys stop working properly, a dialysis machine can do the job.

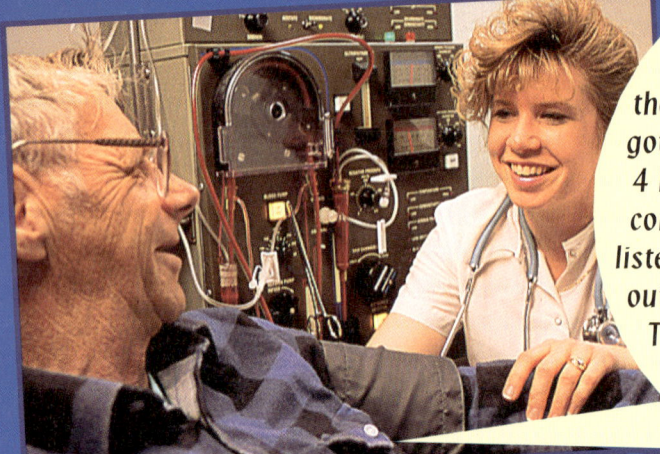

> "I'm waiting to get a new kidney, so for the moment I need dialysis. I've got used to it now. It takes about 4 hours each time and I have to come here 3 times a week. I can listen to music or read, but I miss out on some things because of it. The fact is that I have to keep on getting plugged in to stay alive."

How a dialysis machine works

A person's blood supply is linked up to the machine, which has membranes inside. Blood flows on one side of a membrane and a special dialysis solution flows on the other side.

Water, salts and waste pass from the blood through the membrane, balancing both sides. The dialysis solution carries away the wastes and blood passes back into the body.

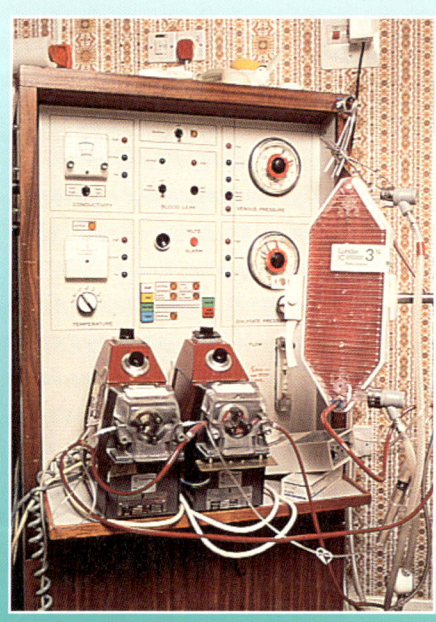

Going mobile with dialysis

CAPD is the short way of saying 'continuous ambulatory peritoneal dialysis'. This type of dialysis can go on all the time, while someone is on the move or fast asleep. With CAPD, the dialysis solution collects waste substances that filter through membranes inside the body. The solution is changed regularly via a plastic catheter

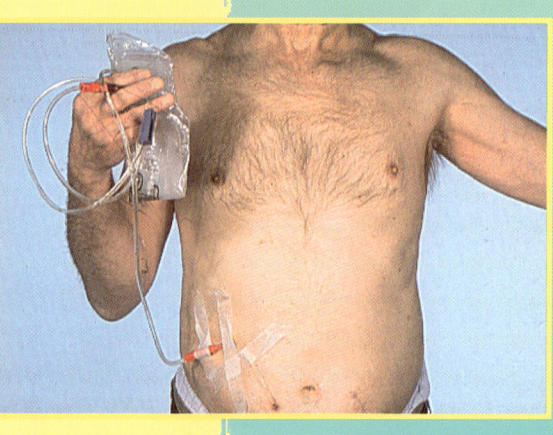

USEFULL ADDRESSES

British Kidney Patient's Association
Borden
Hants

Help The Aged
St James Walk
London
EC1R OBE

Controlling body temperature

Getting cold can mean more than just feeling uncomfortable. Keeping warm in very cold climates is a major challenge. A hazard of travelling in such conditions is frostbite. Frostbite happens when extremities, such as fingers and toes, go so cold that the blood stops flowing through them, and some cells die.

Because they can't always keep on the move, the elderly may get too cold quite easily. It's called **hypothermia**, which means 'low temperature'. Hypothermia is dangerous because people don't usually realise what's happening. If the body doesn't warm up again, the person dies.

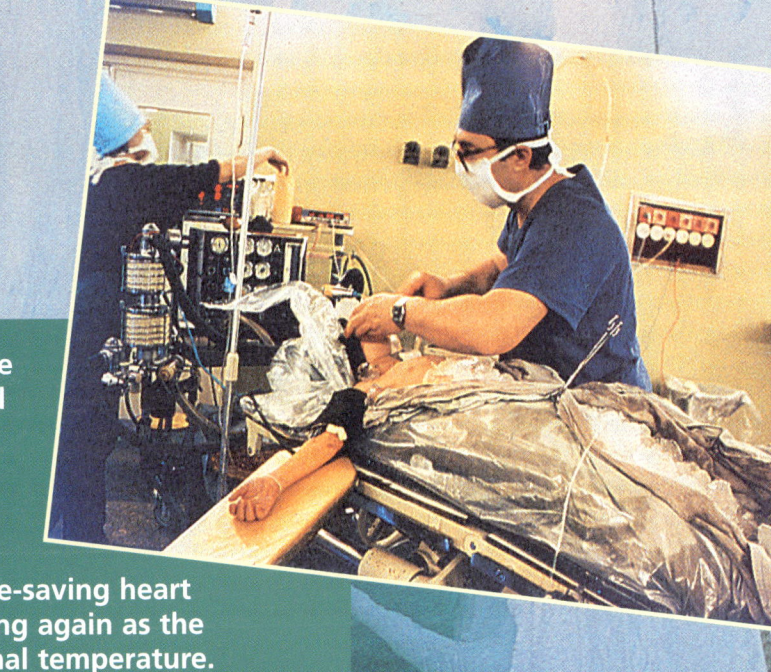

Chilling bodies is a cool technique for surgery. This person is packed in ice, so their body temperature drops. At this temperature the body slows down and the heart stops beating.

Surgeons can then carry out a life-saving heart operation. The heart starts beating again as the body slowly warms up to a normal temperature. The advantage of doing this is that no special equipment is needed to keep the person alive during surgery.

The gift of life

Carrying a donor card means someone has offered to give their organs to another person after they die. You can carry a donor card if you're under 18 years old, but your parent or guardian has to agree as well.

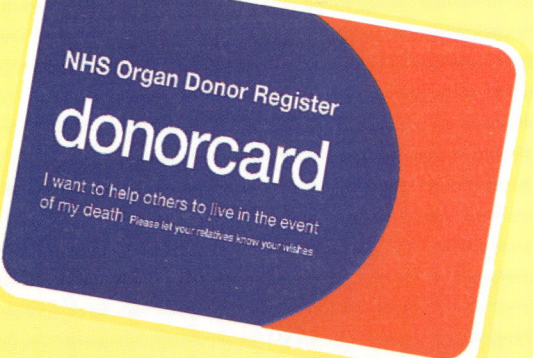

About 1900 kidneys are transplanted each year. 8% of those transplants are from living donors. More kidney transplants would be carried out if there were more kidneys available.

The body in balance

Summary

- Homeostasis means keeping the conditions in the body constant. Cells work best in constant conditions, e.g. at a steady temperature or pH.

- Osmoregulation is the control of water levels in cells of the body. The water taken into the body is balanced with the amount of water it loses.

- Thermoregulation is the control of body temperature. Only birds and mammals can keep body temperature fairly constant.

- Endotherms are animals that get most of their heating from within the body, e.g. by transferring energy from food. Endotherms can control their body temperature closely.

- Ectotherms are animals that get most of their heating from outside the body, e.g. from lying in the sun. Ectotherms cannot control their body temperature closely.

- When blood passes near the surface of the skin it cools. One way of controlling body temperature is to control how much blood goes near the surface of the skin.

- Sweating and panting cool the body.

Questions

1. A person quickly drank one litre of water on Thursday. Samples of urine were collected for approximately four hours after drinking. The room temperature was 20°C.
The procedure was repeated on Friday when the room temperature was 30°C.
The results are shown in the graph.

Explain the differences in the amount of urine collected on Thursday and Friday.

London

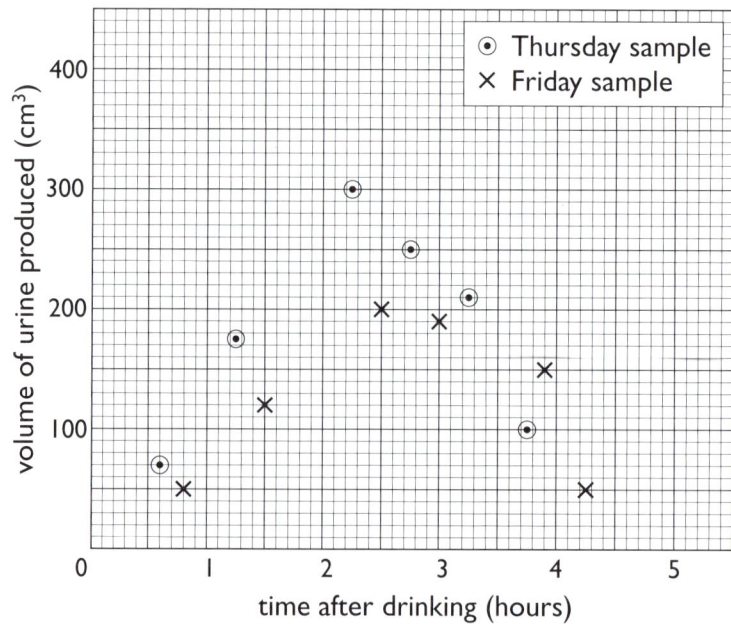

Questions continued

2 The graph shows the volume of urine released by a man over a period of several hours. The urine was collected every half hour and its volume measured. At point X the man drank a litre of cold water.

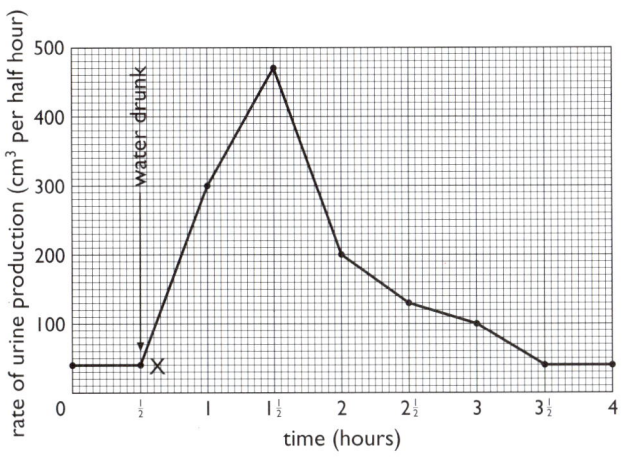

a) i) What was the rate of output of urine per half hour before the man drank the water?
   ii) Describe precisely the effect on urine production, over the $3\frac{1}{2}$ hours **after** drinking the water.
   iii) How long did it take his rate of urine production to return to normal after having the drink?
   iv) What was the largest amount of urine formed in half an hour?
b) This investigation was carried out in cold conditions during winter.
   i) If the investigation was repeated during a hot summer's day, give **two** differences which you would expect the graph to show compared with the above.
   ii) Briefly explain the reasons for these differences.   WJEC

3 The diagram shows a type of artificial kidney.

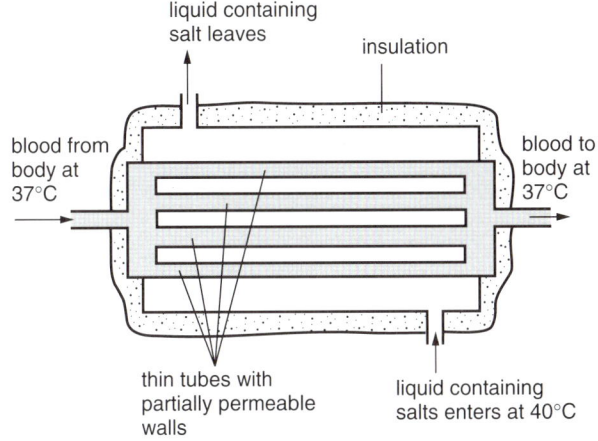

i) Name **one** chemical which will be removed in large amounts from the blood as it passes through the artificial kidney.
   ii) Why is it necessary to remove this chemical?
b) Suggest why many thin tubes are used in the artificial kidney.
c) How does the design and operation of the artificial kidney enable the blood to be returned to the body at the right temperature?
d) The table shows the cost of different types of treatment following kidney disease.

method	Cost in £s in first year	in each following year
A dialysis of the blood at the patient's home	13500	6000
B dialysis of the blood in hospital	12500	12500
C dialysis of other body fluids in a hospital	7000	6000
D successful transplant	15000	1200

i) Which method **A**, **B**, **C** or **D** would cost most in the first year of treatment?
   ii) Which method **A**, **B**, **C** or **D** would cost least over a total of three years?
   iii) State **two** reasons, other than cost, why not every person in need of a kidney transplant can have one.

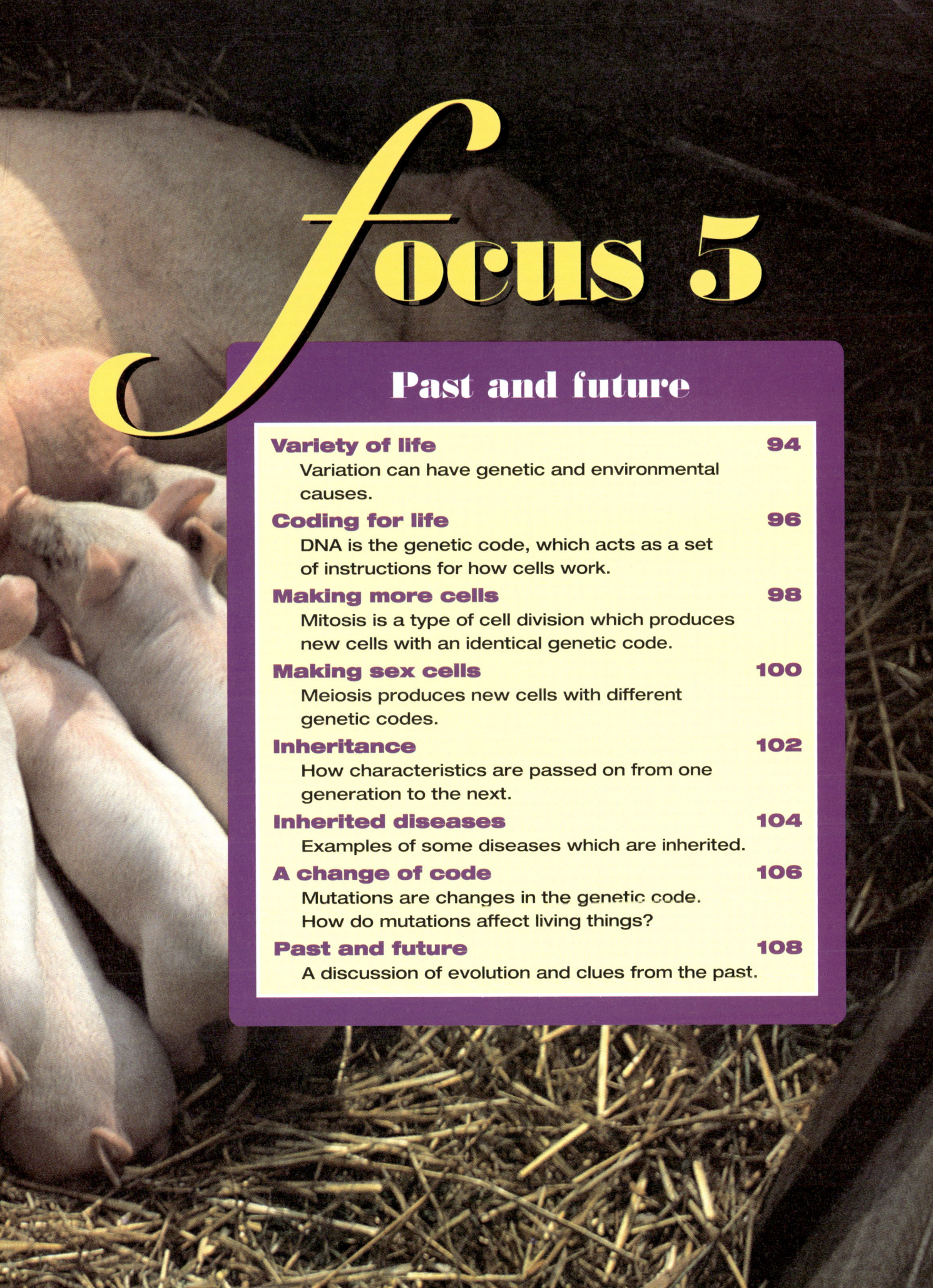

focus 5

Past and future

Variety of life — 94
Variation can have genetic and environmental causes.

Coding for life — 96
DNA is the genetic code, which acts as a set of instructions for how cells work.

Making more cells — 98
Mitosis is a type of cell division which produces new cells with an identical genetic code.

Making sex cells — 100
Meiosis produces new cells with different genetic codes.

Inheritance — 102
How characteristics are passed on from one generation to the next.

Inherited diseases — 104
Examples of some diseases which are inherited.

A change of code — 106
Mutations are changes in the genetic code. How do mutations affect living things?

Past and future — 108
A discussion of evolution and clues from the past.

Variety of life

It takes all sorts ...

A visit to an animal wildlife park reminds us of the huge **variation** between living things. Plants and animals come in all shapes and sizes, with very varied features. Picture 1 shows some of the features of a few animal groups. Within each group there are many species.

A species is a group of plants or animals that all have very similar features, and they can breed together. Even so, there may be some noticeable differences. Picture 2 shows that members of the human species are not exactly the same. The differences between two species, and between members of the same species, are called **variation**.

It's unusual for two individuals from different species to mate, but it does happen sometimes. For example, if a horse and a donkey mate, they may produce an offspring called a mule. This is unsuccessful in some ways, since a mule is not fertile and can't reproduce itself (Picture 3).

mammals have fur or hair, and can produce milk

fish live in water

birds have feathers and beaks, and lay eggs with a hard shell

amphibians have wet skins, and need water to breed

reptiles have dry, scaly skin, and also lay eggs

Picture 1 Some of the main animal groups.

Picture 2 Humans share lots of features in common, and all belong to the same species.

Genetic variation

Looking at snapshots can show just how similar people are within the same family. Brothers, sisters and cousins can look very alike. For example, they may share a **characteristic** such as hair colour. But what decides whether you look like your mother or your father? The information is carried by the genes, and different genes control different characteristics.

Genes are passed on from one generation to another in sperm cells and egg cells. Each sperm and egg cell has its own set of genes. An offspring gets half its genes from the mother and half from the father. So the characteristics of the offspring depend on which particular sperm fertilises an egg cell.

Identical twins are an exception to this rule. They are identical because they have the same genes. One egg is fertilised by one sperm, but the fertilised cell divides into two shortly after fertilisation, and each part develops into a baby.

Picture 3 A mule is the result of mating between two different species.

Past and future

Variation and the environment

Over the last few hundred years, people in the UK have got bigger. If you've been into old houses, you may have noticed how short the doorways are. Accurate records of peoples' height back this up too.

Picture 4 Can you see inherited likenesses?

What has caused this variation over that period of time? Probably environmental factors, that mean people are more healthy and grow more now. The quality and quantity of food that people eat is much greater, but medical science has made a huge difference too.

Picture 5 Light is an important environmental factor for plants.

Some environmental factors are more important than others, such as light in the case of plants. Supplying enough minerals to allow maximum growth is vital too, which is why people use fertilisers on crops and houseplants.

Questions

1 a) What is variation?
   b) Why is there variation between brothers and sisters?
   c) Non-identical twins develop when two sperm cells fertilise two egg cells at the same time. The twins develop in the same uterus.

   Why are non-identical twins not identical?

Picture 6 Identical twins.

2 a) What differences can you see between the twins in Picture 6?
   b) Do identical twins have the same or different genes?
   c) Suggest reasons for the variation between these twins.

3 Sort out these examples of variation into those that are caused by differences in the environment, and those that are caused by differences in the genes, or a combination of both. Examples:

   a) Lizzie feeds her hamster more than Fozia feeds her hamster. The hamsters are different sizes.

   b) A woman collects seeds from one poppy head. When she grows the seeds, they develop into plants which flower later. The plants all produce flowers that vary in colour from each other and the parent plants.

   c) A hamster has six young, which all have different coloured coats.

   d) All the plants in one tray are placed on a window sill. Another tray of the same type of plants is placed in the garden shed. In one tray the plants grow a lot taller.

Coding for life

The nucleus

The nucleus of a cell was first described in the last half of the 17th century by Antony van Leeuwenhoeck, who used a simple lens to examine cells. Since then, the contents of cells have been studied in great detail. Improved light microscopes and the development of electron microscopes have helped in this study.

The **nucleus** is made of DNA (deoxyribose nucleic acid) and contained within an envelope of membrane. The membrane allows some materials to move in and out of the nucleus. The functions of the nucleus are:
- to control the chemical reactions which happen in cells (it does this by providing instructions for making enzymes, which act as catalysts – see pages 34–35)
- to divide at the start of cell division (this means that each new cell has a nucleus and characteristics are inherited).

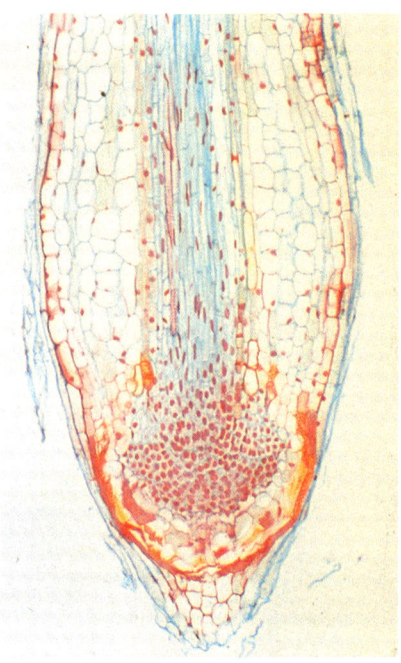

Picture 1 Nuclei can be seen clearly in these root tip cells, as pink coloured circles. A nucleus is roughly spherical, and about 10–20 thousandths of a millimetre in diameter. The plural of nucleus is nuclei.

DNA – the genetic material

Picture 3 shows the structure of DNA which is a large molecule. A simple way of describing the molecule, is that it's rather like a twisted ladder. The bases form the 'rungs' of the ladder.

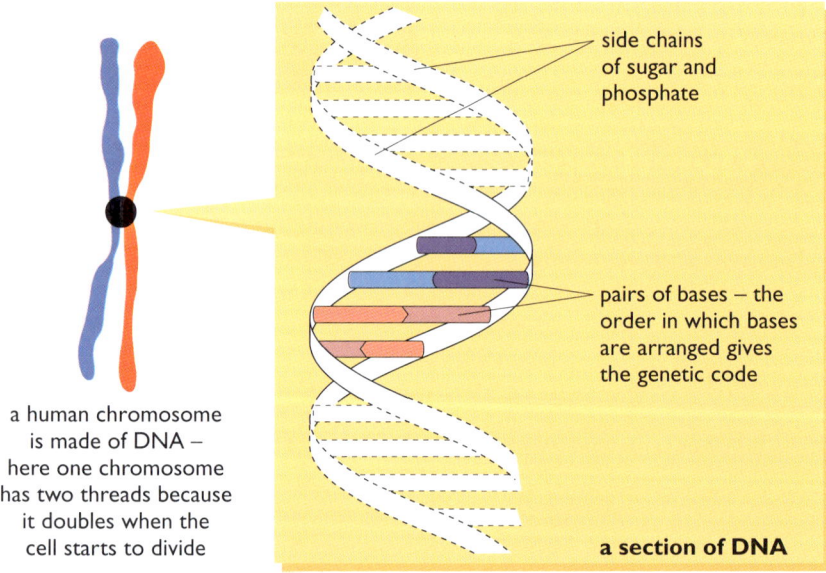

Picture 3 DNA is really a genetic code.

Some of the time DNA threads are loosely arranged in the nucleus. When the cells are about to divide the DNA packs up tightly, forming **chromosomes**. In most human cells there are 23 pairs. A **gene** is a short length of DNA making up part of a chromosome. There are thousands of genes on a chromosome.

A gene acts as a code for a particular characteristic, say brown eye colour in humans. But there are also some sections of DNA that don't seem to code for any characteristic.

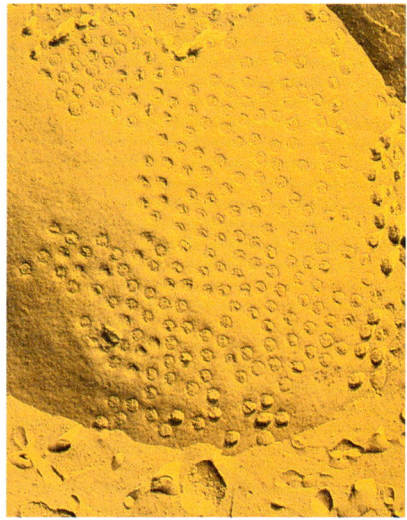

Picture 2 A close-up view of the surface of the nucleus shows that there are pores in the membrane. This picture was taken using an electron microscope.

Past and future

One pair of chromosomes is to do with gender – whether someone is male or female. A female has two X chromosomes, and a male has one X and one Y chromosome. You can see these chromosomes marked in Picture 4.

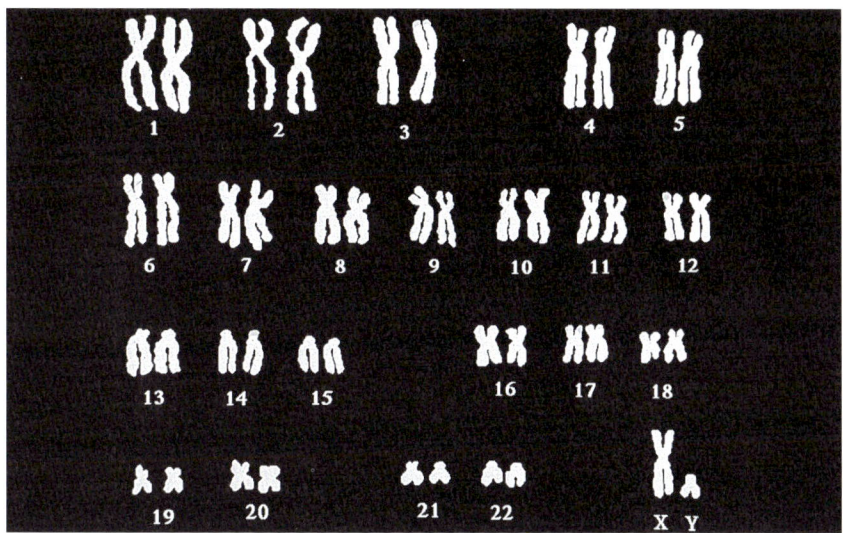

Picture 4 The key to inheritance is in the genes which make up the chromosomes.

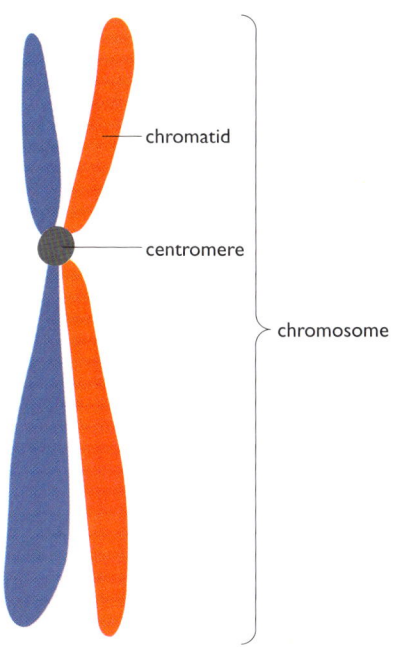

Picture 5 The structure of a chromosome.

Passing on the code

The interesting thing about DNA is that it can form another double strand exactly like itself. This process is called **replication**. The nucleus replicates when cells divide during growth. The type of cell division involved in growth is mitosis (see pages 98–99). Mitosis is happening at the root tip in Picture 1, which is why the nuclei are easy to see. As nuclei divide and new cells form, the root tip grows.

A special sort of cell division is meiosis. Meiosis happens when sex cells form, such as eggs and sperms in animals, and ovules and pollen in plants. There is more about meiosis on pages 100–101.

Questions

1 How did people discover that cells contain nuclei?

2 Why are enzymes important in cell reactions? You may need to check pages 34–35 to answer this.

3 a) What is a gene?

   b) How are genes passed from one generation to another?

4 a) What features of the nucleus can you see in Picture 2?

   b) Why is this feature important to the way the nucleus works?

5 a) What difference can you see between an X and a Y chromosome in Picture 4?

   b) What is replication?

   c) Why is replication important in cell division?

Making more cells

Making new cells by mitosis

Mitosis happens when living things are growing, for example when skin cells are replaced. Mitosis happens at the tips of stems and roots, which are growing points in plants. After mitosis, the contents of new cells increase until they reach adult size. So growth is a combination of cells dividing and cells expanding.

When a nucleus divides during **mitosis**, the two new cells that form have exactly the *same* genetic code as the original cell. These new cells develop identical characteristics to each other and to the parent cell. Picture 1 shows the stages in mitosis.

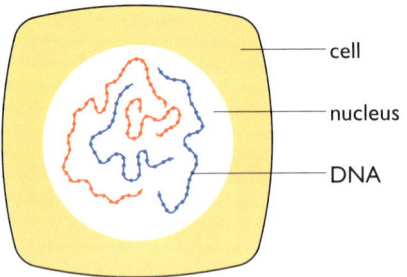

1 DNA is loosely arranged in the nucleus

2 DNA packs up tightly into chromosomes, and replicates so each one is now double

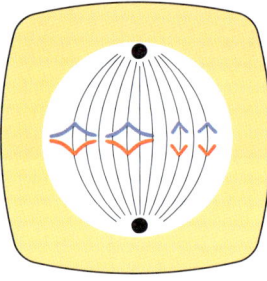

3 the double chromosomes line up at the centre of the cell, and move apart along the spindle giving two sets of chromosomes

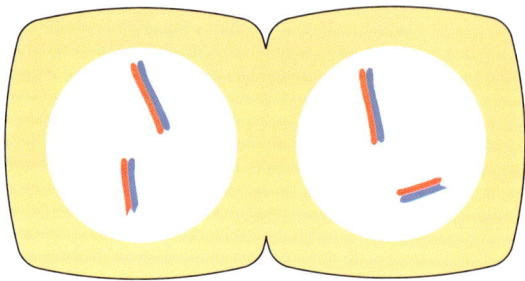

4 the cell divides to form two new cells: mitosis continues DNA replication

Picture 1 Mitosis passes on exactly the same genetic code.

Making new offspring asexually

Here are some key points about asexual reproduction (meaning 'without sex'):

- there is only one parent
- cells divide by mitosis
- all cells have the same genetic code
- all the new individuals have the same characteristics as each other and as the parent.

In **asexual reproduction**, part of a parent develops to form a new individual. Picture 2 shows a one-celled *Amoeba* dividing to give two new *Amoeba* cells. The new cells have exactly the same genetic code as the original one, because the nuclei have divided by mitosis. Mitosis is the cell division happening in Picture 3 too.

Several examples of asexual reproduction are shown in Picture 3. The new plants that form from the original one are called **clones**, because their genetic code is identical.

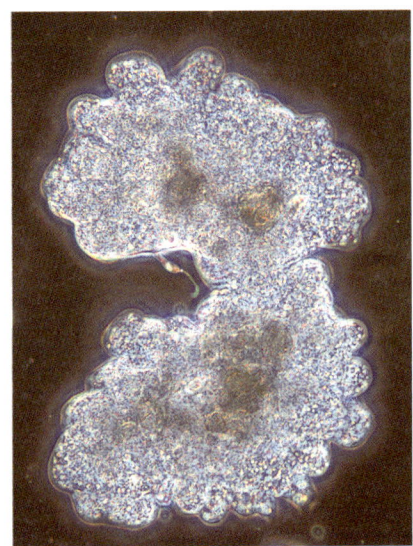

Picture 2 Mitosis is involved in asexual reproduction.

Past and future

Picture 3 a) A spider plant makes many new copies of itself from buds at the end of long stems called runners. Strawberry plants do this too.

b) A potato forms at the end of a stem. It has a starchy food store inside, and several buds. Each bud can grow into a new potato plant.

c) 'Cuttings' are the tips of shoots. Gardeners cut off a shoot just below a leaf stalk. The cutting develops new roots when it is planted, and grows into a whole new plant.

Cloning – taking advantage of good characteristics

Plant growers can work for years to breed a good variety of plant, e.g. a cauliflower. Seeds can be collected from that cauliflower plant. However, the plants that grow from those seeds won't all have the same characteristics. How can the grower be sure to get good cauliflowers the following season? The answer is to clone the first cauliflower, and get many more identical ones. Cloning has been used to grow new types of many crop plants, all around the world, e.g. oil palms in Malaysia. Picture 4 shows how cloning can be done.

d) A bulb is made of fleshy leaves on a very short stem at the base. Buds develop from the base into new bulbs. These can be taken off and grown into new plants.

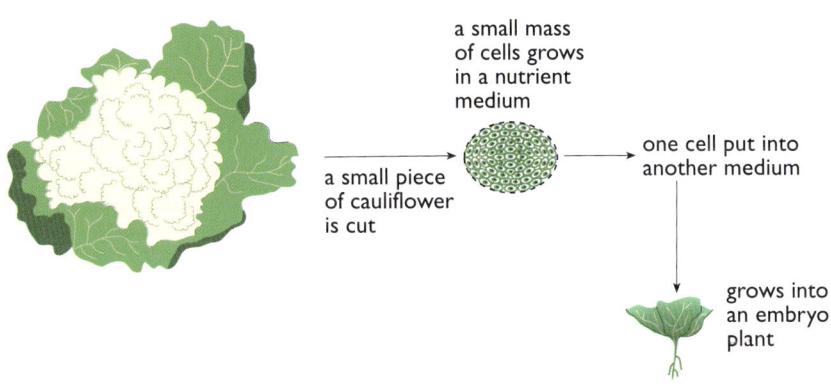

Picture 4 Cloning guarantees the successful characteristics.

Questions

1 Why do the offspring produced by mitosis have

   a) the same amount of genetic material as the original?

   b) the same genetic code as the original?

2 **a)** What are the advantages of cloning plants?

   b) Suggest any problems that growing cloned plants might cause.

   c) Do you think that growers will stop making new seeds now that cloning can be used for many crops?

3 Simple cloning experiments have been done with frog's cells.

   a) Do you think it is a good idea to clone animals?

   b) In what situation might cloning animals not be appropriate?

Making sex cells

Making new cells by meiosis

Meiosis is a special type of cell division. It only happens when cells that are involved in sexual reproduction are made. These cells are called sex cells. Table 1 gives the names of sex cells and sex organs for plants and animals. Pages 64–65 describe the human reproductive system in more detail.

Table 1 Sex cells and sex organs.

	Plants	Animals
male	pollen made in the anther	sperm made in the testis
female	ovule made in the ovary	ovum (or egg) made in the ovary

Picture 1 The female sex cells (called ovules) in this pea plant have been fertilised by pollen. They are developing into seeds inside the pod. The pea seeds won't grow into identical plants because they all contain a different genetic code.

The details of meiosis are quite complicated, but the main points are:

> Meiosis makes a difference to the combination of chromosomes.

This means that each new sex cell has different genes, and so any offspring resulting from fertilisation will have different characteristics.

> Sex cells are unusual because they have only half the number of chromosomes that other cells do.

For example, in humans, sperms and egg cells have 23 single chromosomes rather than 23 pairs. Sexual reproduction involves the nucleus from a female sex cell joining with the nucleus of a male sex cell, during fertilisation.

Sexual reproduction

Here are some key points about sexual reproduction:
- two parents are involved
- sex cells have half the number of chromosomes of other cells in the body, as well as a new genetic code
- sex cells combine during fertilisation to form a new offspring
- the genetic material in the offspring comes partly from each parent.

During fertilisation, the nucleus of a sperm cell enters the egg and fuses with the nucleus of the egg. Each sex cell gives 23 chromosomes to the new offspring. The fertilised egg contains 23 *pairs* of chromosomes.

Picture 2 Pollen grains are male sex cells in plants. Pollen may have to make a long journey from one flower to another. This journey will probably be helped by the wind or animals such as bees. You can see that the bee in this picture has pollen stuck to its body and so might carry it to another flower.

Past and future

Focus 5

Sperms pair up in the race to fertilise

 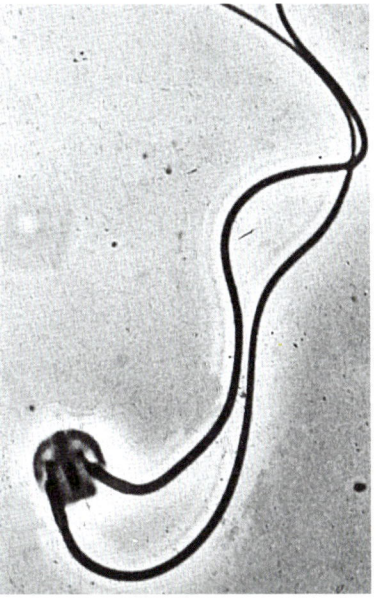

Picture 5 Paired opossum sperms cope well with swimming in thick mucus.

Scientists studying pouched animals such as the opossum, have noticed that 80% of their sperm pair together before they leave the male's body. As they watched the sperm swimming they could see the tails of the sperm cells moving together, rather like the leg kicks of a frog. Their experiments showed that pairs of sperm cells can swim better than single ones through thick liquids. Since the mucus inside the female's reproductive tract is very thick, this gives the sperm cells more chance of fertilising an egg. Only one sperm cell nucleus actually joins with the opossum egg.

Picture 3 These two frogs are mating. The female is laying eggs into the water and the male is laying sperm cells on top. Soon after, jelly swells up around the eggs, protecting them. Fertilised eggs develop into tadpoles.

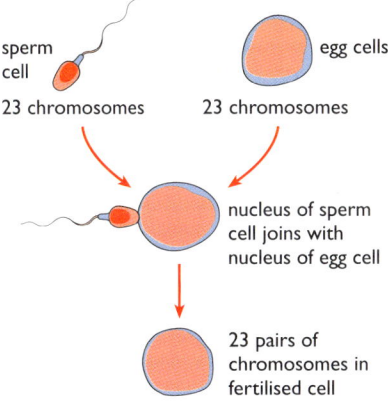

Picture 4 Fertilisation involves two sex cells each with their own combination of chromosomes.

Questions

1. a) Which of the following events A–D involves meiosis?
   - A cells divide in a root as it grows longer
   - B ovules form inside a daisy flower
   - C a leaf bud opens and leaves develop from it
   - D sperms form inside the testis.

2. Why is there variation between the puppies in Picture 6?

3. What is fertilisation?

4. a) How many chromosomes are in a human egg cell?
   b) How many chromosomes are in a human liver cell?
   c) Why is it important that meiosis halves the number of chromosomes?

Picture 6 Puppies in a litter.

Inheritance

The basis of inheritance

It's easy to see in Picture 1 that Gregory looks like his mum, and Chloe is like her dad. In fact, both children inherited 50% of their genetic material from one parent and 50% from the other. So why do brother and sister look so different? It all depends on the genes.

A **gene** is a section of DNA that codes for a characteristic. We know that chromosomes come in pairs, one set from each parent. It follows that for each characteristic, there is at least one pair of genes. A pair of genes that code for a particular characteristic are called **alleles**.

Since a child gains one allele from the mother and one from the father, the alleles may not be the same. Picture 2 shows an example of this.

Picture 1 Both these children have inherited characteristics from their parents.

Meiosis happens when sperms and egg cells are produced, so each has one allele for a particular characteristic. When a sperm cell fertilises an egg cell, the combination of alleles decides what the person actually looks like. In Picture 2, Gregory inherited two alleles for red hair, and so he looks like his mum.

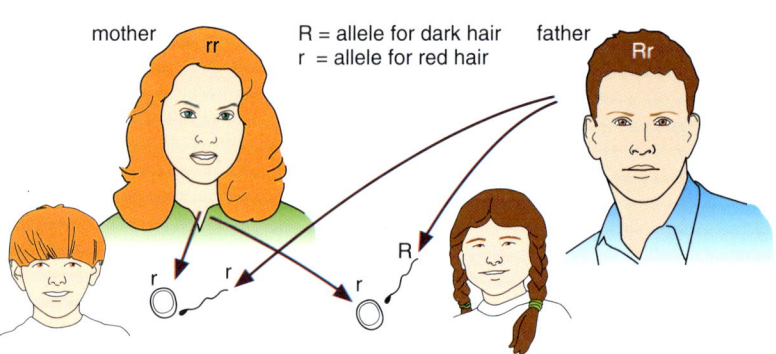

Picture 2 The inheritance of alleles for red hair colour.

Dominant and recessive

In Picture 1, you may have noticed that Chloe had brown hair like her dad, even though she had one allele for red hair colour (Picture 2). Why didn't she have half red hair? The reason is that the allele for brown hair colour is dominant, and it hides the allele for red hair colour.

In other words, it's the **dominant** allele that shows in the appearance of the person. The allele that is hidden (such as red hair colour) is called **recessive**.

Picture 3 shows a simple way of setting out what chances there are of inheriting a characteristic. It's called a checkerboard. Along each side you write the alleles for the parent. Notice that the dominant allele has a capital letter and the recessive allele has a small one. To fill in the squares, read along each row and put in the alleles which an offspring might inherit. This example involves blue and brown eye colour.

B ('big B') stands for the allele for brown eye colour and b ('little B') stands for the allele for blue eye colour. Brown eye colour, B, is dominant to blue eye colour, b. A brown-eyed person can have the alleles BB, or the alleles Bb. This doesn't make any difference to their eye colour, but it does make a difference to the alleles they can pass on. To have blue eyes, a person must have two alleles for blue eyes, bb.

Past and future

Which gender – male or female?

The checkerboard in Picture 4 shows the inheritance of **gender**. In this case it's a whole chromosome that is responsible for inheritance of a characteristic, not just one allele.

Since a female has two X chromosomes, all egg cells that form must contain an X chromosome. On the other hand, males produce 50% sperm cells with an X chromosome and 50% sperm cells with a Y chromosome. Fertilisation is completely random since all sperm cells have an equal chance of fertilising the egg. If a sperm cell with an X chromosome fertilises the egg, a girl is conceived. If a sperm with a Y chromosome fertilises the egg, a boy is conceived.

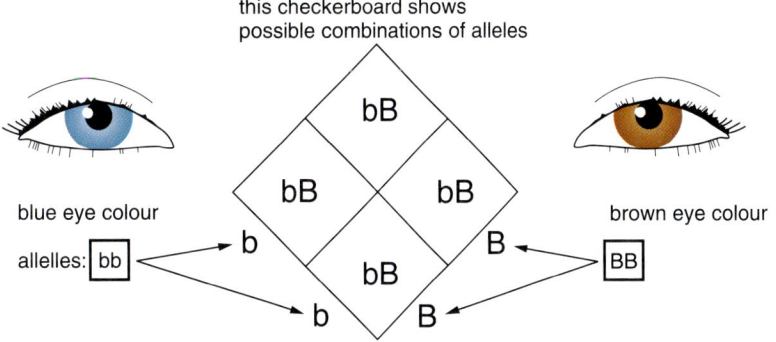

Picture 3 Eye colour inheritance.

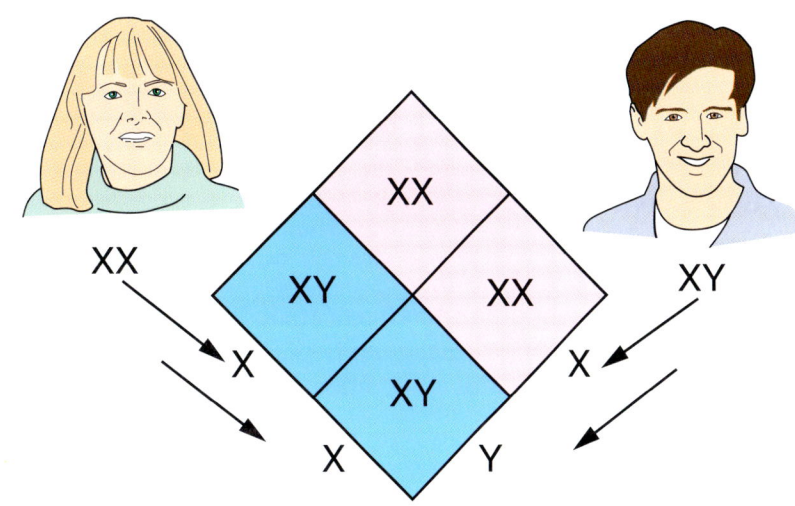

Picture 4 An equal chance for both genders.

Questions

1 Imagine that the parents in Picture 2 have their first child.

   a) What is the percentage chance of the child having dark hair?

   b) What combinations of alleles could a dark-haired child have?

   c) What two alleles would a red-haired child have?

Sue   Huw   Jacinta

Picture 5 Freckles?

2 Picture 5 shows three children. The allele for freckles is F and the allele for no freckles is f. Freckles is a dominant characteristic.

   a) What is meant by the terms dominant and recessive characteristics?

   b) Which of the children has the alleles ff?

   c) Suggest which combinations of alleles the other children might have.

3 Copy a checkerboard. Imagine that a couple decide to have children. Both the parents have the alleles Bb for eye colour.

   a) What colour eyes do the parents have?

   b) Complete the checkerboard. What percentage of their children are likely to have blue eyes?

4 A town has a population of 800 000 people. Roughly how many people are likely to be male? Give a reason for your answer.

Inherited diseases

focus 5

Common illnesses such as chicken pox or a cold are caused by microbes such as bacteria, or by viruses. But not all diseases are caused by microbes. Some diseases are caused by the genes that a person inherits, or even by the lack of a gene. In some cases, scientists have been able to find out which gene causes a disease.

The case studies in this section consider the causes and effects of some inherited diseases.

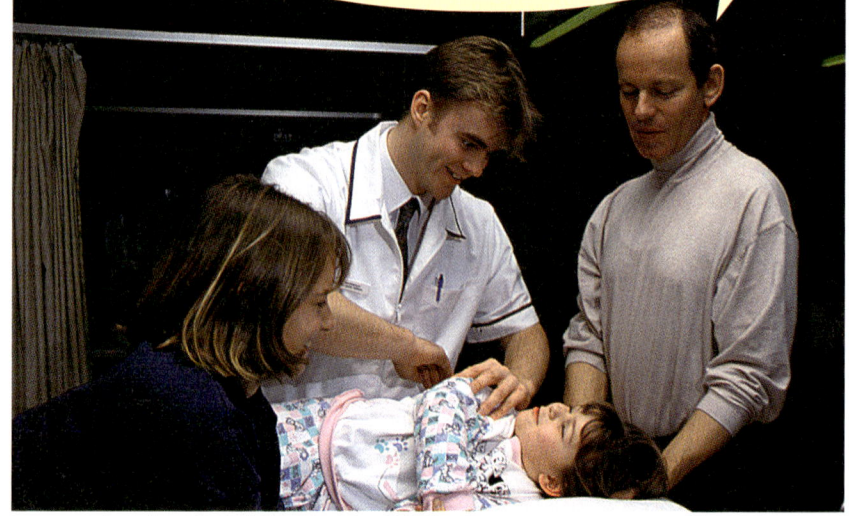

Now we know that we are carriers, and what risk there is of us having a child with cystic fibrosis. It's a difficult decision to make, but we have decided not to have more children in case they develop it too. Since 1989, there's been a test for the cystic fibrosis gene. Knowing about the risks gives people a chance to talk over what the options are.

Case study 1: Cystic fibrosis

Picture 1 Every day Rosalind has physiotherapy, to help move mucus out of her lungs. Her treatment includes taking medicines too.

In Europe, about one person in every 20 carries one allele for cystic fibrosis. They suffer no effects at all, because the gene is recessive. As long as one normal gene is present, they may never know that they are carriers of cystic fibrosis.

It was a total surprise to Elly and Jim when their daughter developed cystic fibrosis. As a family, they have all learned to cope with the daily help that Rosalind needs. Because the mucus in the lungs is much thicker than normal, the lungs get blocked up easily. This makes breathing difficult, and makes it more likely that Rosalind will get chest infections. Thick mucus in the gut can lead to digestive problems too.

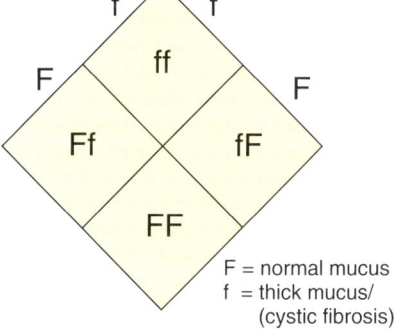

F = normal mucus
f = thick mucus/ (cystic fibrosis)

Picture 2 What are the chances of two people with the cystic fibrosis gene having a child with the condition?

Case study 2: Sickle cell anaemia

Sickle cell haemoglobin does not carry as much oxygen as normal haemoglobin. Also, you can see that the red blood cells are a curved (sickle) shape. They easily block up blood vessels, stopping blood supply and causing damage to organs.

The sickle cell allele is neither dominant nor recessive. A person who inherits two alleles for sickle cell generally dies from the condition, because all their haemoglobin is abnormal. On the other hand, a person with one allele has only 30–40% abnormal haemoglobin. They have a mild form of the condition called sickle cell trait.

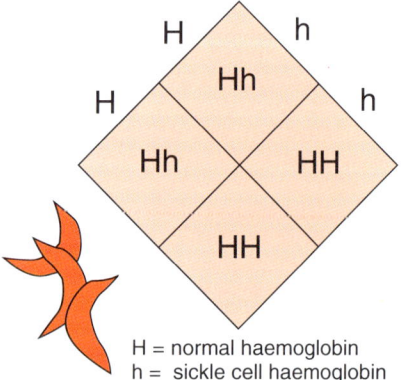

H = normal haemoglobin
h = sickle cell haemoglobin

Picture 3 The unusual shape of some of these red blood cells is due to mutation in one gene, causing abnormal haemoglobin. The checkerboard shows the risk of two people with sickle cell trait having a child with sickle cell anaemia.

Case study 3: Haemophilia

A haemophiliac lacks one clotting factor and so may bleed to death from cuts. Even exercise can cause bleeding inside the

Past and future

body, because of breaks in small blood vessels around the joints. Pages 40–41 explain the process of clotting.

Edie's brother is a haemophiliac. She remembers what a difficult time her childhood was. 'At that time very little could be done. I remember that John had endless blood transfusions and spent a lot of time in hospital. Later on, John was given clotting factor once it became available.'

Edie has a son, David, who also has haemophilia. He has been using clotting factor since he was three. 'We've learned how to use clotting factor according to the activities that David has coming up. Even so, he sometimes gets a bleed, which is a concern. But, overall, coping is easy in comparison to how it was for my brother.'

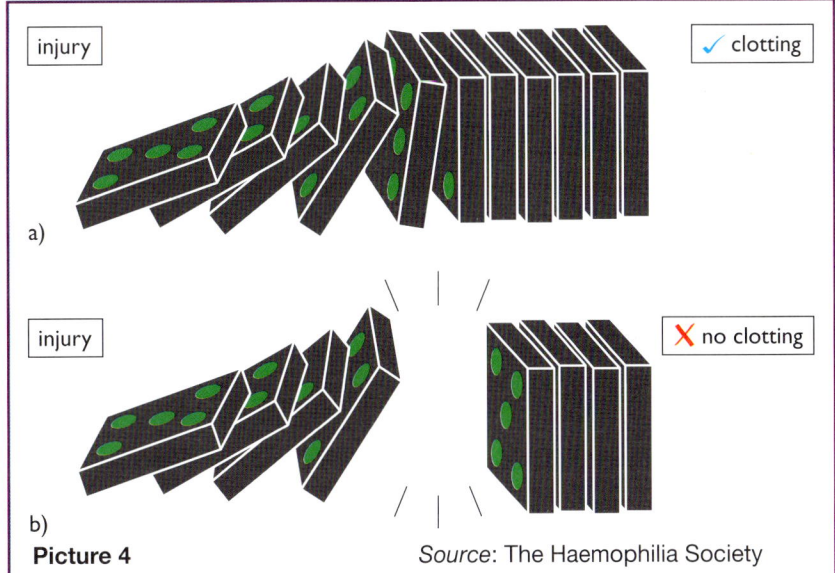

Picture 4

Source: The Haemophilia Society

A person with haemophilia does not bleed more, or bleed faster, than normal – they simply bleed longer. Normally, clotting factors act like a row of dominoes, reacting to each other in turn, creating a chain reaction (Picture a). If a factor does not work, this chain reaction cannot proceed (Picture b).

People with haemophilia have an allele missing on each X chromosome. This allele instructs cells to make a clotting factor. Since the allele for haemophilia (h) is on an X chromosome, it's called **sex-linked** (page 103 explains about the inheritance of gender). The allele (H) for making the clotting factor is dominant.

The checkerboard in Picture 4 shows the chances of a couple having children with haemo-philia. The two possibilities if they have girls, are that one is normal (HXHX) and the other is a healthy carrier (HXhX). But one of the two possibilities for sons is haemophiliac (hXY). In other words the chances are that 50% of any sons they have will be haemophiliac.

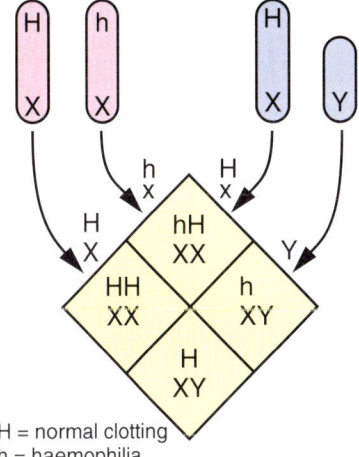

Picture 5 Sex chromosomes and the allele for making a clotting factor.

H = normal clotting
h = haemophilia

Questions

1 Why is the test for cystic fibrosis useful for people with a history of the disease in their family?

2 Suggest reasons why the allele for sickle cell remains in a population.

3 **a)** Haemophilia is a recessive characteristic, and is linked to the X chromosome. Why does this make it more likely for a male to suffer from haemophilia?

b) Copy a checkerboard from Picture 4. Work out the chances of a normal female (HXHX) and a haemophiliac male (hXY) of having a normal child.

A change of code

Focus 5

Code changes

DNA is the code that instructs all of a cell's activities. The code passes into new cells during cell division, when DNA replicates. A new individual inherits the code through sperm and egg cells.

Generally, DNA is a very stable molecule. But sometimes there is a sudden change in the code, for no obvious reason. A change in the DNA code is called a **mutation**. Certain chemicals and ionising radiation can damage DNA, causing mutations (Picture 1).

One effect is that the damaged DNA makes the cells divide over and over again, forming a tumour. This is what happens when people have cancer.

Another effect is that the body reacts as if the cells with a new genetic code are not part of it. It's similar to how the body responds to bacteria. This means that the body's immune system might kill body cells that have changed DNA.

Neither of these effects would be inherited. However, if the DNA of cells which make sperms or egg cells is damaged, this is inherited by offspring.

A change in a gene

Picture 3 shows light and dark forms of peppered moths. A change in a gene caused a moth to produce offspring of a darker colour. In some places, the dark colour makes the moths more difficult to see, e.g. against dark buildings or bark.

As they don't show up against the background, dark moths are less likely to be eaten by birds, and more likely to survive and reproduce. They pass on the dark colour to their offspring, and so the population of dark moths increases.

This is an example of **natural selection**. A characteristic gives a plant or animal an advantage in its environment. In some places, being a lighter colour might be an advantage and then natural selection would cause an increase in the lighter moths. Page 109 gives more information on natural selection.

Picture 1 In 1986 a nuclear reactor in Chernobyl exploded, releasing ionising radiation. This has led to an increase in childhood cancer in the region.
Source: New Scientist 1.4.95.

Table 1 Thyroid cancer in children around Chernobyl (average per million children under 15 years).

Place	1981–5	1986–90	1991–4
Gomel	0.5	10.5	96.4
North Ukraine	0.1	2.0	11.5
Bryansk/Kaluga	0	1.2	10.0

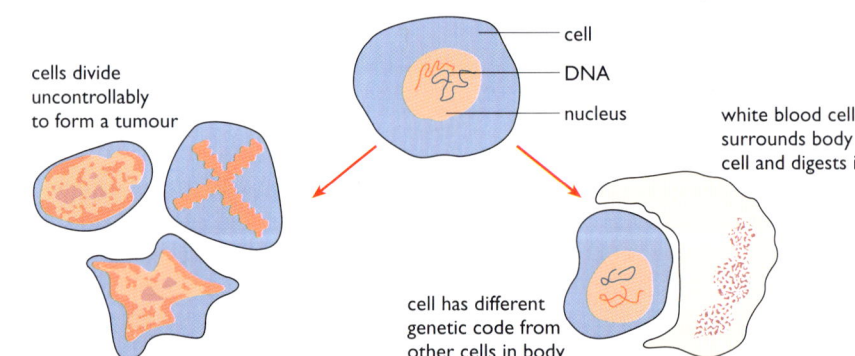

Picture 2 Some effects of changed DNA in body cells.

Picture 3 A mutation caused this new dark colour of peppered moth.

Past and future

A change in a chromosome

DNA changes might also involve whole chromosomes, which is the case in Down's syndrome. A child with Down's syndrome has moderate or severe learning difficulties, but often a very affectionate personality.

Picture 4 These chromosomes are from Paul, a child with Down's syndrome. What difference can you see from a normal set? Compare with Picture 4 on page 97, if you're not sure.

Questions

1 Pictures 5A–D show different animal cells. If the DNA in these cells altered, which cells might pass on the change to the next generation?

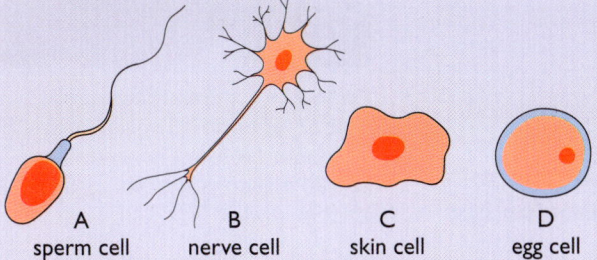

A sperm cell   B nerve cell   C skin cell   D egg cell

Picture 5

2 Picture 6 shows an X chromosome from someone with a mutation called 'Fragile X'.

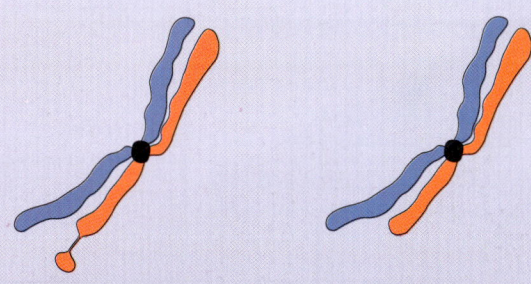

fragile X chromosome   normal chromosome

Picture 6 An X chromosome from a person with Fragile X.

a) What difference can you see between this X chromosome and a normal one?

b) Is this condition likely to be passed on from one generation to another? Give a reason for your answer.

3 The beak shape of different species of finch varies, as shown in Picture 7.

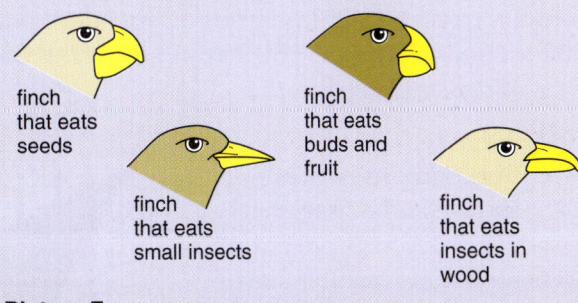

finch that eats seeds   finch that eats buds and fruit   finch that eats small insects   finch that eats insects in wood

Picture 7

a) How does beak shape relate to a finch's diet?

b) If the fruit crop failed one year due to disease, how might natural selection affect which finches survive?

c) One year there is a bumper crop of grass seeds. How might natural selection affect the finch population?

Past and future

Fossils – a key to the past?

Fossils are fascinating clues to the past. They can tell us tiny fragments of what happened many millions of years before humans existed on Earth. Picture 1 shows three different types of fossil.

Some fossils are preserved remains, like the insect in Picture 1a. Amber, peat and ice can preserve animals and plants after they die. In fact the amber preserved these insects so well, that bacterial spores were still inside their stomachs. Some spores were taken out and given nutrients. After a time delay of many millions of years, they started to grow!

Surface structures like feathers, scales, leaves and footprints can make an impression in layers of rock as they form. Picture 1b shows a dinosaur footprint found in Arizona.

As materials turn to rock, a space can form where the remains of a dead plant or animal once lay. Sometimes the space fills with other materials, giving a stony replica. The trilobite in Picture 1c is a replica of the original, which lived millions of years ago.

You can tell roughly how old a fossil is by looking at the layer of rock it is found in. Older rock layers are found deeper, so younger fossils tend to be in the top layers of rock. But this doesn't give exact ages, and anyway layers of rock move and change over millions of years. Another technique measures traces of radioactive elements in rocks (see *Physical Processes* pages 132-133).

Picture 1 a) Bees preserved in amber for up to 40 million years. b) Dinosaur footprint in sandstone, up to 190 million years old. c) Trilobite cast in stone.

Life on Earth

Conditions on Earth have been changing ever since it formed. It's these changes that have affected what lifeforms exist. For example, oxygen built up in our atmosphere around 2500 to 1500 million years ago. This happened at the time that the first living things appeared in the oceans.

Since then millions of years have passed, land masses have moved, and oceans have risen and fallen. Temperatures have changed dramatically too. If living things can't adapt to changes in the environment, they die out and become **extinct**.

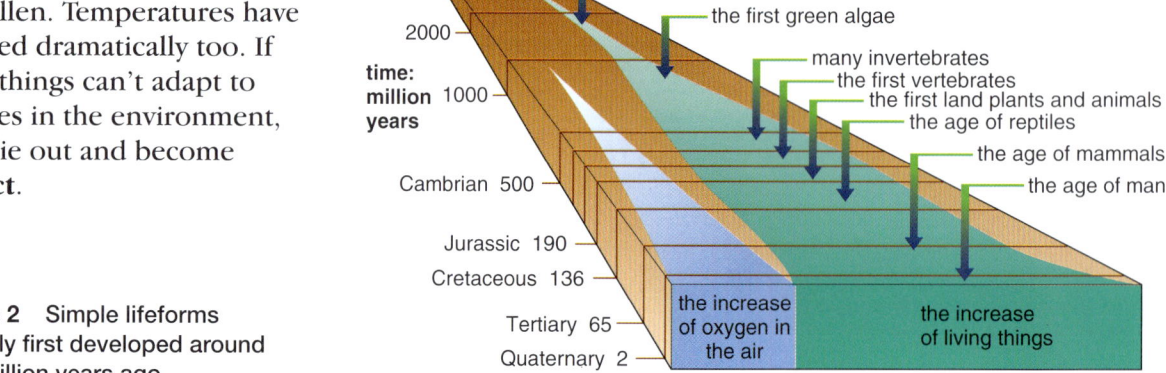

Picture 2 Simple lifeforms probably first developed around 2500 million years ago.

Past and future

Evolution – fact or fiction?

In the 1830s, the naturalist Charles Darwin sailed around the world, studying many plants and animals. At that time, many people believed that plants and animals had been created in their present form by God. But Darwin became convinced that the wide variety of living things was due to evolution. **The theory of evolution** is that:

- in the wild, there is a **struggle for existence**, since living things compete for food, and may face predators
- **variation** happens within a species
- some characteristics make an individual better adapted for surviving in the environment – called **'survival of the fittest'** (not the strongest or fastest, but the best *adapted* to that environment)
- the living things that survive pass on their characteristics when they reproduce. This is called **'natural selection'**
- over many generations, the characteristics of a species changes as it **evolves** into other species.

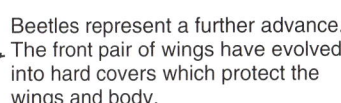

Picture 3 Dead as a dodo? The dodo lived on the island of Mauritius in the Indian Ocean. It had no wings and so couldn't escape humans that hunted it for meat.

Most scientists today believe in evolution. Even so, there are plenty of unanswered questions. Can the theory of evolution also fit in with the idea of God's creation? It depends on each person's own interpretation.

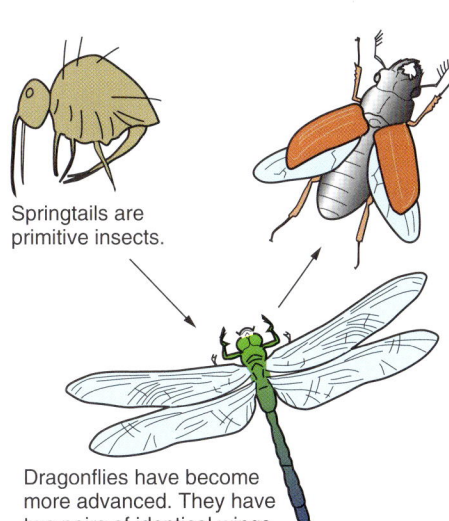

Springtails are primitive insects.

Beetles represent a further advance. The front pair of wings have evolved into hard covers which protect the wings and body.

Dragonflies have become more advanced. They have two pairs of identical wings.

This beetle cannot fly but has clearly evolved from a flying beetle. It is well adapted for living on land.

Picture 4 Evolution of some insects.

Questions

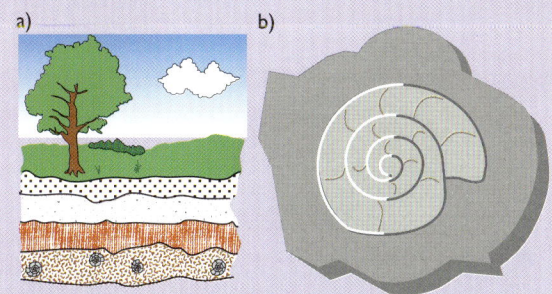

Picture 5 a) Layers of rock. b) A fossil.

1 a) Which layer of rock in Picture 5a is the oldest? Give a reason for your answer.

b) Which layer of rock do you think the fossil in Picture 5b was found in?

c) How can people estimate the age of fossils?

2 a) In what ways are the conditions on Earth changing?

b) How are changes in the environment linked to the evolution of new species?

3 What type of evidence about plants and animals do you think Charles Darwin collected on his trip around the world?

Past and future

Activities

How did the horse evolve?

Picture 1 The evolution of the horse.

Fossils are the ancient remains of living things. Over millions of years they can show how a species has changed (Picture 1). This slow change is called **evolution**.

1 What changes can you see between horses 60 million years ago and horses today?

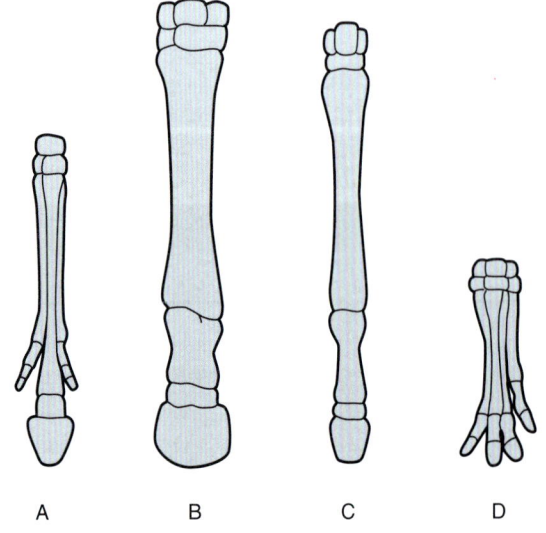

Picture 2 Horses' legs have changed over millions of years.

2 Put the fossils shown in Picture 2 in the correct order, starting with the oldest first.

Selective breeding

Take a tomato that tastes nice, and another that ripens well to a beautiful red, and one that resists disease. Is it possible to get all these desirable characteristics in one tomato? The aim of a selective breeding programme is just that, to breed in the desired characteristics.

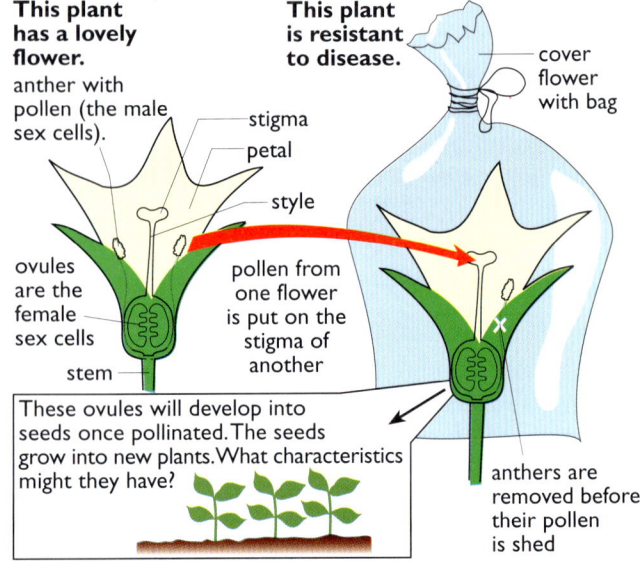

Picture 3 Pollen fertilises the ovules. The pollen and the ovules both contain characteristics for the new seed.

With tomatoes, that means taking pollen from a plant that has tasty fruit, and fertilising the ovules of a plant that resists disease. The seeds that form then have to be grown, before it's possible to see which characteristics have been inherited. The most promising new plants are selected and the process is repeated.

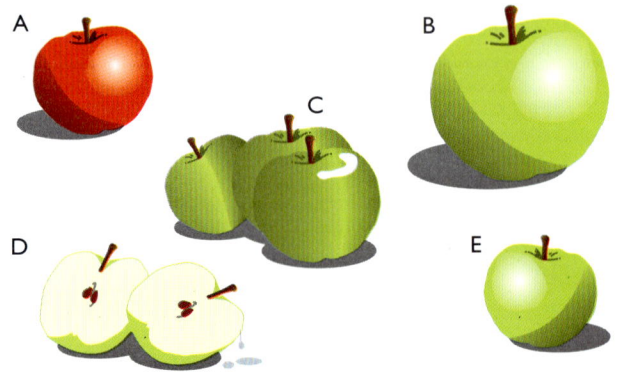

Picture 4 A red fruit   B big fruit   C lots of fruit   D juicy fruit   E keeps well.

3   a) What are the male sex cells of a strawberry plant?

   b) What are the female sex cells of a strawberry plant?

   c) What is fertilisation?

4 How would you set up a breeding programme to make a new type of strawberry plant which has lots of large, juicy fruit?

5 Why is selective breeding a relatively slow process?

6 Why is it impossible to be certain of success in a selective breeding programme?

Being too selective

7 Young dogs were screened for early signs of the disease. How could this information be used to help stop the disease passing on to new dogs in the future?

8 Diseases like PRA increase if there is breeding between closely-related dogs (**inbreeding**). Why does in-breeding make the problem worse?

Genetic engineering

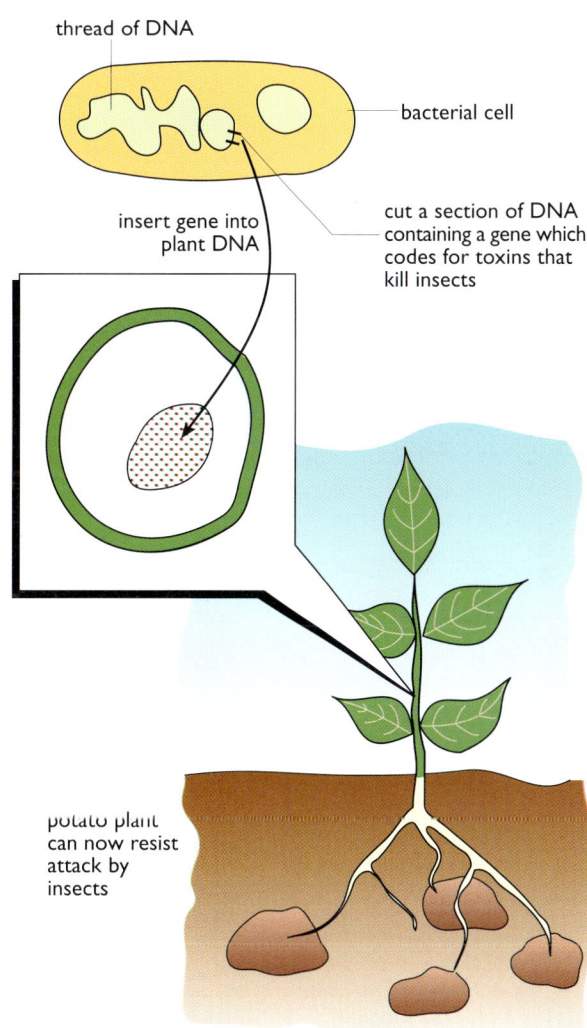

Picture 5   Guide dogs go blind . . .

Many of the dogs bred by the Guide Dogs for the Blind Association in the 1970s and 1980s, suffered from a disease called PRA. PRA (progressive retinal atrophy) made the dogs go blind by the time they were middle-aged. This is an inherited disease, caused by a mutation in a single gene (see pages 104–105).

Picture 6   Genetic engineering is a way of giving living things new characteristics.

Genes from one living thing can be given to another living thing by **genetic engineering**.

9 Both selective breeding and genetic engineering give offspring new characteristics. What are the main differences between these two processes?

THE GENETIC LINK

Scooby Doo signs in DNA

In days gone by people were known to sign in blood. Nowadays, the latest in designer signatures involves using DNA. The American cartoonist Joe Barbera signs frames from recordings such as *The Flintstones* and *Scooby Doo* with his own DNA pen. Since each person's DNA is different, a collector can check that the frame is not a fake.

Scooby Doo holds the DNA code.

This is how it works. DNA is taken from tiny pieces of hair. More of the same DNA code is made from the original piece, using a series of chemical reactions. The DNA is mixed with ordinary ink and used to sign a frame.

A scanner detects the unique pattern reflected back by the artist's DNA, rather like a barcode. It may be possible to develop this system to stop people making counterfeit driving licences or passports.

Clue into fossils

Fossils are rather like the parts of a jigsaw. With enough pieces in place you can start to see the picture. But the whole picture only becomes clear when *all* the pieces fit together.

Just 200 kilometres from Sydney is the Wollemi National Park. Hidden in the depths of the park, are forty pine trees of a previously unknown species. Trees like these may well have been living alongside dinosaurs.

The trees were discovered by David Noble. He abseiled down a 600 metre gorge and found the trees at the bottom. He took a branch back to Sydney, where scientists examined it.

They first thought it came from a fern, not a pine tree 40 metres tall.

Now it has been identified as belonging to a family which includes the Chilean Monkey Puzzle tree. Scientists used a fossil of an extinct species to help them identify it. Exactly how this species fits into the evolution of pine trees is not known.

A newly discovered pine tree species.

One problem is that a fossil record is not often complete. This means that scientists work out their ideas according to the clues they have available. But a new find can change their ideas altogether.

Using 'nonsense' DNA to stop cancer cells

Cancer cells divide more rapidly than normal cells, producing tumours. A protein called PKA1 triggers cell division. Cancer cells make more PKA1 than normal cells, which is why they divide faster.

Scientists in the USA are testing out an idea. They have injected cancer cells with DNA. The DNA contains a 'nonsense' code that blocks the production of PKA1. 'One injection was enough to inhibit tumour growth in mice for two weeks' said scientist Yoon Cho-Chung. She now hopes to test this new treatment on human volunteers.

Using genes to treat cystic fibrosis

People with cystic fibrosis produce 'thick' mucus in their lungs and gut. Apart from problems with digestion, breathing is more difficult. They tend to get lung infections easily, and usually die young. At present the best treatment is having physiotherapy every day.

Cystic fibrosis is caused by a recessive allele. Now scientists are working on ways of giving normal copies of the allele to people with cystic fibrosis. So far, spraying tiny droplets containing the alleles up people's noses seems to be working well. In the lungs the alleles cause cells to make normal mucus.

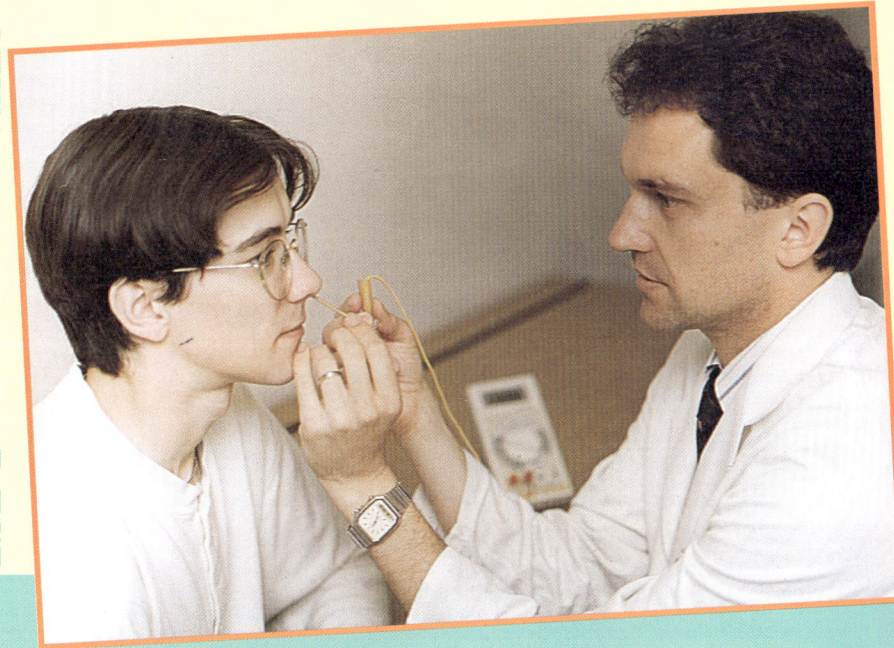

Sleeping beauty?

In 1982, archeologists were digging up a 2000-year old settlement in Japan. They found that the farming people who once lived there stored grain in small pits. Among the remains of some grain was a different seed. When it was planted it sprang to life – it was a Magnolia tree. The Magnolia flowered 11 years later, each flower having 6–9 petals. Scientists don't yet know if this is the sole survivor of an ancient species.

Flower of the magnificent Magnolia tree.

Past and future

Summary

- A species is a group of living things with very similar features, that can breed together.

- Variation means that there are differences between members of the same species, and between different species.

- Variation can have genetic and environmental causes.

- The nucleus of a cell is made of DNA. DNA is the genetic code that acts as a set of instructions for how cells work. DNA can make extra exact copies of itself by a process called replication.

- A gene is a section of DNA that acts as a code for a characteristic. There are thousands of genes on one chromosome.

- Chromosomes are in pairs in all cells except sex cells such as egg cells. This means that a pair of genes, called alleles, are needed for a characteristic to be inherited.

- Mitosis is a type of cell division that gives rise to new cells which have the same genetic code as each other and as the original cell.

- Mitosis happens during asexual reproduction, which only involves one parent.

- Meiosis is a type of cell division that gives rise to new cells which have a different genetic code from each other and from the original cell. The new cells have half the number of chromosomes as the parent cell.

- Meiosis happens during sexual reproduction, which involves two parents.

- A checkerboard is a way of working out inheritance of a characteristic.

- Sex chromosomes are responsible for the inheritance of gender. A female inherits two X chromosomes. A male inherits an X chromosome and a Y chromosome.

- A mutation is a change in the genetic code.

- Evolution is a gradual change in species which happens over millions of years, so that new species develop.

- Fossils are a record of species that existed in the past. They are clues to how evolution has happened.

Questions

1. **a)** Plants and animals may be bred selectively.
   i) Describe the process of selective breeding.
   ii) Suggest **two** characteristics a farmer may want to improve by selective breeding of his wheat crop.
   iii) Give **one** problem which can be caused by selective breeding.

   MEG

2. **a)** New Begonia plants can be produced from cuttings taken from an existing plant.
   A gardener produced some new plants from a healthy, fully-grown plant which was 30 cm tall and had dark green leaves.
   A leaf was cut into thin strips.

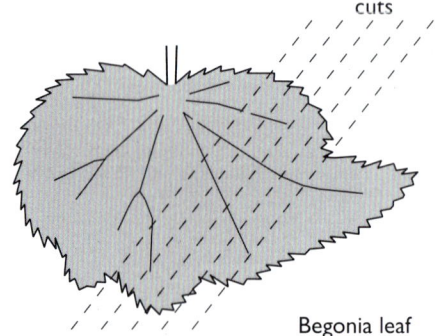

Begonia leaf

Each strip was planted in a separate pot of the same compost.

Questions continued

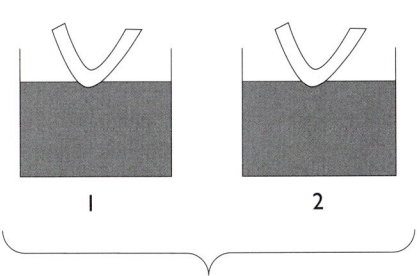

grown in a greenhouse under controlled conditions

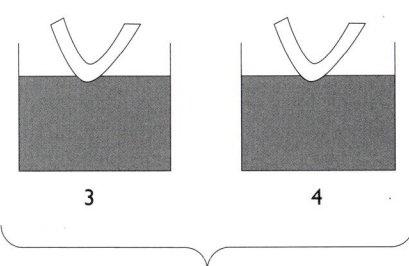

left outside to grow

Pots **1** and **2** were kept in a greenhouse where conditions such as temperature, water and nutrients were controlled.
Pots **3** and **4** were left outside in the open.
i) Explain why a new plant can be produced from only a small strip of leaf.
ii) The cuttings in pots **1** and **2** grew well. Predict how these new plants would compare in appearance with the original parent plant.

MEG

3 The beaks of four different types of birds are shown.

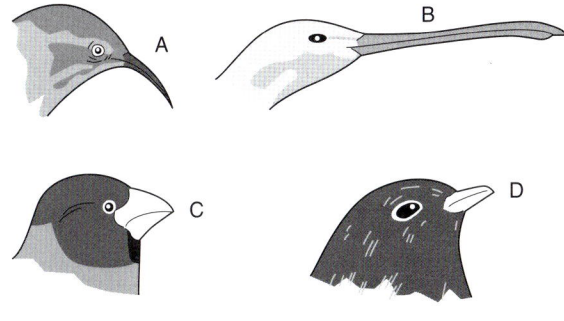

Which of these birds **A**, **B**, **C** or **D** is best suited (adapted) to
i) cracking open nuts?
ii) scooping food from mud?
iii) probing for insects?

MEG

4 a) Choose, from the list below, words or numbers to complete the following passage. You may use each word or number once, more than once or not at all.
**allele inherited mutation nucleus sperm
23   46**
A gene is a unit of _____ information found along a chromosome. The _____ of each human body cell has _____ pairs of chromosomes but the _____ and ovum each contain _____ chromosomes. Each gene may have more than one form, e.g. one producing brown eyes and one producing blue eyes. Each form of a gene is called an _____

b) In humans, brown eye colour (B) is dominant to blue eye colour (b). The incomplete family tree below shows how eye colour was passed through the Jones family.

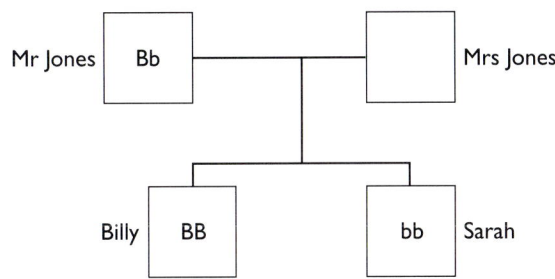

i) Write the correct letters for eye colour into the empty box for Mrs Jones. Explain your answer.
ii) Sarah (bb) and Tom (BB) are having a child. Copy and complete the diagram below to predict the eye colour of their child.

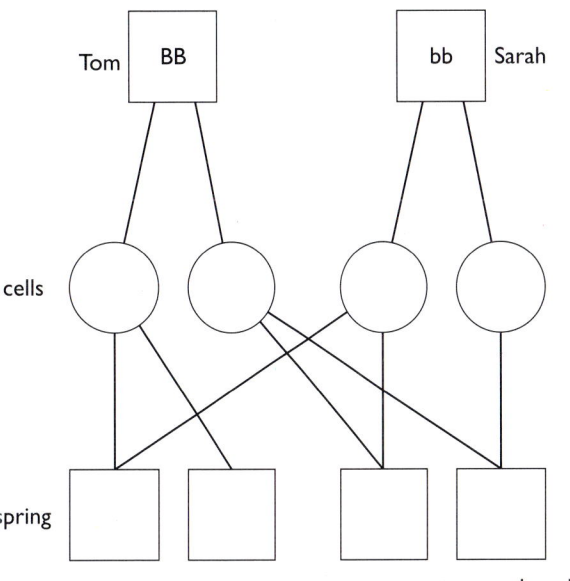

London

focus 6

Ecosystem Earth

Spread around the world — 118
About the world's major ecosystems.

Ecology — 120
Living things interact with each other and their environment.

Adapting, competing and surviving — 122
What makes a species successful?

Predator and prey — 124
Some animals are well adapted for catching food, others are the ones being caught.

Human impact on the Earth

1 Pollution — 126
Pollution changes the environment and has an effect on living things.

2 Using the land — 128
Farming, building and cutting down trees has an impact on the balance of nature.

Protecting the planet — 130
Being responsible about our world.

Spread around the world

The world and wildlife

An **ecosystem** consists of living things and their environment, and the interactions between them.

Looking from space, you can see the whole planet. Together, Earth and its inhabitants make up the largest ecosystem, the **biosphere**. Within the biosphere are several **major ecosystems**.

The land provides **terrestrial** ecosystems. Picture 2 shows some major terrestrial ecosystems. It is mostly the climate and type of landform that determines what lives there.

Picture 1 Vast but vulnerable – Earth from space.

Coniferous (Boreal) Forest
The trees in coniferous forests have cones containing seeds. They have needle-like leaves that drop onto the soil making it slightly acid.

Hot Desert
A desert gets very little rainfall and there is limited plant life. The temperatures can be extremely hot in the day and cold at night. But, suprisingly, invertebrates and mammals have adapted to life in these harsh conditions.

Savannah
Dry tropical grasslands called savannah provide food for grazing animals, animals that prey on them and many invertebrates. These merge into tropical woodlands where there is more rainfall.

Picture 2 Major ecosystems within the biosphere.

Ecosystem Earth

Temperate Forest
Temperate forests grow in cool but mild conditions, where temperatures are not extreme. There are fewer species than in a tropical rainforest, but both evergreen trees and trees which drop their leaves live there.

Tundra
Tough grasses, moss and lichen are the main plant species in the tundra, which is found on the highest mountains and in the Arctic. Conditions are very cold, and much of the water exists as ice. But many migrating birds and animals use the tundra during the short summers.

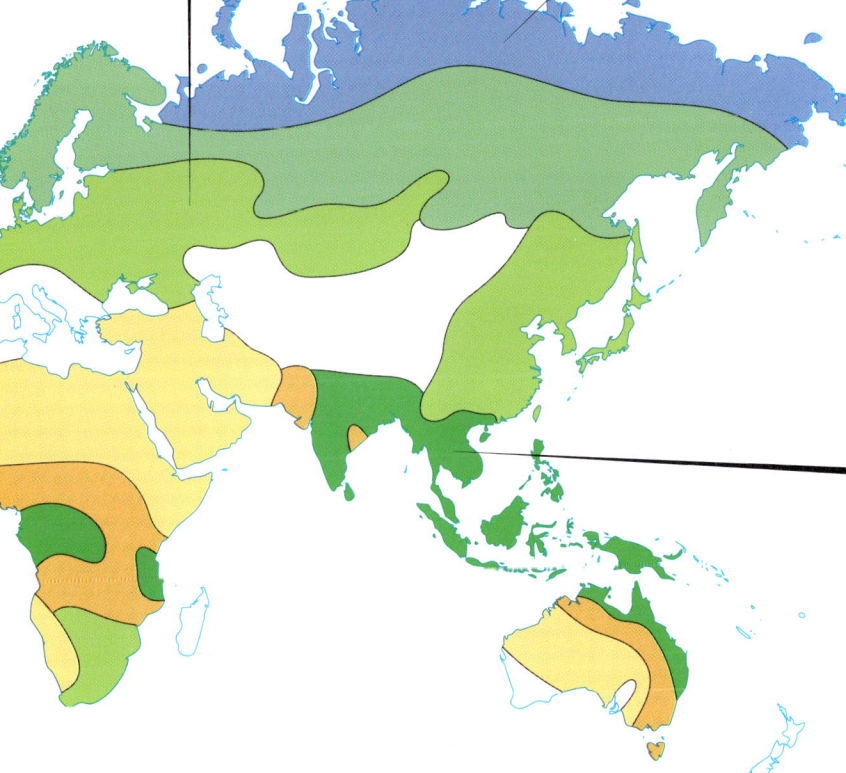

Tropical Rainforest
High rainfall all through the year and warm temperatures are ideal growing conditions for plants. Trees grow very tall, creating a canopy of leaves 40m or so above the ground. The canopy cuts out light so few plants grow at ground level. But the trees support other plants such as vines. Animals live in the canopy, and also down at ground level. The rainforest contains a vast range of different species.

Questions

1. Use an atlas to find out a place where each of the ecosystems occurs.

2. What factors mostly influence whether the type of forest growing is

   a) rainforest

   b) coniferous forest

   c) temperate forest?

3. Which conditions make desert a harsh environment?

Ecology

Living space – a habitat

The places where living things spend their lives are called **habitats**. Almost everywhere in the biosphere is a habitat – on land, in water, in the air and under the ground. Even living things can be a habitat for others. After all, we share our bodies with millions of bacteria.

The **environment** is the set of living conditions in a particular habitat. Temperature, how much water is available and the other living things are some of the conditions making up the environment.

All the living things in a habitat are called a **community**. A community is usually a mixture of different species. Each species has its own population. For example, a seashore community may include populations of seaweeds, limpets and crabs. Ecology is the study of communities, and how they interact with one another and with their habitat.

Elephant ecology

This is a story about a game reserve in Botswana, Africa. Chris Styles is a scientist studying the veld ecosystem. He questions whether elephants are really the masters in this environment.

Picture 1 A ragworm's habitat is a sandy beach. It's a wet and salty environment.

Picture 2 The veld is an ecosystem.

The veld is mostly tropical grassland, with many mopane bushes and trees. Mopane trees are key to the ecology of the veld. With unusual leaves that can fold in hot weather, a tree exposes less surface to the burning sun's rays, and so survives extreme heat.

Animals such as impala, kudu, eland, giraffes and elephants eat mopane trees. This browsing has reduced some mopane trees to little more than shrubs. Wardens in the game park are concerned about damage caused by animals, particularly elephants, which also strip bark. The stripped areas may let in insects and fungi that can kill trees.

Ecosystem Earth

Yet the mopane soon floods the stripped area with protective resin.

Where elephants have caused damage, termites sometimes get in and build a nest up against the trunk. They bore out the heartwood, leaving the tree alive, although the trunk is hollow. Later, ants move in after the termites leave. They protect trees from being eaten, by swarming over the lower branches. The ants bite the animals, and smear repellent chemicals on their mouths. Other species such as bees build nests in hollow trees too.

Picture 3 Elephants eat the mopane trees.

Chris Styles was interested to find that the smaller mopane shrubs develop leaves a month or so earlier than undamaged trees. These young leaves, which contain less tannin than leaves on taller trees, are easier for animals to digest. So they provide food for animals at the end of the dry season, when there's very little else around.

What else eats mopane? Caterpillars of the mopane emperor moth (called 'mopane worms' locally) can strip trees of leaves in summer. But if rain falls soon after the leaves are eaten, the trees put on a spurt of new growth. This is a benefit to animals which feed on the new leaves in the dry season. What's more, the mopane worms excrete, fertilising the ground.

number of elephants	14
total food eaten in a year	307 tonnes
time mopane worms live for	34 days
total food eaten in this time	779 tonnes

Source: BBC Wildlife, March 1995

Table 1 Some estimated data for a 4000 hectare plot in the game park.

Picture 4 A tasty dish for tribespeople who eat these caterpillars, mopane 'worms' are a cash crop, and a good source of protein.

Questions

1 a) Describe the habitat in the game park.

   b) What climate factors influence this environment?

   c) List five important populations that are part of the community described in this story.

   d) Make notes on the effects that the invertebrates mentioned in this story have on the veld.

2 Some people might argue that elephants do not damage the veld, although others are concerned that they do. Put forward reasons to support both sides of this argument.

3 Elephants are strong and few animals pose a threat to them. Do you think that they are 'masters of the veld'?

Adapting, competing and surviving

Competing for limited resources

In any ecosystem, the **resources** needed by living things are limited. This means that populations cannot go on increasing forever. In fact there is fierce **competition** for the resources. Picture 1 shows a pond ecosystem. The individuals in this community have to compete for their share of the resources, or they die.

The main resources that living things need are food, space to breed, and suitable conditions to live in. Light is a vital resource for plants, since they transfer it as chemical energy in their food.

In Picture 1, you can see that *Asellus* is food for both fish and leeches. If more *Asellus* are eaten by fish, then there are less for leeches. An organism that is successful at getting food is more likely to reach reproductive age, and have young. This can affect the size of a population.

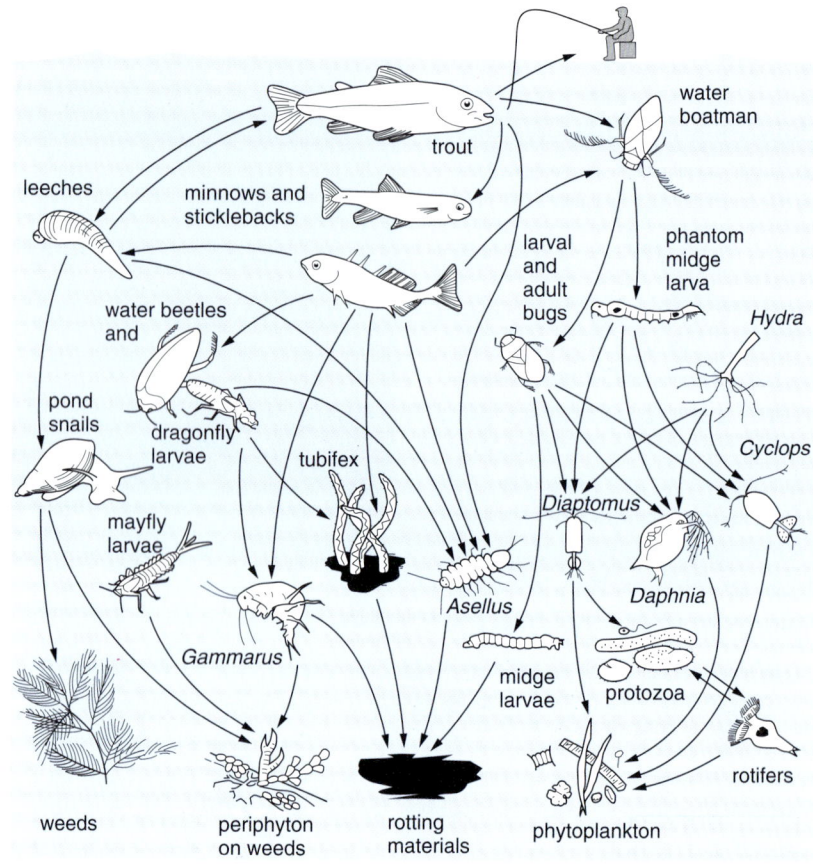

Picture 1 Competing in a pond.

A space to live in

Living space is an important factor too. In this century, thousands of kilometres of hedgerows have been lost in the UK. Small mammals such as mice, and many birds and invertebrates such as insects and snails, have decreased. This is because they have lost living space, food and shelter from this habitat.

Sea birds often nest together in vast numbers (Picture 2). But if too many birds crowd into an area, egg production drops and so does the population.

Plants also compete for living space. Their roots need space in the soil to anchor the plant, and absorb water and minerals. Picture 3 shows how beech leaves form a pattern that means they get a maximum amount of light shining on their surfaces.

Picture 2 Gannets nesting on rock ledges.

Ecosystem Earth

Increasing the chances of survival

Adaptations are ways in which living things are suited to living in an environment. Focus 4, *Controlling change*, describes how animals are adapted for living in hot and cold climates, and for stopping too much water loss.

If an animal is well adapted to its environment, it will be more successful at competing, and more likely to survive and increase the population. For example, in 1879 grey squirrels were introduced to the UK. Since then their population has soared, overtaking the red squirrel population (see page 132).

Since drought reduced the food supply in the outback, eastern grey kangaroos have invaded the Australian capital, Canberra. They have adapted their behaviour and diet in order to survive.

Picture 3 When some leaves and stems of this plant are bitten, they squirt out a fine jet of toxic liquid. Cattle and goats soon learn to steer clear of Bursera.

Adapting to disease

Rabbits do a huge amount of damage to crops each year. They breed fast and are very successful mammals. In 1950, a virus disease called myxomatosis was introduced to rabbits in Australia. The virus attacks a rabbit's nervous system, killing it.

The population of rabbits dropped dramatically. But some rabbits inherited different genes, and they survived the myxomatosis virus. Now the population of rabbits has increased again, but this time the rabbits are **resistant** to this disease. In 1995, another virus called calcivirus escaped from an experiment, which was carried out on an island, onto the south coast of Australia. It began to infect rabbits, killing 90% of them.

Picture 4 An Eastern grey kangaroo searches a rubbish bin in Canberra, Australia.

Questions

1. **a)** What is meant by limited resources?

    b) List the main resources that living things require.

    c) Why do plants and animals compete for resources?

    d) Give examples of living things in Picture 1 that are competing for resources.

    e) Look back to page 80. How are cacti well adapted for surviving a hot, dry climate?

2. An Eskimo lives in a very cold climate. An African tribesman lives in a very hot climate. Suggest ways in which their body types are adapted for living in different climates.

3. **a)** Why does resistance to disease give a population more chance of surviving?

    b) Why might sheep farmers be pleased that the rabbit population drops when a new disease infects it?

    c) Some farmers raise rabbits for fur. How might they feel about the escape of calcivirus onto the mainland?

Predator and prey

Catch or be caught!

Some animals are **predators**, as they catch other animals and eat them. The animals they catch are called their **prey**. Predator and prey interact in their ecosystem, each affecting the population size of the other. What are predators like, and what features help prey escape them?

Picture 2   Rabbits are prey for other animals such as foxes.

Picture 1   An owl is a predator of small mammals.

Both predators and their prey rely on their senses to survive. Some predators, such as the owl in Picture 1, have very sharp sight. In dim light their eyes can detect tiny mammals moving at a great distance. The eyes are towards the front of their heads, making their sight more accurate.

A rabbit, on the other hand, has excellent hearing. It's large ears can be swivelled to make detection even better. Notice that the rabbit's eyes are on the side of its head. This position means that it has a very wide field of view, so it can see all round. What's more, rabbits can run extremely fast. As their white tails bob up and down, they warn other rabbits of danger.

Other predators like the terrier in Picture 3 have a very good sense of smell. Like wolves, foxes and dingos, they pick up many chemical signals through receptors in their noses.

Many predators develop special techniques for catching prey. The spider is an example, since it weaves a web as a trap. The rock python in Picture 4 suffocates its prey with its muscular coils.

Picture 3   Nosing his way through life? A terrier has a terrific sense of smell and can sniff out its prey.

Population data

A population changes in size because of births and deaths. If there are more births than deaths, the population increases. If there are fewer births than deaths, the population decreases. In Picture 5 you can see how the population of predators follows the pattern in the population of prey.

As the number of prey increases, so does the food supply for the predators. They catch more prey and more survive to reproduce. This means that the predator population increases.

Picture 4   A rock python starts to swallow a whole gazelle.

Ecosystem Earth

But the effect of this increase is that more prey are being caught, and their population declines. So the food supply for the predators decreases and then their numbers fall too.

Over a period of time, the two populations rise and fall, although the prey population is always greater than the number of predators. Environmental changes might alter this picture. For example, a record wet and warm summer might mean more plant growth, providing more food for the aphids which suck plant sap. Ladybirds are predators of aphids. If there are more aphids in one year, the number of predators would rise too.

Many predators have more than one food source. As one food source is finished, a predator will hunt for others. Clearly the feeding relationships between living things are complex.

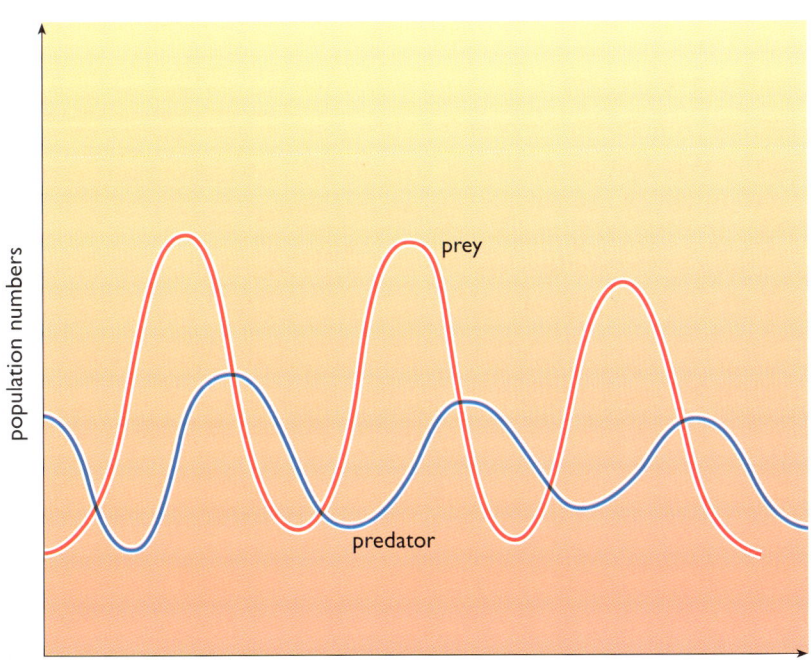

Picture 5 A general pattern for predator and prey populations.

Questions

1. **a)** Which of the following animals in Picture 7A–D do you think are predators and which are prey? Are any both predator and prey?

A   B   C   D

Picture 7

Population	Births/week	Deaths/week
A	10 200	9875
B	6.1 million/year	6.4 million/year
C	4.4×10^3	16×10^3

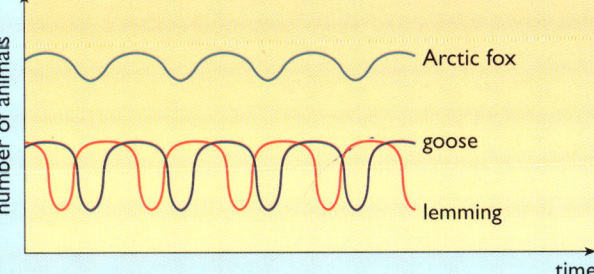

b) Suggest features that help the predators catch prey.

c) How do the prey try to escape capture by a predator?

2. Which of the following populations A–C show an increase and which show a decrease?

3. The picture above shows how the population of Arctic foxes changed over a period of years. Arctic foxes eat geese and lemmings.

a) Why is the number of geese less than the number of predators?

b) Suggest a reason why the number of Arctic foxes doesn't vary as much as the pattern shown in Picture 5.

Human impact on the Earth 1

Pollution

Using fuels

Learning to make fire was an enormous milestone in the development of humans. Having fire meant humans were able to keep warm, to fend off enemies and to cook food.

Today most fuel is used to generate electricity, burned to provide heating or power vehicles. Using fuels is a part of daily routine for most people, although some people use a lot more fuel than others (Picture 1).

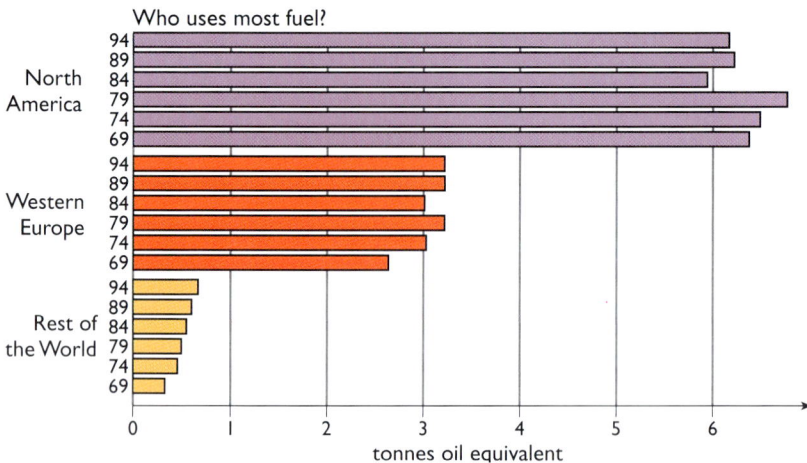

Picture 1 Energy consumption per capita.
Source: BP Statistical Review of World Energy, June 1995.

Fuels cause pollution

Burning fossil fuels such as coal, oil and gas is one of the major reasons for pollution. The problem with fossil fuels is the waste gases that are produced. The main culprits are:
- acidic gases such as sulphur dioxide and nitrogen oxides
- greenhouse gases such as carbon dioxide and hydrocarbons.

Acid gases cause acid rain

Sulphur dioxide and nitrogen oxides dissolve in rainwater, making it acidic. When the rain soaks into the ground or drains into waterways, it makes them more acid too. Because air currents move from country to country, acid gases made in one place can cause acid rain in another (see *Materials*, page 64).

Picture 2 shows that buildings and stonework can be damaged by acid rain. Trees are also damaged if the soil is too acid.

Picture 2 The Sphinx's nose has been slowly eaten away by acid rain.

Greenhouse gases and global warming

The atmosphere around Earth filters out many of the light waves reaching it from the sun. However, some shorter wavelengths pass through, and are absorbed by Earth's surface. Other longer wavelengths are radiated back towards space from Earth. But longer wavelengths cannot penetrate the atmosphere, so remain within the biosphere and cause a heating effect (see *Physical Processes*, pages 70-71).

This is a model called the **greenhouse effect**, because it is similar to the heating effect that happens in a greenhouse. This greenhouse effect keeps Earth warm enough to support life as it is today. But what if it gets warmer?

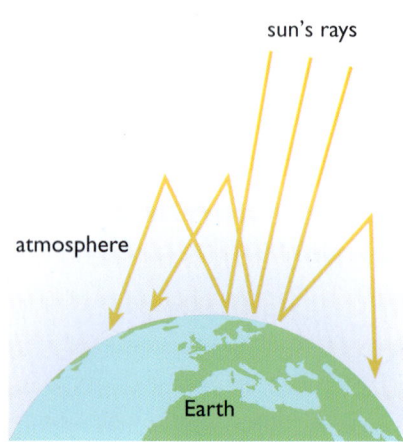

Picture 3 The greenhouse effect.

Ecosystem Earth

Although the rise in average temperatures shown in Picture 4 may not seem like a lot, the effects are significant. Scientists are still not sure what will happen, although most predict climate changes.

An increase in greenhouse gases, particularly carbon dioxide, is thought to be the main reason for global warming (Picture 4). Carbon dioxide is the main greenhouse gas, but methane from cows and rice fields contributes too. Even ozone at low levels in the atmosphere acts as a greenhouse gas.

The latest power stations which burn fossil fuels now produce less nitrogen oxides and less sulphur dioxide. Catalytic converters on cars also help reduce these gases. But carbon dioxide is still a problem, and one solution may be to use nuclear power stations, instead of ones that burn fossil fuels.

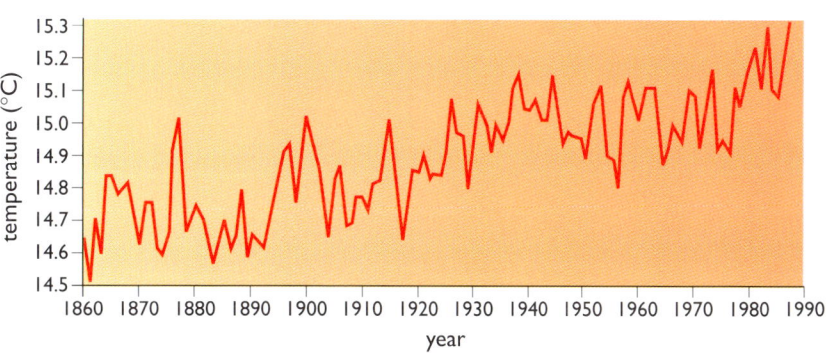

Picture 4 Global temperatures are rising, (about 0.3–0.7°C over the last 100 years). This is called **global warming**.

Sewage pollution

An increase in the human population naturally means an increase in sewage. Most sewage is treated before it is fed back into waterways, but some is let out into the sea untreated. This causes a health hazard on beaches and to wildlife in the sea.

Chemical pollution

Chemicals from many manufacturing processes, as well as pesticides and fertilisers used to improve yields in farming, find their way into soil or waterways. CFCs are hydrocarbons that contain fluorine and chlorine. They are used in aerosol cans as propellants – the gases that carry the product out of the can. CFCs damage 'the ozone layer', which is a layer of ozone at high levels in the atmosphere.

The ozone layer absorbs a lot of the penetrating waves that pass towards Earth. In the late 1980s, scientists measuring ozone concentration realised that this layer is getting thinner, particularly over the icecaps. As a result, more ultra-violet (UV) light is reaching Earth. People need to use sunscreen when exposed to the sun, because the increased level of UV means more chance of burning the skin. Skin damage by the sun can lead to skin cancer.

Questions

1. **a)** In which countries do people use most energy?

   b) Which of your daily activities uses an energy source?

   c) Why does burning fossil fuels cause
   i) acid rain
   ii) global warming?

2. The spread of plants and animals around the world may change if climate changes. Explain this idea using the data in Picture 4.

3. **a)** How might individuals help to slow down global warming?

   b) How might governments help control levels of carbon dioxide in the atmosphere?

   c) Fossil fuels will all be used up one day in the future. Suggest other sources of energy which humans might use.

4. How does the ozone layer help to protect living things on Earth?

Human impact on the Earth 2

Using the land

How life has changed

Early humans were hunters and gatherers. They found whatever food was around them. Few people live like this today, most rely on farming to give a constant supply of food. This has brought a huge increase in the standard of living and in how healthy people are. Farming involves using the land for growing crops and raising animals.

Picture 2 A commercial wheat field.

Picture 1 Only 3% of British hay meadows remain, so many plant species have been lost. How might the number of different plant species in a field of wheat the same size compare to the number in a hay meadow?

Farmers are now using intensive farming methods to produce more and more food from the same area of land. This makes food cheaper and, as the world population increases, governments have encouraged it. But intensive farming requires more use of pesticides to stop crop damage, and more chemical fertilisers to help crops grow. Left alone, the land in the UK would slowly return to woodland. Although this might look nice, it wouldn't feed as many people.

Wheat, maize, coffee, bananas, rubber trees, sugar cane and oil palm are just a few of the crops which are grown across vast areas of land, in different parts of the world. This means that the types of plants and animals living there have changed dramatically, since the land was wild. Pictures 2 and 4 show how farming can influence the land.

Apart from farming, building takes up a lot of space. People need homes, and industries need offices and factories. Motorways and other roads are needed for faster transport. All these activities use up materials and energy. At the same time, we are producing more waste in our homes and in industry. The oceans are polluted and land is used up when we dump waste.

Picture 3 In Malaysia, many rubber tree plantations have been removed, and oil palms planted instead. The oil palm nuts are attractive food for rats. Barn owls are increasing in these plantations because the rats are an easy food source. An average-sized family of barn owls eats 1300 rats per year. Nesting boxes have been put up so more owl pairs can breed, and less rat poison is used.

Ecosystem Earth

Losing major ecosystems

Tropical rainforests are very productive, and contain a huge number of different living things. The forests formed over millions of years. They cover a relatively small area of land, and yet they are very important in

- absorbing carbon dioxide from the atmosphere
- putting water vapour into the air, causing rain
- keep Earth's temperature more stable
- as a source of genetic material, in the many species of plants and animals found there.

By 1980, over 40% of the world's rainforest had been cut down, partly for timber. But a lot of it is burned to clear space for farming. The soil quickly becomes useless because heavy rains wash minerals and topsoil away. Settlers then have to move on to new areas. If destruction continues at the present rate, there will be no rainforest left in about 90 years time.

Picture 4 Cattle will graze where this forest once grew. Cattle are raised for the beefburger trade. Much of the money gained through this trade will go to big companies, often outside the country.

The balance of nature

Natural ecosystems are in a very delicate balance. Changing one part of an ecosystem, say introducing one new species of plant or animal, can have unexpected effects. Picture 3 on this page, and pages 134–135 *Interacting, competing and adapting* give examples of this.

Questions

1. **a)** Why is more food needed in the world today than was needed 300 years ago?

   b) What are some of the advantages and disadvantages of intensive farming?

   c) What difference is there between the number of species found in a crop field compared to a wild area?

   d) Which ecosystem in the world has the widest diversity of species?

2. **a)** Deforestation is the loss of forest. Which major ecosystem is being lost because of deforestation?

   b) Why do local people want to use land that forests grow on?

   c) Why does the use of the land not necessarily give wealth to local people?

   d) Why is deforestation such an important issue for everyone, not only the people living in the deforested areas?

Protecting the planet

Taking responsibility

Living things interact with each other and with the environment, making up Ecosystem Earth – the biosphere. Because of these interactions, a change in one part of the ecosystem can affect living things in other parts. Often it's impossible to predict exactly what will happen as a result of changes in the natural environment.

Picture 1 Protesting about something you disagree with can make a difference.

We get lots of information about what's happening all around the world, through the television and other media. It's easy to think that problems such as pollution are happening somewhere else, and someone else will deal with them. But in the end, who is responsible for taking care of the planet? If no-one takes responsibility, what will happen?

The good news is that everyone can make a difference to what happens in the future. After all, people can help at all levels:
- as individuals, everyone can take responsibility for their own actions
- within a country, decision-making by industry and government
- internationally, through agencies such as the United Nations.

Here are some stories about projects that are helping to protect the planet.

Worms help deal with Bombay's rubbish

Earthworms are India's secret weapon against growing mountains of rubbish. The rubbish attracts rats, and the rats carry plague. A city such as Bombay makes 5800 tonnes of rubbish a day, and at present most of it is burned or buried.

The Green Cross Society of Bombay has started a large number of clear-up projects, using a species of deep-burrowing worm. The worms can chomp their way through rubbish, turning it into useful compost. Now the city authorities are looking into using worms on a larger scale.

Picture 2 Wriggling out of trouble – worms deal with the rubbish problem.

Ecosystem Earth

Laikipia rhino project

Rhinoceroses (rhinos) are killed for their horn. The horn is ground up and used in medicines, or carved into dagger handles. Rhinos have little defence against modern weapons, and in the last 20 years the black rhino population has crashed.

On a privately-owned ranch in Laikipia, is the largest undisturbed 'wild' population of black rhino. Four males and two females are fitted with radio ear-tags. The ear-tags emit radio waves which can be tracked over large distances. The idea is to find out more about how the rhinos live, in particular their mating habits.

Radio tracking is useful because it has made it easier to collect more urine samples. The urine samples are tested for reproductive hormones. This knowledge will help in managing captive herds. Since rhinos will breed in captivity successfully, the hope is to prevent them becoming extinct.

Picture 3 The rhino's finest possession is also its worst enemy when it comes to poachers, who kill rhinos for horn.

Fishing

Thirty years ago, children in Newfoundland, Northern Canada, could dip a basket into the ocean to catch fish. Now not a single school of cod is left in what was once the world's richest fishery. The Grand Banks cod has been destroyed.

Since the 1950s, scientists have been responsible for setting the level of cod catches which are 'safe'. But by 1992, they realised that there were almost no adult cod left. How could experts get their estimates so wrong?

Scientists made their estimates using a standard method: cruising the area randomly, and counting how many fish were caught, recording their ages, and how long they took to catch. Other data came from fishing vessels, but their estimates were higher because they knew when and where to fish for the best catches.

Picture 4 A successful herring catch. The Canadian government banned fishing on the Grand Banks. The ban is likely to remain for at least a decade to allow young fish to mature, and for cod populations to increase. Now more thorough ways of sampling fish stocks will be used.

Protecting the planet — Ecosystem Earth

focus 6

Sustainable forestry?

Catherine Barr of Greenpeace states that 50–90% of the world's species live in forest habitats. Yet many people tend to think of forests as 'sources of timber, rather than ecosystems' she says.

What have governments done to protect forests so far?

- In 1985 the Tropical Forestry Action Plan was launched by the World Bank, the United Nations Development Programme and other agencies.
- In 1992 there was an Earth Summit in Rio de Janeiro: two international treaties were declared, including the Convention on Biological Diversity.

Sustainable forestry means using the forest in a way that does not damage it. One key point is that only some selected trees are removed from a particular area, and that an area is not cropped more than once in a 25 year period. But also an important point is that native people can live in the forest, and support their traditional lifestyle. This may mean selling some forest products for cash.

Sarawak covers roughly 15 million hectares (about the size of England and Wales). Officially 9 million hectares are described as forest, yet much has been logged. Over half of the forest is managed by sustainable forestry.

In October 1994 the Malaysian government announced its intention to take over 4 million hectares. They will fell natural trees and turn the area over to tree plantations. Although a planted forest will support wildlife, there will not be such a wide number of species as in the original mixed forest.

Picture 5 Tree felling in Sarawak, Malaysia.

Ecosystem Earth

Activities

Reds and greys – the furry type

These days, very few people in the UK have seen a red squirrel in the wild. Yet a hundred years ago they were common in all British woodlands. In contrast, grey squirrels have steadily increased since they were released in the UK, first in 1879.

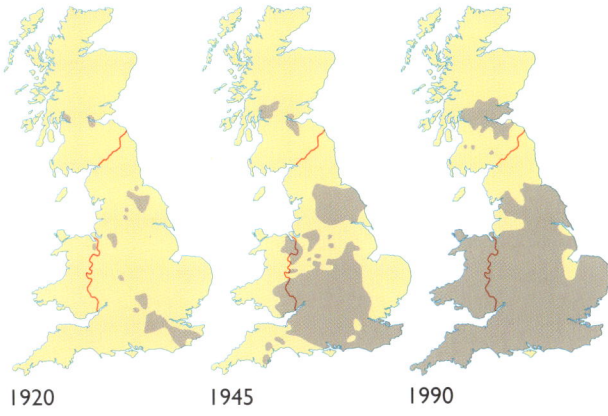

Grey squirrel

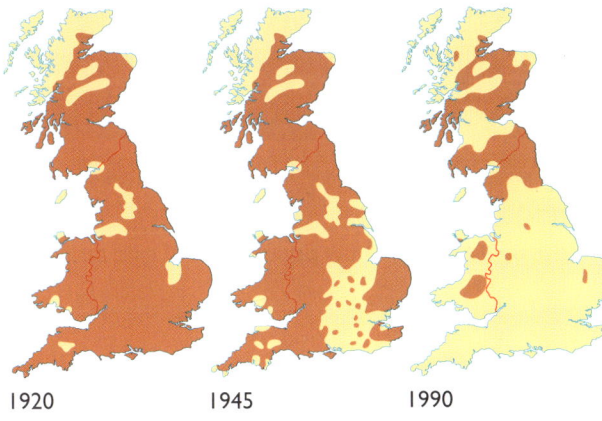

Red squirrel

Picture 1 The spread of grey squirrels and decline of reds.
Source: Biological Sciences Review, November 1993; Derek Yaldon.

There are many ideas about why red squirrels are decreasing. Here are some facts about the ecology of red and grey squirrels and their woodlands:
- Greys have a mass of about 550 g, and reds 300 g.
- Greys and reds may live close to each other.
- Red squirrels disappeared from areas once greys had also been established there for around 15 years.
- In some areas red squirrels disappeared before greys became established.
- Red squirrels are not decreasing so fast in areas with pine forests.
- Much natural woodland has been lost in the UK.
- Recently, most of the trees planted for timber are pines.
- Grey squirrels can digest acorns better than reds.
- Every 10 years or so there is a 'bumper crop' of acorns and chestnuts.
- Cones on pines take up to 2 years to mature and may be present all year round.
- Red squirrels spend more time up in the tree branches than greys that feed more at ground level.

Picture 2 a) The red squirrel is a native of Britain. b) Grey squirrels were introduced from America.

Work in a group with two or three other people in your class. Discuss the information in this activity. Then write notes on why your group thinks that red squirrels are decreasing in the UK. You may be asked to give a short talk about this topic. These questions may help you:
- Is the difference in size between red and grey squirrels important? If so, why?
- Why is there a time lag between greys appearing and reds disappearing?
- What are the different food sources and feeding habits of reds and greys?
- How have Britain's forests changed since the early 1900s?

Fish farming

In recent years, fish farming (in particular salmon) has increased greatly (Picture 3). The young fish are raised in freshwater farms, and later moved to sea farms.

Farming can provide a steady supply of food, and help to stop over-fishing of wild stocks. What's more, fish farming provides employment. However, there are some concerns about how fish farming affects the environment.

Ecosystem Earth

Activities continued

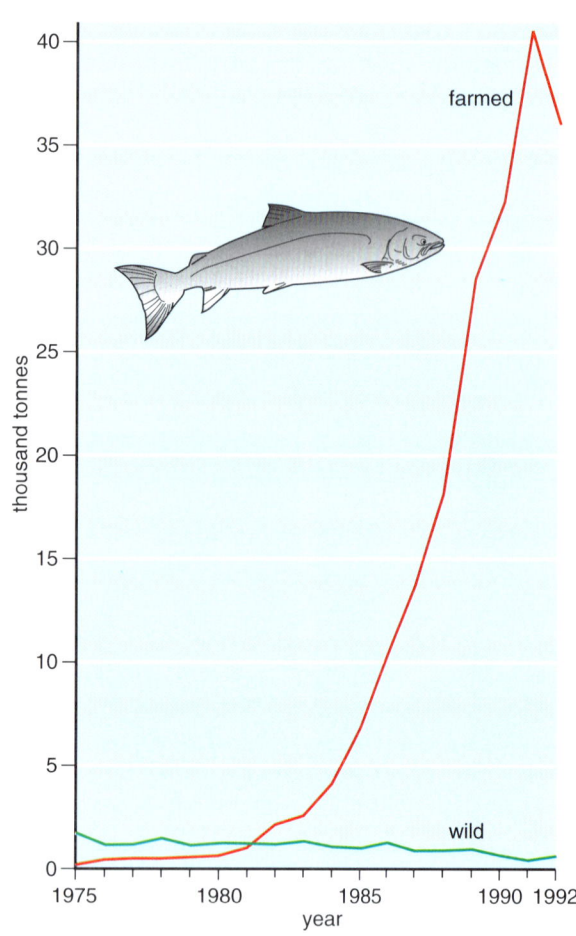

Picture 3 Salmon catches – from the wild and from farms.
Source: Biological Science Review, Jan. 1994

1 For each of the following points, suggest what environmental concern there might be:

a) Waste fish food, and the urine and faeces of the fish drop through the fish cages into the water. These wastes use up oxygen from the water as they decay.

b) Because fish are more crowded in farms than in the wild, disease spreads easily. Fish escape from farms into the wild.

c) Fish farmers use disinfectants and anti-biotics to cut down the amount of fish disease.

2 What are the advantages and disadvantages of fish farming?

3 How might fish farming be controlled to make it less damaging to the environment?

Catch or be caught

Graph 1 is data provided by the Hudson's Bay Company in Canada. The Hudson's Bay Company is a fur trading company.

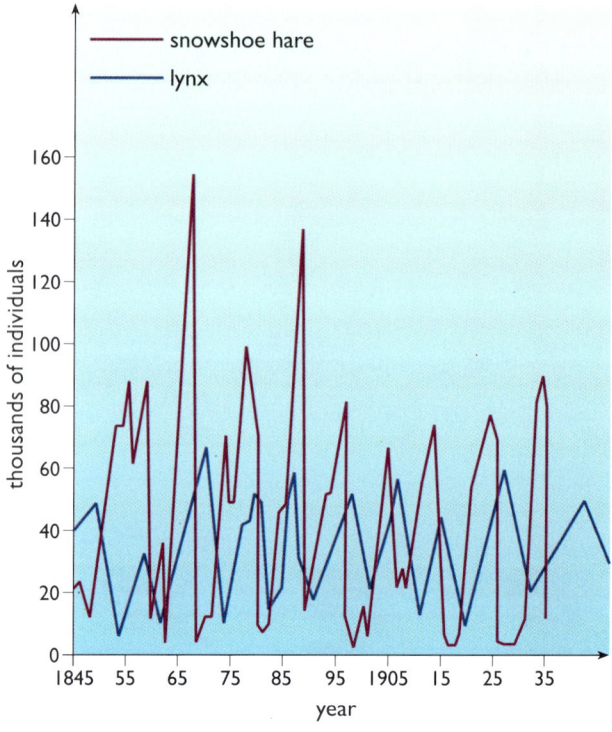

Picture 4 Graph to show populations of lynx and snowshoe hare.

1 a) Which animal is

   i) the predator

   ii) the prey?

b) Use your school or local library to find out more about these animals.

2 What has happened to the size of each population during the ninety years in which data were collected?

3 Describe a pattern in population size which is true for both the lynx and the snowshoe hare.

4 Which environmental factors might affect the number of snowshoe hares?

Acid in the loch

Loch Fleet is a small inland lake in Scotland, which was famous for trout fishing in the 1930s and 1940s. But by the end of the 1950s very few trout had survived. Scientists discovered that the water falling as rain and draining into the lake from the land, had become acidic. Page 126 describes the causes of acid rain.

Lime is a base which neutralises acid. Lime pellets were scattered in the area in 1986 and 1987, and trout were put back into the loch.

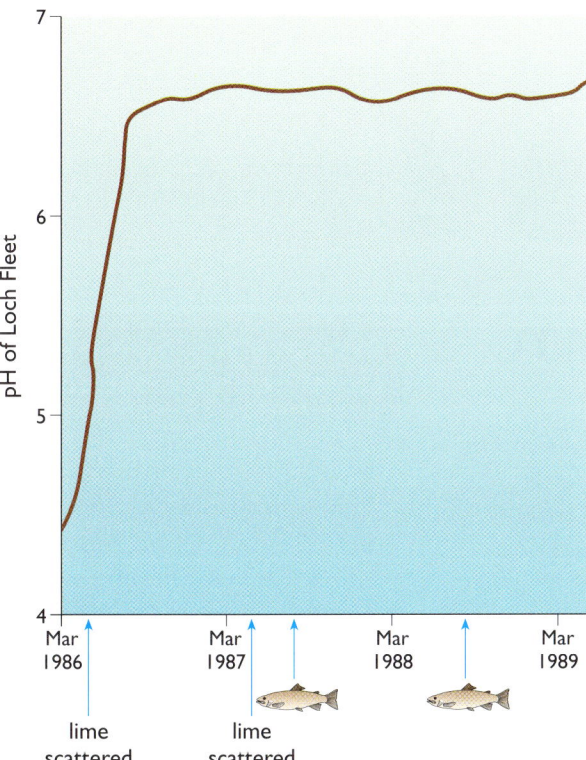

Picture 5 This is a record of the brown trout population in Loch Fleet.

1 What is the link between pH and the size of the trout population.

2 Suggest reasons why lime

a) was added to the land rather than directly to the water.

b) was added as pellets rather than a powder.

3 What evidence is there that the lime treatment was successful?

4 Suggest some ideas for a longer term solution to the problem of acid rain.

Predicting is an uncertain business

This map has been produced with the help of a computer. Existing data is the starting point for predicting what might happen in the future. There is more than one set of predictions and no-one knows if any are exactly right. Even so, the general trends are useful.

The main climate changes which seem likely are:

- Some parts of the world will get cooler and others warmer.

- There may be more extremes in weather conditions.

- As the temperature rises overall, the icecaps at the North and South Poles will melt, causing an increase in sea level and a loss of land surface.

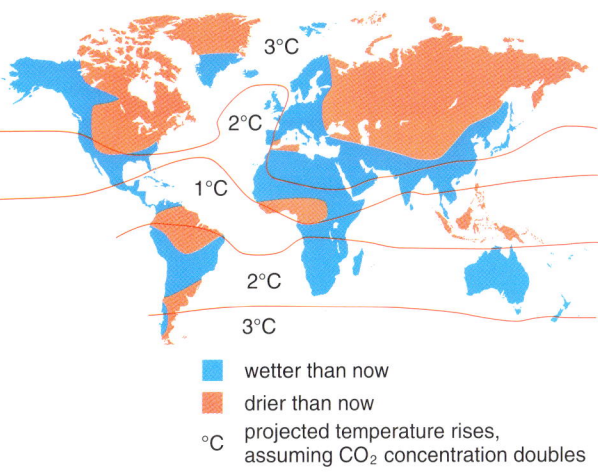

Source: Satis Atlas, ASE 1992

Picture 6 Possible climate changes, assuming that carbon dioxide doubles, which might happen between 2015 and 2050.

1 Read pages 126 and 127 to help you answer this question. Why does an increase in carbon dioxide have an effect on climate?

2 a) Which parts of the world might alter most in temperature?

b) Why is temperature increase at the North and South Poles particularly important?

c) Why would an increase in sea level affect many people around the world?

3 What can you as an individual do to try to prevent further global warming?

INTERACTING, COMPETING AND ADAPTING

Cuckoo – carefree parent and an ultimate competitor

A cuckoo uses another bird's nest to lay its egg in. The cuckoo egg hatches earlier than the other eggs. Within an hour of hatching, the cuckoo chick follows an instinct – to get rid of the competition. It pushes each egg up the side of the nest, until they fall out.

The adult bird can't resist feeding the open mouth of the cuckoo chick, even when the chick is several times bigger than it is itself.

a) A cuckoo chick throws out the competition, and then b) takes all the food it can get from the tiny willow warbler

Foxes feel fine about town

Foxes have learned to live in and around many towns in the UK. Professor Stephen Harris has spent 25 years studying them, and is still enthusiastic about these lovable rogues. They eat a wide variety of food, including fruit, fungi, insects such as beetles, worms, birds and small mammals. In London, 50% of a fox's diet is likely to be food scraps raided from bins or left out by humans.

He points out that they live near to humans because of the shelter and food available. However, if foxes get into a cellar they don't make good neighbours; 'The stink of urine, faeces and rotten food permeates the whole house.' What's more, foxes can do a lot of damage by chewing pipes and cables.

Town foxes have adapted to a very different environment from country foxes

Protecting our planet now for the future

In 1992, 153 countries signed The Framework Convention on Climate Change. Signing the agreement means a country commits to reducing the level of greenhouse gases to whatever the level was in 1990, by the year 2000. The UK is confident of meeting the target, and expects to do better than this by 5–10%.

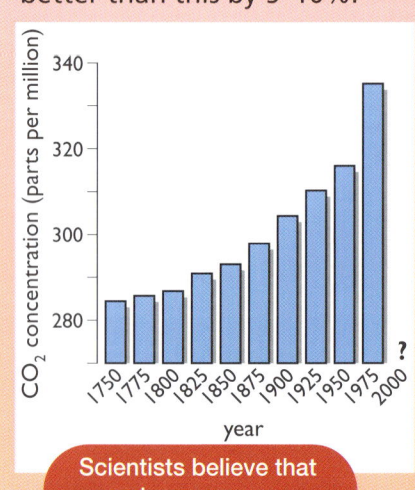

Scientists believe that greenhouse gases cause global warming

Gaining ground

When a new species is introduced into an area, it is not easy to predict exactly how it will spread. Whether the species will survive, and how it will affect other living things, are uncertain too. The maps show how the European Starling spread across the United States. In 1890, 10 were released in Central Park, New York City, 10 more were released the following year.

More recently, the New Zealand flatworm moved into Europe. It probably arrived on some plant materials that escaped a careful check. The slimy flatworm coils around an earthworm, injecting it with enzymes which digest and kill it.

The flatworm was first found in Northern Ireland in 1963, in Scotland in 1965 and in England in 1993. Sightings of the flatworm show that it is steadily working its way south. There seem to be no natural enemies to check the spread.

A new species can upset the balance in an ecosystem

What damage will this invader cause? Earthworms are important because they take dead plant material underground, where it rots and fertilises the soil. Their burrows let air into the soil too. Farmers are seriously worried about this pest.

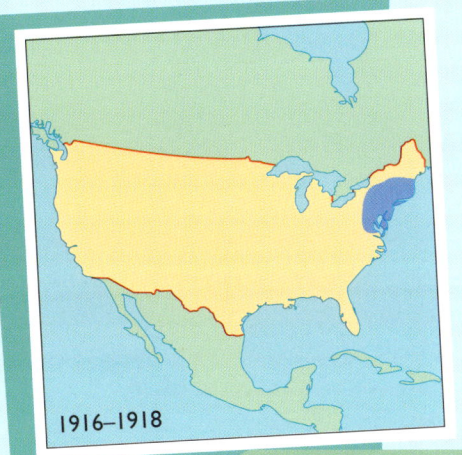
1916–1918

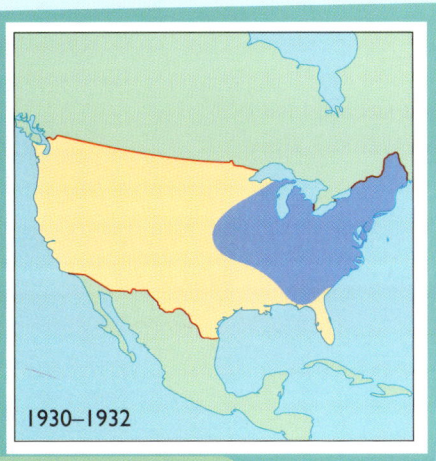
1930–1932

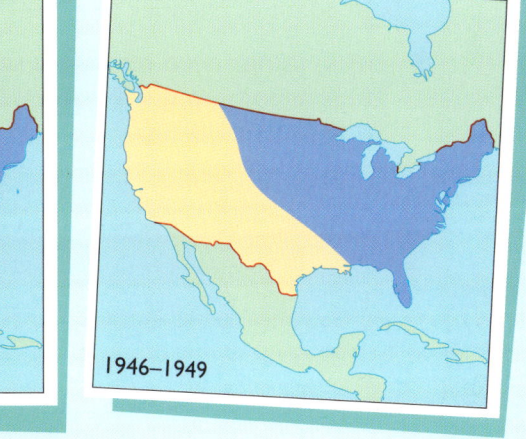
1946–1949

Starlings wing their way across America.

Dying for a cup of coffee?

In the 1970s, the Brazilian government encouraged people to move into the Amazon and farm the area. Coffee was planted on a large scale, but in the 1980s many workers moved on.

Amazonian Indians of the Surui tribe took over the care of coffee plantations. They use machetes rather than hoes, and so work close to the ground, which is dusty work. It seems that the Indians inhale soil particles, and a yeast-like fungus that lives in the soil. The fungus infects skin and the lining of the lungs.

Since coffee became the main crop of the area, the Indians' traditional farming methods have collapsed and they depend on cash for buying food. Many have malnutrition and are more likely to die from malaria.

Humans are part of Ecosystem Earth. Their way of life can be disrupted because of the actions of other humans

Ecosystem earth

Focus 6

Summary

- A habitat is a place where living things live.
- The environment is the set of living conditions in a habitat.
- A community is made up of all the living things in a habitat.
- The living things and their environment, and the interactions between them, make up an ecosystem.
- The planet Earth is an ecosystem called the biosphere. Within the biosphere there are major ecosystems such as the rainforest.
- An organism survives in an environment if it can adapt to changes that happen.
- Living things need resources such as food. There is competition between living things for limited resources.
- A predator is an animal that catches other animals and eats them. The prey is the animal that a predator catches.
- Pollution is caused by human activities such as burning fuels.
- A greenhouse gas is a gas that stops radiation passing back out through Earth's atmosphere.
- Global warming means that there is a very gradual increase in the average temperature at the Earth's surface.
- Human activities such as farming and cutting down forests, have an effect on the land and living things.

Questions

1 Farmers often spread fertiliser over their fields.

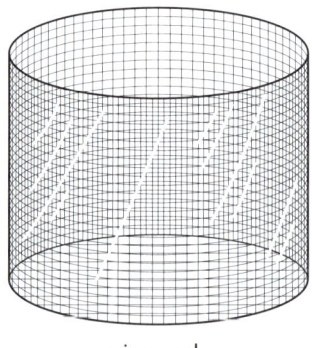

a) i) Why is fertiliser put on the soil?
   ii) Sometimes the fertiliser gets into nearby streams. Suggest how this can happen.
b) If fertiliser does get into streams it can cause a thick layer of green algae to grow on and near the surface of the water.
   i) What effect do the algae have on
      1. the amount of oxygen at the bottom of the stream?
      2. the fish that live in the water?
   ii) Explain why the layer of algae causes many of the plants that grow on the stream bed to die.
   iii) Suggest what can be done to get the water back to normal again.

c) Gardeners often use compost as a fertiliser. They make the compost from rotting plants in containers like this.

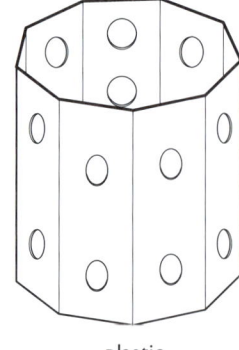

wire mesh   plastic

i) What **type** of organism makes the plants rot?
ii) Suggest why the containers have holes in them.
iii) What happens to the temperature of the compost as it starts to rot?
iv) Suggest **two** advantages of using compost instead of artificial fertiliser.

d) Pests can be killed using chemicals called pesticides.

Questions continued

Organic farmers prefer to use *natural methods of pest control*.

  i) Suggest why using pesticides may cause problems if used on fruit and vegetables.

  ii) Suggest why it may be better to kill pests by *natural methods*.

MEG

2 Read the following newspaper article.

> **SEAL DEATH HORROR**
> **POLLUTION BLAMED**
>
> Reports have been coming in from the east coast of hundreds of dead seals being washed up or found dying at sea. The seals appear to have died from a type of flu. Scientists think that the seals' immune system may have been damaged by chemicals polluting their food.
>
> The local fishing crews are said to be pleased because their catches of cod have increased. Their spokesperson said: "Less seals eat fewer cod so there are more for us." With the summer weather causing rapid growth of tiny plants called plankton, the number of small fish on which the cod feed are also increasing.

Scientists have been studying a number of chemical pollutants now being found in the sea. A report card on a group of chemicals called PCBs is shown below.

> **PCB REPORT CARD**
>
> FEATURES OF CHEMICAL:
>
>   Does not dissolve in water;
>
>   Can dissolve in fats/oils;
>
>   Excellent electrical insulator;
>
>   Very stable chemical, does not easily break down.
>
> USED IN THE MANUFACTURE OF:
>
>   Paints;
>
>   Electrical equipment;
>
>   Flame proofing.

a) Explain why flu was killing so many seals when normally most would have survived this disease.

b) Fill in the boxes to show the food chain described in the newspaper article.

c) Why are PCBs used in the manufacture of electrical equipment?

d) Why can PCBs cause a long-term pollution problem in the sea?

e) Seals are mammals and so feed their young on milk. PCB pollution kills more baby seals than adult seals. Use the information from the report card to explain this.

f) Scientists are working to reduce PCB pollution. Suggest **one** way in which this pollution could be reduced.

MEG

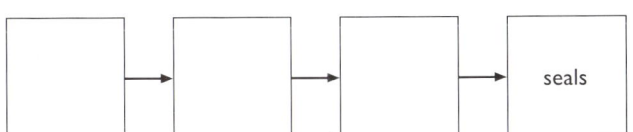

Glossary

Look up the meaning of an *italicised* word in another part of the glossary.

abdomen
lower body cavity containing many organs

active ingredient
the part of a medicine which affects the body

active site
part of an enzyme molecule where a reaction takes place

AIDS
(acquired immune deficiency syndrome)

allele
a form of a gene which codes for a particular characteristic

amino acids
small molecules which make up proteins

anaemia
a lack of iron in the blood

antibody
substance which causes antigens to 'clump' together

antigens
proteins on the surface of a cell, which act as specific markers

axon
a thread of cytoplasm which forms part of a nerve cell

balanced diet
all the types of food the body needs in the right amounts

biosphere
the Earth as an ecosystem

cambium
a layer of growing cells in plants which adds to the girth of the plant stems

carbohydrate
contains carbon, hydrogen and oxygen

carnivore
a meat-eating animal

catalyst
speeds up a chemical reaction

cell
a tiny unit of life

cell body
most of the cytoplasm of a nerve

cell membrane
layer which controls movement of substances in and out of cells

cell wall
a layer of material around a cell, gives support

cellulose
a carbohydrate which makes up most of plant cell walls; provides fibre in the diet

chloroplasts
structure in a plant cell that carries out photosynthesis

chromosomes
section of DNA which contains the code for many characteristics

community
a group of different organisms which live together

cone
receptor in the retina sensitive to different wavelengths of light, giving colour vision

cytoplasm
part of a cell where chemical reactions occur

diabetes
a disease in which the level of blood sugar is not controlled

diaphragm
fibrous and muscular sheet separating chest cavity from abdomen

diffusion gradient
a difference in concentration of solutes

digestion
breaking down big particles into smaller ones, often food

dominant allele
an allele which hides the appearance of another characteristic

ecosystem
living things and their environment

effector
part of the body that carries out an action, or responds to a stimulus

environment
the set of conditions in the surroundings of an organism

enzyme
molecule which is a catalyst in living cells

epidermis
surface layers of cells, e.g. in skin, on a leaf

evaporation
a change of state from liquid to gas

evolution
the change in characteristics of a species over a very long time scale

excretion
getting rid of waste

fertilisation
the fusion of sex cells

gene
a section of DNA that codes for a characteristic

genetic engineering
altering the genentic code of a cell by giving it DNA from another organism

geotropism
growth response of a plant to gravity

global warming
rise in global temperature

glucose
a simple carbohydrate, a sugar

greenhouse effect
tendency of the atmosphere to stop infra-red rays radiating back out to space from Earth

growth
a permanent increase in body size

haemoglobin
substance which combines with oxygen, transports oxygen in red blood cells

haemophilia
a disease in which blood does not clot

hallucinogen
a substance that causes imaginary images to appear real

herbivore
animal that eats plant material

HIV
(human immunodeficiency virus)

homeostasis
keeping conditions constant

hormones
chemicals that co-ordinate body processes

Glossary

hydrotropism
growth response of a plant to water
immunity
the body's defence against disease
leukaemia
a type of cancer which affects the blood
meiosis
cell division which happens when sex cells are produced
menopause
the time when menstruation stops completely
menstruation
loss of blood as the lining of the womb is shed from the body; a 'period'
microvilli
projections on the outside of cells
mitosis
cell division that happens when organisms are growing, or replacing cells
mutation
a change in the genetic code
natural selection
inheritance of characteristics that give an organism an advantage in an environment
negative feedback
a control mechanism which brings a condition back to the right level
neurones
nerve cells
nutrition
getting a source of energy and raw materials from food
organ
a special structure usually built of several tissues, performs particular function
organic
substances which mainly contain carbon
osmoregulation
balance of water intake and water loss
ovaries
make egg cells
ovule
female sex cell in plants
ovum
female sex cell in humans

pH
scale of acidity
phagocytes
white blood cells that can engulf and digest particles eg. bacteria
photosynthesis
process that plants use to make food from carbon dioxide and water
phototropism
growth response of a plant to light
plaque
a sticky film containing food and bacteria that can coat teeth
plasma
the liquid part of blood
pollen
male sex cell in plants
predator
an animal that catches and eats other animals
prey
an animal that is caught and eaten by another
puberty
a set of physical changes that happen between childhood and adulthood
pulp cavity
living tissues inside a tooth
receptors
detect change, may be part of a single cell, or grouped in a sense organ
recessive allele
an allele which codes for a characteristic which is hidden by another allele
reflex action
an action which does not require conscious thought
replication
the doubling of DNA to produce an exact copy
reproduction
the process of making new lives
respiration
transfer of energy in food to the body
retina
light sensitive layer, lining the eye
rods
receptor cells in the retina which operate in low light conditions

sedative
a substance which slows down the nervous system
selective breeding
breeding plants or animals to obtain desired characteristics
sensitivity
being able to detect change
sickle cell anaemia
an inherited form of anaemia resulting from abnormally shaped red blood cells
species
a group of living things which have similar features and can breed together
stimulant
a drug which speeds up the nervous system
stimulus
a change detected by a receptor
substance of abuse
a drug which changes mood or feeling
substrate
particles whiich react at the active site of an enzyme
synapse
the gap between two neurones
testis
male sex organ, makes sperms
thermoregulation
control of body temperature
tissue
group of cells of the same type
urea
a waste material made from excess amino acids, excreted in urine
urethra
tube leading from bladder to outside the body
urine
a watery liquid containing body waste
vacuole
part of a plant cell, containing a watery solution
variation
differences between living things
vascular tissue
transport tissue in plants
villi
tiny protuberances on the inside of the small intestines, which increase surface area

Index

A
abcess 31
abdomen 12
absorption 28, 33
acid rain 126, 134
active ingredient 58
active site 34
adaptation 123
addiction 58
AIDS 41
alleles 102, 104-105
amino acids 25, 34
anaemia 40
   sickle cell, 41, 46, 104
antibody 37-39
antibody cells 37
antigens 38-39
anus 28
asexual reproduction 98
axon 52-53

B
balanced diet 26
biosphere 118
blood 12, 36, 43, 46
body system 9, 10-13, 16-17, 20
brain 55
breathing system 11

C
caecum 28, 42
cambium 17
canine 30-31
capillaries 14
carbohydrate 24, 46
carnivore 31
cell 8,
   antibody 37-38
   blood 36
   body 52-53
   membrane 8
   neurones 52-53
   wall 8
cellulose 8, 42
chloroplasts 8
cholesterol 27
chromosomes
   96-97, 107, 114
ciliary muscle 56-57
clone 99
clotting 37, 40, 46
community 122, 136
competition 122, 136
conditioned reflex 55
cones 56-57
contraception 67, 74
control
   in general 78-79
   of blood sugar 60
   of heart rate 55
   of temperature 82-83
   of water 80-81
cornea 56-57
cystic fibrosis 104
cytoplasm 8

D
decay (of teeth) 30-31
diabetes 27, 60-61
dialysis 86
diaphragm 11
diet 24, 26-27, 43
diffusion 33
digestion 6, 28, 34, 42
digestive system 12, 28
DNA 96-97
Down's syndrome 107
drugs 74

E
ecosystem 118-119, 128-129, 136
ectotherm 82-83
effector 50-51, 52-53
ejaculation 65
elephants 87, 120-121
enamel 30-31
endotherm 82
environment 120, 136
enzymes 25, 33-35, 46
epidermis 14
evaporation 14
evolution 109
   of horses 110, 114
excretion 7, 20, 81
extinction 108
eye 56-57, 74

F
fibre 24
fibrin 37, 40
fibrinogen 37, 40
fossil 108, 114
fossil fuels 126

G
gender 103
gene
   for insulin production 61
   in variation 94-95, 114
genetic engineering 111
geotropism 68-69
global warming 126, 136
glucagon 60-61
glucose 24
gluten 27
greenhouse effect 126, 136
growth 6

H
habitat 120, 122, 136
haemoglobin 36, 38, 46
haemophilia 40, 46, 104
hallucinogen 58-59
herbivore 42
HIV 41, 46
homeostasis 78-79, 80
hormone 60-61
   at puberty 62-63
   in farming 66
   in fertility 66-67
   in reproduction 64-65
   summary 74
hydrotropism 68-69

I
immune memory 39
immunisation 39, 46
immunity 37, 38, 39
in vitro fertilisation 66
inbreeding 111
incisor 30-31
inheritance 102-105
insulation 25, 85
insulin 60-61

K
kidney 81, 86

L
lacteal 32, 33
large intestine 28, 42
learning 55
leukaemia 41, 43, 46
life processes 6
lipid 35
liver 12
lungs 11

M
medicine 58
meiosis 97, 98-99, 100, 114
menopause 63
menstruation 62-63, 74
microvilli 32
minerals 26
mitosis 97, 98-99, 114
molar tooth 30-31
movement 7
mucus 33, 104
muscle 10, 28
mutation 106, 114

N
natural selection 106, 109
negative feedback 61
nerve impulses 50-51
nervous system 10, 51, 70, 74
neurones 52-53, 54-55
nucleus 8, 96, 114
nutrition 6

O
oesophagus 28
oil gland 14
organ 9, 20
organic molecules 24
osmoregulation 80-81, 90
ovaries 13
oviduct 63, 64
ovule 17
ovum 13
ozone layer 127

P
penis 65
phagocytes 37
photosynthesis 6, 16
phototropism 68-69
placenta 64
plaque 30
plasma 36
platelets 36
pollen 17
pollution 126-127, 136
population 124-125
predator 124-125
pregnancy 64
protein 25, 35, 46
prey 124-125, 133, 136
puberty 62-63, 74
pulp cavity 31

R
receptors 14, 15, 50-51, 52-53
red blood cells 36
reflex action 54-55, 74
replication 97
reproduction 7, 62-63
reproductive system 13
resistance 123
respiration 6
retina 56-57
rods 56-57
root hairs 16-17

S
secondary sexual characteristics 62-63
sedative 58
selective breeding 110
sensitivity 7, 50-51, 74
sex-linkage 105
sex organs 13
sexual reproduction 64-65, 100
sickle cell 41, 43, 104
skeletal system 10
skin 14-15
small intestines 28, 32-33
species 114
squirrel 123, 132
starch 24
stem 16
stimulants 58-59
stimulus 50
stomach 28
stroke 71
substance of abuse 58-59, 64, 74
substrate 34-35
support 10, 17
survival of the fittest 109
sweat gland 13
sweating 13, 85
synapse 52

T
target organs 60
teeth 30, 43, 46
   decay of 26, 30
testes 13
thermoregulation 84, 87, 90
tissue 9, 20
tropism 68-69

U
umbilical cord 65
urea 7
urethra 13
urine 7, 13
urine system 13
ultraviolet (UV) 127

V
vacuole 8
vagina 13
variation 94-95, 114
vascular tissue 16-17
villi 32-33
vitamins 26, 35

W
withdrawal symptoms 58